Asymmetric Deregulation: The Dynamics of Telecommunications Policy in Europe and the United States

edited by

Eli M. Noam
Columbia University

Gerard Pogorel
France Telecom University

Ablex Publishing Company
Norwood, NJ

Copyright © 1994 by Ablex Publishing Corporation

Printed in the United States of America.

Library of Congress Cataloging-in-Publication Data

Asymmetric deregulation : the dynamics of telecommunications policy in Europe and the United States / co-editors, Eli M. Noam and Gerard Pogorel.

    p. cm.

   Includes bibliographical references.

   ISBN 0-89391-696-X (cl); 1-56750-003-X (ppb)

    1. Telecommunication policy—Europe. 2. Telecommunication policy—United States. I. Noam, Eli M. II. Pogorel, Gerard.

   HE8085.A85 1994

   384'.068—dc20   93-43433

                                            CIP

Ablex Publishing Corporation
355 Chestnut Street
Norwood, New Jersey 07648

Contents

About the Authors   v

Introduction   1

1 Is Telecommunications Liberalization an Expansionary   7
  Process?
  Eli Noam

2 Multilateral Cooperation in International Telecommunica-   17
  tions: Sources and Prospects
  Henry Ergas and Gerard Pogorel

3 Oligopoly in International Telecommunications   33
  William Sharkey

4 Financial Agreements for Jointly Provided International   59
  Services
  Robert E. Dansby and Thòmas R. Luciano

5 Reconciling Competition and Monopoly in the Supply of In-   75
  ternational Telecommunications Services: A U.S.
  Perspective
  Evan Kwerel

6 Industrial Organization for the Telecommunications Sector: 107
  Main Scenarios
  Jacques Arlandis

7 Competition, Concentration, and Competitiveness of the   119
  European Manufacturing Industry
  Godefroy Dang Nguyen

8 Asymmetric Deregulation and the Transformation of the   137
  International Telecommunications Regime
  William Drake

9 Asymmetric Re-regulation of Telecommunications Under   205
  European Community Law
  Joachim Scherer

10 Departing from Monopoly: Asymmetries, Competition Dy-   237
   namics, and Regulation Policy
   Laurent Benzoni and Raymond Svider

Author Index   259

Subject Index   261

About the Authors

Jacques Arlandis is Scientific Director of IDATE, France. Prior to IDATE he worked at the Forecast Unit of France Telecom, where he was Head of the Strategic Analysis Department. His recent work at IDATE has covered the economics of VANS, the introduction of ISDN in Europe, and integrated broadband communications. He has a Ph.D. in economics from ECSP (Paris Business School).

Robert Dansby is Division Manager of Regulatory Economics and Pricing Theory at Bellcore Laboratories.

Evan R. Kwerel has been a senior staff economist in the Office of Plans and Policy at the Federal Communications Commission since 1983. In 1976, Mr. Kwerel joined the Department of Economics of Yale University as an assistant professor. In 1981, he spent a year at the Department of the Interior as a Brookings Economic Policy Fellow. From 1982 to 1983, he was a senior staff economist with the President's Council of Economic Advisers. He received a Ph.D. in economics from the Massachusetts Institute of Technology in 1976 and a B.A. in economics summa cum laude from the University of Pennsylvania in 1972.

Thomas R. Luciano is District Manager of International Settlements at AT&T.

G. Dang Nguyen holds a Ph.D. in economics from the European University Institute in Florence (Italy) and an engineer's degree from Ecole des Mines de Paris. He is Professor and Head of Economic Department at Ecole Nationale Superieure des Telecommunications de Bretagne in Brest (France). His research is related to telecommunications economics and policy, in particular in the European framework. He has been consultant to the European Commission and Economic Advisor to the Ministry of Post and Telecommunications in France.

Eli M. Noam is a professor at the Columbia University Graduate School of Business. He has served as a member of the New York State

Public Service Commission from 1987 to 1990, while on leave. At Columbia, he was Director of the Center for Telecommunications and Information Studies. He has also taught at the Columbia Law School and Princeton University. Among his publications are more than 100 articles and the edited or co-edited books *Telecommunications Regulation: Today and Tomorrow; Video Media Competition; The Impact of Information Technology on the Service Sector; The Economics of Libel Law; The Law of International Telecommunications in the United States*. Recent work includes the two-volume monographs *European Telecommunication and Television* (Oxford University Press) and the forthcoming edited studies *Telecommunications in the Pacific, International Trade in Film and Television*, and *Asymmetric Liberalization*. He serves on the editorial boards of the Columbia University Press and of several academic and professional journals. He was a member of the Advisory Board for the federal government's FTS-2000 telephone network and of the National Academy of Science's review of the IRS computer system.

Professor Noam received an A.B. (1970, Phi Beta Kappa), a Ph.D. in economics (1975), and a J.D. law degree (1975) from Harvard University. He is a member of the New York and D.C. bars, and a licensed radio amateur, Advanced Class.

Gerard Pogorel is Professor of Economics and Policy Advisor, France Telecom University. He has served as a consultant to OECD, the EEC, and several institutions involved in formulating public policy in France and Europe. His research has focused on communications management and policy, with applications for the management of technology, transborder data flows, and government and business policies in the area of data banks and international communications. He received honors degrees in business administration from the Ecole des Hautes Etudes Commerciales (HEC Paris, 1966), in sociology from the Sorbonne (1970), and holds a Doctorat d'Etat in economics from the Université de Paris I (1973).

Joachim Scherer is partner of Baker & McKenzie (Döser Amereller Noack) in Frankfurt/Main and a Professor of Law at the University of the Armed Forces in Munich. Previous to joining Baker & McKenzie, he was an assistant professor at Johann Wolfgang Goethe-Universität and a visiting professor at Philipps Universität Marburg and at Universität Hannover. He specializes in administrative law, telecommunications law and European Community law. He is the author of several books and law review articles in these fields. He has been appointed as a consulting expert on telecommunications law by the Commission of the European Communities. He received his Dr. jur. from Johann Wolfgang Goethe-Universität and his LL.M. from Columbia University Law School, New York City.

William W. Sharkey has been a member of technical staff of the Economic Research Group of Bell Communications Research (Bellcore) since 1984. From 1973 to 1983 he was a member of the technical staff of AT&T Bell Laboratories. During these years he also taught briefly at the University of Pennsylvania and the University of Arizona. Dr. Sharkey is the author of *The Theory of Natural Monopoly* and is currently working on a second book, *Theories of Government Intervention into Economic Activity*. His research interests include applied game theory, industrial organization, and the economics of regulated industries. He received a Ph.D. in economics from the University of Chicago in 1973.

Introduction

For almost a century, relatively smooth cooperation characterized transatlantic communications; problems mostly involved technical compatibility and were resolved by technologists of the monopolistic telephone organizations on either side of the Atlantic. In recent years, however, numerous developments have rapidly changed the nature of international communications, their institutions, and their collaborative arrangements.

In the United States, technological and institutional change have reduced the extent of a core natural monopoly, and this has brought out entrepreneurial initiatives, a restructuring of the industry, and reduction of government involvement. In Europe, similar underlying technical developments have often led to a stiffening of the coalition protecting the governmental PTT system. Telecommunications policy has also often been used as industrial policy and served as a central element in developing an advanced electronics industry.

The clash of different policy approaches was particularly acute in the field of telecommunications services. Historically, U.S. policy in international telecommunications had been to carve up the market into distinct segments, each assigned to different types of carriers. The United States, however, restructured the rules of the game radically within a short period, thus confronting its correspondent countries with the necessity of responding to a new situation. At the same time, the PTTs, as a result of U.S. deregulation, were in a position of a monopsonist as far as their domestic market is concerned and could attempt playing off American carriers against each other. This "whipsawing" lead to U.S. responses that are far from deregulatory.

There is a great variety in the patterns of ownership and usage of telecommunications across different countries. The United States has followed up its domestic deregulatory policies with a variety of

1

initiatives in economic and diplomatic areas and proposed an evolution of the present framework in international telecommunications. European nations have selectively adopted parts of this framework, but have also taken certain defensive measures to control the impact of foreign policies on their domestic market.

This difference has led to a disequilibrium in the world telecommunications market and raises a complex of important issues:

- Can evolving domestic deregulation be reconciled with an international regulatory regime? How does international trade regulation affect multinational governmental cooperation? How does it affect private collaboration?
- Is competition viable in all sectors of the international telecommunications industry? Does competition require a significant scale, and then does it produce reasonable substitutes and permit entry on an international level? Are there cost penalties from the loss of economies of scale in domestic and international telecommunications?
- What has happened to the price of services after they are no longer tied to a monopolist? What costs are incurred by the user after the initial shift from a monopolistic environment to a competitive one? How does asymmetric deregulation affect trade and trade imbalance? What is the role of regulation, both domestically and internationally, in combating trade imbalances in telecommunication.

This volume brings together work from major scholars and researchers from the fields of economics, political science, and law. They discuss issues specific to European countries and the United States and, more generally, offer an analysis of regulatory policy, trade, and pricing issues in the context of international telecommunications.

In the first chapter, Eli Noam, of Columbia University, asks the question whether liberalization is a contagious process in the sense that instability in one part of an internationally interconnected system would spread throughout the entire system. This raises the question whether deregulation can be contained geographically or functionally. The American experience has been that partial deregulation leads to pressure at the functional boundaries, to arbitrage, substitutions between network and user equipment, and between equipment and services. His analysis is based on a model of interactions between diversely regulated economies. Various levels of competition and monopoly are assumed where policies can be reactive to each other, dynamic interactions can occur, including oscillations.

Given the increase in the interactive parameters, Noam expects it to become increasingly difficult to conduct national policies.

In the second chapter, Gerard Pogorel, of Universite de Compiegne and now with France Telecom University, and Henry Ergas, of OECD and now at Monash University in Australia, argue that the growing pace and complexity of technological change, combined with the increase in the number of parties in multilateral cooperation, might already be jeopardizing the process of international negotiations and regulation itself. This is exemplified by the rising difficulties of the standardization process, and in the tendency toward bilateralism.

In Chapter 3, William Sharkey of Bell Communications Research discusses how deregulation in the United States represents a sudden and radical departure with implications not only for market structure in the United States but also for the international network. Sharkey considers several models of a deregulated telecommunications industry. First is an application of sustainability theory to the specific technology of network transmission. It is shown that sustainable prices need not exist, but that network externalities suggest that nonexistence is not a real problem. Therefore, free entry itself is unlikely to create inefficiency as is theoretically possible. Next, a model of competition is considered in which the network is fragmented, for example, by a political boundary. In this case, it is argued that equilibrium is likely to be inefficient or fundamentally unstable. On the whole, the author emphasizes the unpredictability and instability of the outcomes that can be expected as more and more countries allow competitive entry into telecommunications markets, thus creating an oligopoly in international communications. If this is an alternative to monopoly conditions, however, the competition enhances consumer welfare.

Robert Dansby and Thomas Luciano, both of AT&T, discuss in Chapter 4 how the dramatic changes in the structure of the international telecommunications market require that the financial terms and conditions of international agreements be reexamined. Major factors that contribute to this evolution include: competitive entry, technology innovations, and changes in traffic patterns. These market fundamentals have induced changes in the marketing and pricing strategies of service providers. Of particular interest are the implications these changes have for the structure of the international settlements process. This chapter focuses on a discussion of the settlements process and alternatives to current accounting rates policy. Financial terms and conditions which are incentive compatible and better serve the economic interest of all partners in international joint agreements are discussed.

Next, Evan Kwerel, of the Office of Plans and Policy of the Federal Communications Commission, discusses the impact of growth in competition in international telecommunications on interexchange carriers' relationship with foreign telecommunications authorities. PTTs have a monopoly on access and may be willing to exercise their market power in order to provide revenues to subsidize domestic telecommunications. The position of foreign telecommunications authorities (relative to U.S. carriers who wish to interconnect) is analogous to that of U.S. local exchange carriers (relative to interexchange carriers) except that foreign telecommunications authorities are not subject to the jurisdiction of any U.S. governmental body. Mechanisms and policies are examined that might reduce the incentives to foreign telecommunications authorities of using such competition to extract undue concessions from interexchange carriers.

In Chapter 6, Jacques Arlandis of IDATE, the major French telecommunications research organization, proposes an assessment of possible communications scenarios (ISDN, VAS, VANS, and Private Networks) based on an evaluation of the costs and benefits of market and hierarchy type organization. He shows that these scenarios entail very different allocations of the value-added, among equipment manufacturers, network operators, and the producers of telecommunications services.

In Chapter 7, Godefroy Dang Nguyen of the Ecole Nationale Superieure des Telecommunications (ENST) Bretagne and the policy planning Mission a la Reglementation, French PTT, presents a method of computation of the potential gains of strategic alliances among public switching equipment manufacturers. He diagnoses a certain level of "myopia" among European manufacturers (and policymakers), which prevents them from choosing the optimal development path at the right time. The implementation of ISDN is offered as an example that may allow them to do so.

Next, William Drake, formerly at the Center for International Affairs at Harvard University and now at University of California, San Diego, suggests that the regime of international cooperation in which the International Telecommunications Union (ITU) originated and flourished was feasible due to a universal commitment among its members to monopolistically control their respective telecommunications networks. In this environment, free of "the rigors of competitive entry," the telecommunications authorities could readily cooperate and interconnect. As a result of the divestiture and progressively increasing deregulation of the U.S. telecommunications market, this formerly stable regime faces an environment of asymmetric regulation which creates momentum for members to change their regulatory structures in order to compete more effectively. Drake contends that this is an evolutionary process. To reveal its dynamics, he traces ITU's historical and political roots, examines the current power structure, and then looks forward to the directions in which current policies are forcing changes.

Joachim Scherer, University of Frankfurt, in Chapter 9, analyzes divergent national deregulatory practices from the broader perspective of European trade laws. From the beginning, the regulation of telecommunications trade and standards were a highly internationalized affair. For a long time, a few international organizations were used to shore up domestic arrangements. These included the ITU, CCITT, and CEPT. More recently, efforts to deregulate have involved many new players, and the growing number of national, regional, and international organizations that have a stake in the standardization process have made international cooperation more difficult.

Laurent Benzoni and Raymond Svider, both of Ecole Nationale Superieure des Telecommunications (ENST), investigate in Chapter 10 the problems of deregulation as they apply to the telecommunications industry in France. The authors first present a model that simulates the entry of a new firm in to the monopolistic French long distance market. Based on this model, an analysis follows of the asymmetries within the market and the effects of the newly created competition. Finally, the authors discuss effective regulatory policies for such a newly competitive market in France.

This volume is a result of a project and conference collaboratively undertaken by the Columbia Institute for Tele-Information at Columbia University and the Universite de Compiegne, France. The Institute received a National Science Foundation award through the U.S.–France Cooperative Sciences Program, and the Universite de Compiegne received a parallel grant from the Centre National de la Recherche Scientifique. The principal organizers were Eli Noam (Columbia University), Henry Ergas (OECD), and Gerard Pogorel (Universite de Compiegne).

The editors would like to thank those who contributed to this volume and to the organization of the project. At Columbia University, Douglas Conn and Christopher Dorman were instrumental, as were Maryline Potel, Pascal Fresch, and Patrice Geoffron of Universite de Compiegne. The editorial production of the book was supervised by Douglas Conn. At the National Science Foundation we would like to thank Charles Brownstein and Lawrence Rosenberg, and at the Centre National de Recherches Scientifique, Claire Girault and Laurence Ratier-Coutrot. The editors would also like to thank Thierry Vedel of CNRS, who hosted the seminar and helped with its organization.

Chapter 1
Is Telecommunications Liberalization an Expansionary Process?

Eli M. Noam

A look across countries and across different economic sectors shows a spreading in the liberalization of previously strictly controlled economic activities. In the U.S., deregulation has expanded *functionally* from one line of business to adjoining ones, such as in transportation from airlines to railroads and then to trucks, or in telecommunications from equipment to long distance service, local transmission, and central office functions. Liberalization has also spread *geographically*. In telecommunications it has moved from the U.S. to the U.K., Japan, and to some extent to continental Europe. In air transportation, too, it proceeded from the U.S. to Britain and Europe. One should note that, in other historical periods, the opposite trends have occurred, and regulation has expanded. In the United States, for example, state railroad regulation led to federal railroad regulation in the 1880s, which in turn spread in the 1920s and 1930s to trucking, buses, and airlines. In financial services, regulation of savings and loan banks expanded to commercial and investment banks and brokerage services. In telecommunications, national telegraph regulation of European countries was extended in the 1850s to international arrangements, and later to telephone service.

This leads to the question why these long-term trends are taking place. Is it a change in *ideology,* in which the Chicago School of Economics follows, e.g., the Fabian Society? Or is it the political *dominance* of one country, which is then reflected in international trends of policy? Or is it a dialectic cycle, in which the inevitable shortcomings of any policy lead in time to the adoption of another?

More likely, these factors are the symptoms or catalysts of change rather than its causes. While they all play a role, there is a more structural cause for regulatory change. This force is the instability of interaction. That is, the more interrelated countries and economic activities are, the less likely are there stable solutions to separate policies. And where instabilities exist, they ripple throughout the entire system. It becomes increasingly difficult to control all of the elements in such a complex matrix of interrelations. Ultimately, overarching control over many countries and many economic activities is necessary. And since this power does not exist, or is usually not deemed desirable, regulatory strictness unravels.

The following will provide a simple framework to analyze a regulation in its intersectoral and international dimensions. We start by narrowly defining regulation as the setting, by a regulatory body, of a price vector R for a set of economic activities. A total prohibition is an infinite price; total laissez-faire approach by the state means a vector of market prices; most regulation, however, is somewhere in between and can be viewed as a way of making an economic activity costlier (as in pollution control) or cheaper (as in residential telephone usage). Various interest groups are affected by the setting of these prices, and they seek favorable Ps by exercising pressure through the political process.

Where will R be set? This depends on the optimizing function of the regulator. For purposes of the model, it is not necessary to specify this function, except to assume that regulatory behavior is affected by the groups according to their power and stake in the outcome. Let us assume two interest groups A and B, each with with a "political weight" of W_A and W_B. Each group is affected by the regulation R, with the effect E described by $E_i = g_i(R)$. We assume for simplicity that the two groups are impacted differently by regulation, in that one gains from a higher R, while the other loses from it.

$$E'_A \geq 0 \qquad E'_B < 0$$

Each group asserts pressure P_i according to that impact E_i, weighted by the group's political weight W_i.

$$P_i = E_i W_i = g_i(R)W_i$$

The various pressures are in equilibrium when

$$P_A + P_B = g_A(R)W_A + g_B(R)W_B = 0$$

which is where the ratio of the benefit functions is equal to the inverse of the political weights of the respective groups.

$$\frac{g_A(R)}{g_B(R)} = - \frac{W_B}{W_A}$$

Since the W_i and g_i are given, we can determine the expected regulation R in such a system as

$$R = h \begin{bmatrix} g_A & w_A \\ g_B & w_B \end{bmatrix}^{-1}$$

We now introduce a second and related economic activity and denote it by 2. This activity affects both A and B in their activity 1. For example, activity 2 could be telephony, which affects telegraphy (activity 1) and two interests affected by it, carriers and users. Similarly, activity 2 could be functionally the same as 1, but exercised in a different political jurisdiction. The demand and supply for one activity tends to be related to the other, either as substitutes or as complements. Hence, in an interrelated world, the politically optimal regulations may be different than for a single activity in an isolated jurisdiction.

$$R_1 = \delta_1 \begin{bmatrix} g_A & w_A & R_B \\ g_B & w_B & \end{bmatrix}$$

In most instances, we will encounter a cross elasticity C that is positive,

$$\frac{dR_1 \; R_2}{dR_2 \; R_1} = C_1 > 0$$

But in some instances, cross-elasticity of regulation C would be negative. For example, if banking laws are tightened in Italy, they may be lowered in Switzerland, since its banking industry, which benefits from inflows from Italy, would be worse off than before without counterrelaxation. Similarly, if Switzerland lowers the strictness of its banking regulations, Italy may have to tighten up its own to reduce outflow.

This can lead to instability. As Italy successively tightens up, Switzerland keeps liberalizing.

An example in telecommunications are transborder data flow protection laws. The less protected data are in one country, the tighter the other may become in response.

Now for activity 2 the same holds true. Here, too, are two interest groups, denoted by C and D, and an effect of R_1 with a cross elasticity of C_2.

Therefore, we can think of two "reaction functions" f_1 and f_2 which track the response of one regulation to the other's given level.

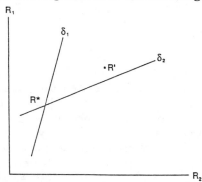

A point such as R′ would denote the two independently set regulatory policies. But once we postulate reactions to each other, there would be a shift to R*.

$$R^*_1 = (R'_1 \cdot R_2^{C_1}) \exp (1/(1 - C_1C_2)).$$

Under moderately sized and positive cross-elasticities, there will be an equilibrium point such that regulation will be lower for desirable activities, and higher for undesirable ones.

Examples include: (a) lower telephone rates, if one wants to attract business from the other jurisdiction; (b) stricter local zoning laws, to prevent undesirable activities from spilling in.

There is no need for *coordination* between 1 and 2; and equilibrium can be reached by unilateral actions and reactions.

However, for an equilibrium to exist requires that the reaction functions 1 and 2 are such that 2 is steeper than the inverse of 1 at the point of intersection, i.e., that δ2 cuts δ1 from below.

If the reverse is true, then there is no equilibrium, and the regulatory strictness either moves successively higher or lower to corner solutions. Examples include "race to the bottom" in state corporation law in the United States. The reverse is the zoning out of chemical waste dump sites. These are instances of corner solutions. For other configurations of the reaction functions, cyclical change is possible.

Instability raises questions of how to prevent it, and therefore leads to the issue of *policy coordination*. But even in stable situations, R* may not be the optimal result for either 1 or 2, or for both, and policies may be sought to affect moving from R* back to R'.

There are several possibilities for such policy coordination:

1. "Supra"regulation. This is an encompassing regulation, either across jurisdictions, e.g., a supranational policy, or across functions, i.e., "supramodal." This expands regulation to a *higher* level of institutions, for example to the European Commission, or to a *wider* institution, such as the Interstate Commerce Commission in the U.S., which regulates all modes of surface transportation.

How is supraregulation set? By analogy to the single jurisdiction case, the two sets of interest groups are assumed to affect the joint jurisdiction in an aggregated fashion, if the suprajurisdiction is answerable to the body politic.

$$R_s = f_3 \left[(P_{1A} + P_{2A}), (P_{1B} + 2_B) \right]$$

This can be higher or lower than uncoordinated outcomes. Supraregulation is not invariably stricter than particularist regulation, for the reasons discussed above. In telecommunications, for example, the regulatory principles of the European Commission are less strict than those of most of the member states. In the United States, the same holds true for the FCC vis-á-vis the state Public Utility Commissions. But the reverse is also often the case, as for example in the regulation of securities.

One question is why interest groups (or a whole country) would consent to supraregulation. Would this not dilute the power of dominant groups? This is indeed true. Therefore, a dominant group will normally consent to a shift to supraregulation only where its favored policy would be enhanced, e.g., if the balance of power of interest groups in the other sector is even more favorable to its concerns. However, for symmetrical reasons, the dominant group in the other sector would then oppose supraregulation lest it dilute its own influence. Lag rolling aside, this then leaves as the primary reasons for mutual joining of supraregulation two cases: (a) when the balance of power is essentially equal in the two sectors, so that supraregulation does not make much difference. This is why policy coordination is easier among Western European countries than, for example, East Asian ones. And, more importantly, (b) when supraregulation establishes a *policy cartel* to avoid separate regulation to affect each other and to lead to results that are considered suboptimal by the dominant groups. This is more likely to be important where the cross-elasticity of regulation is high, which is likely to be the case with sectors or countries that interact strongly with each other.

In other words, the advantage of the elimination of uncontrolled interaction must be greater than the value attributed to control and independence. Of course, *de facto* independence already had been lost through the mechanism of interaction, and supraregulation reflects this.

A related issue is that of uniformity in regulation. Here, the issue is not the strictness per se, but the importance of being identical. There are situations where efficiencies exist in uniformity or connectivity. The width of railroad gauge or protocols in telecommunications are examples.

Technologists tend to favor standardization. Economists have more mixed views, because uniformity has its costs. To have cars with identical pollution controls in both Australia and Japan may not necessarily be optimal for either or for both jointly.

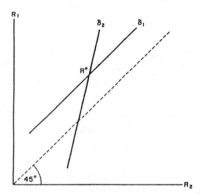

In terms of the model, uniformity is given by the 45° line, which is likely to be off the equilibrium point R*. Uniformity is the dominant policy throughout if at least one reaction functions is sloped at 45°, i.e., where at least one jurisdiction reacts to the other's change by an identical change so as to preserve uniformity. But that is an exceptional situation.

There may be great incentives for one state to be nonuniform. Examples include large countries for whom international interaction may be small in relative terms, such as the United States, which, e.g., affords a nonmetric system of measurements. At the same time, many other examples are small countries, or states: Switzerland in banking; Delaware in corporation law; Hong-Kong in tariff duties; Liechtenstein in taxes; Monaco in gambling; Luxembourg in broadcasting. These examples suggest that small countries have incentives to being nonconforming, probably since the loss in revenue, control, etc. from their own relatively small domestic economies is more than offset by the inflow from the larger countries due to nonconformity. To prevent such nonuniformity, the other states have to impose substantial pressure on the maverick jurisdictions or pay significant compensation.

2. Regulatory Treaties. Another possibility of coordination is to establish interjurisdictional or intersectoral treaties. Here, there is no supraregulation by a suprabody, only an agreement, and, each side must be better off than before to enter into it. Agreement will stop at the point where marginal benefits of marginal regulation will begin to be negative for at least one jurisdiction. Thus, such a system is a convoy travelling at the speed of its slowest ship. It can be extended further where compensation to some participants is possible, which is one of the ways the European Community operates in the agricultural field.

3. Regulatory Colonialism. An extreme example for regulatory coordination could be called *regulatory colonialism,* when one jurisdiction can set regulations for another jurisdiction solely to benefit itself. Britain's imposition of regulations on cotton spinning in India or on opium trade in China are examples. Other illustrations include American railroads imposing regulations on trucking using the Interstate Commerce Commission, or America broadcasters successfully pressuring the FCC to restrict cable television for a number of years. The model can describe the regulatory outcome for such a situation.

Instability

The problem of any coordinated regulatory structure is its instability. First, there may be no equilibrium possible, because the reaction functions do not meet the stability criterion described above. Second, one jurisdiction's adherence to an agreement provides the other with an opportunity of gain by seeking a noncooperative policy. In each jurisdiction there are pressures to seek one's own ideal regulatory level, which is likely to be different from the agreed upon level or from the interactive equilibrium. Going it alone can be due to short-sightedness or lack of understanding of the interaction involved. But it can be based on the rational desire to gain advantages over others by breaking joint policy, at least in the short run.

In telecommunications, for example, communications "havens" are possible and likely to emerge. The example of telex service is instructive. In the 1980s, London-based telex bureaus started to retransmit traffic between North America and continental Europe in defiance of CCITT cartel "recommendations" against such retransmission. It was profitable for U.K. firms to break these rules, since this generated more traffic and made the U.K. more attractive as a business location. In time, the cartel rules were held to be illegal.

It is important to recognize that domestic intersectoral instability is linked to international instability in regulation. A matrix describes the set of intersectoral (vertical) and international (horizontal) regulatory cross-elasticities.

$$c_{11}, c_{12}, \ldots, c_{1n}$$

$$c_{21}, c_{22}, \ldots, c_{2n}$$

$$\bullet$$
$$\bullet$$
$$\bullet$$

$$c_{m1}, c_{m2}, \ldots, c_{mn}$$

Generally, a stable solution is less likely:

1. as the number of jurisdictions (columns) increases.
2. as the number of sectors (rows) increases.
3. when the sectors increasingly overlap (higher vertical cross-elasticities), for example, due to "merging" technology. (Examples: telecommunications, mass media, computers.)
4. when jurisdictions increasingly interrelate (higher horizontal cross-elasticities), for example, due to lower transportation costs.
5. when the relative weight of interest groups in different jurisdictions varies as their economies develop on different trajectories. This can be a self-feeding mechanism, as some countries become specialized in certain sectors.
6. the more the regulatory price set diverges from cost, generating incentives for breaching the set.

These changes lead to unstable situations that affect the entire system. A single inconsistency has multiple secondary effects, which in turn lead to further inconsistencies. At the same time, collaborative regulatory adjustments becomes more difficult, because they cannot be confined to subsectors.

Outlook

Is there anything to stop the process? At some point, the cost of instability and diversity become high enough for a coordinated regime to be reestablished. But this is not likely to be stable over time, especially since no real international enforcement or compensation mechanisms exist, and their absence has domestic reverberations. For example, if international airline cartels break down, domestic ones are threatened. One can fly from Toronto to Vancouver through the United States, if Canadian prices are too high.

Applied to telecommunications, one should therefore expect an overall trend towards liberalization, though accompanied by efforts to stabilize its collaborative aspects. As the matrix of interrelations becomes steadily more cross-elastic, one hence has some oscillations. The overall tendency, in the long term, should lead to reduced regulatory strictness internationally. In that sense, liberalization is an expansionary process. If it is not so much an ideological choice, but as a response to an internal inability to structure a stable equilibrium that serves multiple domestic interests and goals, then one has to predict that similar inconsistencies will spread throughout the system.

Traditional telecommunications operated through national monopolies protected internationally by a cartel arrangement. Now, a challenge to domestic monopolies threatens the international cartel. Conversely, the breakdown in international arrangements threatens domestic stability. It is difficult to see how the simplicity of the traditional system can be maintained or restored. Most likely we are merely at the beginning of a lengthy, dynamic, and untidy process, of which the presently asymmetric liberalization across the two sides of the Atlantic is a manifestation.

Chapter 2
Multilateral Cooperation in International Telecommunications: Sources and Prospects*

Henry Ergas and Gerard Pogorel

The international telecommunications system is among the most successful examples of multilateral cooperation. The standards, rules, and regulations elaborated by the ITU and its subbodies have been widely respected by telecommunications common carriers, and the institutions themselves have avoided the crisis of legitimacy that has more generally affected the United Nations and its specialized agencies.

This chapter seeks to identify structural factors underlying the resilience of international cooperation in this field, and to assess the extent to which they are affected by changes now under way in the telecommunications regulatory environment.

Part I of this chapter outlines a general "structural realist" theory of multilateral cooperation. According to this theory, the extent of multilateral cooperation reflects (a) the *demand* for such cooperation, or the extent of the gains such cooperation can achieve relative to purely bilateral approaches; and (b) the *supply* of such cooperation, or the ease with which the mechanisms for such cooperation can be put into place. The demand for international cooperation is presumed to

---

The analytical framework of this chaptercan be found in Kramer (1983), and especially in Keshane (1983).

reflect the saving in transactions costs of negotiating agreements multilaterally rather than bilaterally; these savings will in turn depend on the degree to which the activity involved must be dedicated to it, and the nature of the contracts on which it rests. Equally, the supply of international cooperation is presumed to involve both first-mover and public good problems; the ease with which these are resolved is expected to reflect the capability of a single country or "club" of countries to internalize the benefits from cooperation, the extent to which negotiators share a common outlook and objectives, and the stability or instability of the technological and economic context.

In Part II, this model is applied to the domain of telecommunications. International telecommunications have traditionally been characterized by factors that resulted in a particularly strong demand for multilateral cooperation. These factors include the fact that given a domestic monopoly at each end, international service could not be provided by a single carrier on an end-to-end basis but had to be provided jointly. Also, for such joint provision to occur, detailed agreements had to be reached between suppliers, and the costs of negotiating such agreements could be minimized by standardizing some features of these agreements on a multilateral basis. At the same time, the supply of multilateral cooperation has been enhanced by the small total number of participants and the high degree of control exercised by each over its environment, by the dominance of an engineering/public service culture, and by a technological context whenever change was evolutionary.

In Part III, we argue that these features, which have provided stability to the international telecommunications regime, now appear in question. The liberalization of entry into domestic telecommunications markets makes end-to-end service by a single entity feasible, at least for the largest customers; together with technological developments, this reduces the need for joint-supply agreements. At the same time, the increasingly competitive nature of the industry's environment and the rapid pace of technological change undermine the gradual, cooperative approach to multilateral negotiation that has characterized international telecommunications.

We conclude that these changes are already affecting the success of multilateral cooperation in telecommunications. This is most evident in the growing difficulties of the standardization process and in the tendency towards bilateralism in the handling of disputes. Adapting international institutions to these changes is the major challenge that lies ahead. Viewed historically, telecommunications has been an outstanding success story of international cooperation. Compared with areas such as trade, finance, or development assistance, international cooperation in telecommunications has been distinguished by the resilience of the institutional mechanisms on which it is based, the widespread acceptance and observance of multilateral rules and regulations, and a relative lack of conflict between the technical function of solving immediate problems and the claims of contrasting ideologies and interests.

Can this distinctive performance survive the major changes now affecting telecommunications worldwide? Does domestic deregulation—and the varieties of approaches to it—threaten the international telecommunications regime? To answer these questions, it is important to first identify the general factors that may contribute to stable and effective international cooperation in particular areas; this is done in Part I. Part II examines the extent to which these factors have been at work in the context of telecommunications, while Part III assesses whether these factors are now operating less fully and derives some implications for the likely course of the international telecommunications regime.

A word of warning is appropriate at the outset. The discussion in this chapter is primarily directed to the ITU and its subbodies, since they are the principal locus of multilateral cooperation in the telecommunications sector; but the conclusions apply, perhaps with even greater force, to INTELSAT and the European Conference of Postal and Telecommunications Administrations (CEPT).

INTERNATIONAL COOPERATION: AN EXPLANATORY FRAMEWORK

The phrase *international cooperation* covers an enormous multitude of phenomena, varying in both the nature of the obligations they create and the degree and form of institutionalization of these obligations. Yet this diversity does not detract from a common theme: sovereign states together entering into voluntary "agreements" that in one way or another inform their domestic policymaking. Within the spectrum of such agreements, a particular variant are those that set out on a multilateral basis rules, regulations, and procedures governing a specific functional area of interaction between monetary systems or the exploitation of marine resources. These "agreements" are generally detailed and established mechanisms for dispute resolution. It is these characteristics that are usually taken to define an *international regime.*

Why would governments enter into such regimes? And why has it proven easier to establish and maintain multilateral arrangements in some areas of policy than in others? It is useful to approach these questions in terms of a *demand* for, and *supply* of, international regimes. The "demand" side refers to the factors that affect the benefits states can obtain from multilateral arrangements; and the "supply" side to the factors that make it either easier or more difficult for these arrangements to evolve.

The Demand for International Regimes

The advantages that can be secured from multilateral arrangements fall into two categories. The first consists of enabling domestic output and investment decisions that would be taken without assurances about future policy in other countries. The second advantage is in the reduction of the costs of actually obtaining these assurances.

The first of these advantages will depend on the extent to which the decisions made domestically are vulnerable to changes in policy in other countries. Thus, if a good or service can only be provided in cooperation with a foreign supplier, and if the return the domestic agent secures from an investment in providing that service depends on the behavior of the foreign supplier, then the domestic agent will have a significant interest in obtaining assurances about the future behavior of the foreign supplier. More generally, domestic agents' interest in controlling the behavior of foreign suppliers will vary according to:

1. the degree of jointness in the supply decisions of domestic and foreign agents; and
2. the degree of sunk costs these decisions involve, and consequently, the domestic supplier's exposure to opportunistic behavior overseas.

Insuring that the gains obtainable from joint supply are realized and the risks of opportunism kept to a minimum requires a framework for cooperation, not only between the agents directly involved in the decision, but also between the states, which can interfere in their action. In principle, such a framework could be established solely through bilateral arrangements between the states. However, multilateral arrangements are likely to prove an effective complement to, or (more rarely) a substitute for, purely bilateral relations when the three following conditions are met:

1. The decisions involved have an inherently multilateral character, in the sense that the benefits country A secures from agreement with country B will at least partly depend on each country's relations with C, D, E and so on;

2. the arrangements themselves are both relatively technical and require fairly frequent revision; and
3. surveillance and enforcement of agreement requires information and approval, not only from the parties directly involved in a transaction but also from others.

Under these circumstances, multilateral agreements will reduce transactions costs relative to purely bilateral negotiations in three respects:

1. They make it easier for participants to discover complex packages of tradeoffs and compensation, allowing each country to secure a better outcome than could be had were compensation only to be provided on a bilateral basis;
2. they allow standardization of the agreements between countries and provide a parallel forum for review, clearly a saving compared with the cost of trying to revise a large number of bilateral agreements one by one; and
3. they can provide for cost-effective enforcement, by encouraging the pooling of information, increasing the visibility associated with noncompliance, and permitting "smaller" agents to coalesce for the purpose of sanctioning "larger" ones.

The Supply of International Regimes

The fact that multilateral arrangements provide benefits to participants is not sufficient, however, to ensure that such arrangements will emerge or survive. The problems are twofold:

1. In practice, such arrangements are likely to resemble clubs in requiring an initial (largely sunk) investment, which it may prove difficult for investor to recoup; and
2. multilateral arrangements may have a quasi-public-good character, such that nonparticipants cannot be fully excluded from obtaining some share of the benefits they provide.

It is a matter of some controversy under what conditions these difficulties are most likely to overcome. Two broad views can be distinguished.

First, some writers have emphasized the role of a "hegemonic" power in initiating multilateral arrangements. This is a role frequently ascribed, at least in the early postwar period, to the United States. Underlying this viewpoint is the argument that the hegemonic power is best placed to "internalize" the benefits arising from the provision of international cooperation as a public good. In turn, its position of political dominance helps it convince other countries to participate fully in the proposed arrangement. Other writers, however, have pointed out that the statistical relation between the existence of a hegemonic power in the world system and the establishment of multilateral arrangements is, at best, a weak one. According to this view, it would be dangerous to treat the special circumstances of the late 1940s and early 1950s as a paradigmatic case of successful multilateralism.

The second approach draws on Mancur Olson's theory of collective action. According to Olson, quasipublic goods will be made available when the supply of these goods can be "bundled" with the supply of a private good (that is, a good with standard excludability conditions), for example, a listener-funded radio station (clearly a local public good) that also runs a social club (a private good). While this approach is appealing, it has not proved of wide applicability in explaining multilateral arrangements.

These differences of approach to the establishment of multilateral agreement notwithstanding, three conditions seem particularly important for their instability.

First, the parties to the agreement must be in a position to provide assurance regarding the behavior of the agents who will actually be involved in the transactions. These assurances may be based on a negotiating mandate received from these agents or on a statutory power of regulation, but must in either case be sufficient to make the negotiation credible.

Second, agreements are most likely to be reached and maintained when they are buttressed by a shared world view. The more the negotiators agree about the way the world works, the greater the similarity in the language they use to describe it, the closer their objectives, and the higher the probability of a successful outcome.

Finally, agreements are not likely to survive if parties are frequently placed in zero-sum situations. As became painfully obvious in discussions about the law of the sea, recurring conflicts over common access resources (that is, resources the property rights of which are not vested in individual owners) are particularly damaging in a multilateral context. Participants have few incentives to correctly signal their preferences, mechanisms for arranging compensation are likely to be rudimentary, and the prospects for enforcement will generally be poor.

In short, multilateral regimes are most likely to evolve when the following conditions are met:

1. Decisions require a high degree of jointness between domestic and foreign agents.

2. The sunk costs involved in these decisions are high, so that domestic agents may be vulnerable to opportunistic behavior by foreign suppliers.
3. The agreements needed to control such behavior entail high transaction costs for the following reasons. One, the extent of the costs and benefits from any bilateral link also depends on circumstances of other links. Two, the agreements themselves must be fairly technical and may need frequent revision. Finally, surveillance and enforcement requires information from a broad range of sources and effective disciplinary action in a number of bilateral relations.
4. Countries can find some way of allocating the fixed costs associated with setting up such an effective multilateral approach, and can make such an approach stable because they have an effective mandate to negotiate on behalf of domestic agents and/or the power to regulate their behavior. Negotiators share a common approach to the world and common objectives, minimizing the frequency of zero-sum negotiating situations.

MULTILATERALISM IN TELECOMMUNICATIONS

The conditions outlined above have for many years characterized international telecommunications. Indeed, international telecommunications have been marked by features that strengthened the demand for multilateral cooperation while at the same time making such cooperation easier to achieve.

The Demand for Multilateral Cooperation

Unlike most other goods and services, international telecommunications have virtually always been provided on a joint basis by a domestic and a foreign supplier. This reflects the historical monopoly status of each service provider (telecommunications common carrier) in its domestic market. Given this monopoly, no foreign firm could provide end-to-end service into the domestic market, having to rely on the monopoly provider in the domestic market for the connecting link.

This jointness of supply also has a multilateral dimension. The most obvious instance is when geography requires that traffic between two points must transit a third country, but it also arises because network costs can be minimized by concentrating traffic from thin onto thick routes and by using multiple routing possibilities to handle traffic peaks and minimize network vulnerability. Likewise, for radio transmission media (which until the 1950s were the backbone of long distance communications) frequency coordination was required to minimize interference between transmission sources. Since such interference can occur over a wide geographical area (and indeed for short-wave radio occurs virtually worldwide), efficient use of the radio spectrum requires multilateral procedures for allocating frequencies to uses and users.

Multilateral supply arrangements not only reduce costs but also increase the value of the network to each user. This is because the value of a network to a user depends on how many termination points representing subscribers can be reached through the network. Given that all supply arrangements must be made jointly (because the existence of domestic monopolies rules out end-to-end provision), the value of international service to a subscriber will depend on the number of joint supply arrangements concluded by its national common carrier.

Together these features have increased the importance for each common carrier of securing a broad range of joint supply arrangements. At the same time, the features of these arrangements have been significantly affected by the investment characteristics of telecommunications networks. In particular, telecommunications investment was for many years largely irreversible in character. Reliance on physical connections, notably cables, for high-quality international transmission, and the relatively limited flexibility of microwave operations meant that once in place networks could not be readily reconfigured. Similarly, the hardwiring of signaling and similar characteristics into exchange equipment meant that formats and protocols were very costly to alter after the early stages of equipment design. These features naturally meant that joint supply arrangements had to be negotiated well before service could start, and they created scope for opportunistic behavior once the investments had actually been made.

A further implication of these technical characteristics was that, to be effective, joint arrangements to provide service had to specify a considerable amount of detail. From a purely technological point of view, this detail included the physical nature of the connections to be used and their electronic and signaling properties. But arrangements also had to be made for the collection and division of revenues, for liability in the event of outages, and so on.

In short, international telecommunications services could not efficiently be provided without a large number of joint supply agreements. Each of these agreements had to specify both detailed technical features of interconnection and provide pricing and accounting guidance, and the agreements had to be reviewed in line with changing technology and demand patterns.

These features created clear cope for multilateral cooperation. To begin with, multilateral control of radio spectrum use was essential if radio technology was to be used effectively, both domestically and internationally. And at the same time, multilateralism could standardize key features of joint supply arrangements and thus reduce the transaction costs involved in established international service.

The Supply of Multilateral Cooperation

While necessary conditions for successful multilateralism, these demand side features cannot be considered sufficient. In particular, it remains to be explained both how the mechanisms for cooperation were put into place and why these mechanisms succeeded in meeting their perceived objectives.

It is conventional, in this context, to separate the question of *regime formation* from that of *regime stability*. The first of these concentrates on the question of how the public good aspects of "supplying" international cooperation are overcome, that is, on why participants cooperate rather than adopting free-rider strategies. Hegemonic explanations do not appear to be particularly relevant to the ITU or its subbodies; indeed, over the longer term, these bodies have been distinguished by a relative equality of power among the major (mostly European) participants. Rather, a more plausible approach could draw on Olsen's *logic of collective action*, that is, a link between the public goods supplied by multilateral cooperation in this field and more classical private goods. Two such private goods are of particular importance: First, the rules set down by the ITU and its subbodies may have reinforced the entry barriers confronting potential rivals to the monopoly common carriers. Second, the main benefits of the technical standardization process may have been appropriable only by those direct participants in that process. But important though these factors may be, they have been buttressed by others that made the system particularly stable and effective once established.

To begin with, the participants in the negotiating process were uniquely wellplaced to make credible commitments. The ITU and its subbodies are organizations grouping the telecommunications common carriers; these carriers are vested with the authority which comes from their status as utilities operating in the public interest, and with the power that comes from their monopoly status. Even in the case of the United States, with its multiple international carriers, AT&T had held a dominant position. Moreover, the 1934 Communication Act's delegation of responsibility for international negotiations to the Department of State has been confirmed by subsequent Executive orders, providing a further element of centralization.

Moreover, the negotiating process has clearly not been zero-sum in character. The carriers involved have almost never been in direct competition; rather, the activity's regulatory structure has kept them out of each other's markets. Even in the area of spectrum allocation, where interests have more frequently clashed, the overriding need to minimize signal interference has kept conflict within fairly tight bounds.

Finally, the participants have shared a common culture and outlook to a highly unusual degree. The telecommunications industry has generally been heavily dominated by engineers, with broadly similar training insuring a strong shared emphasis on *network integrity* (that is, the central role of the common carrier network in providing service to users) and an ideology of public service. As a result, the international negotiating teams have been relatively insulated both from considerations of commercial rivalry between countries and the trend toward politicization of the negotiating process.

These features can be viewed as largely structural, but their effects have been bolstered by their conjunction with two additional factors.

To begin with, for many years the development of telecommunications technology was sufficiently evolutionary for change to be accommodated within the gradual process of international negotiation. The delays needed for standard setting were acceptable, as the lag in the pace at which new technologies were introduced did not threaten carriers' competitive position.

Perhaps most importantly, over the long course of their history, the ITU and its subbodies have proved highly capable of avoiding conflict. This is to some extent a question of history. Partly due to the unique institutional features of the telecommunications industry in the United States (the multiplicity of international carriers and the division of regulatory responsibility between competing agencies of government), the ITU was never dominated by the United States; it was consequently spared the crises arising from the United States' changing role in the world economy. The specific financial provisions for the ITU (whereby contributions are self-assessed rather than levied) reinforced the ITU's independence by limiting the institution's reliance on United States funding. But the international regimes has also been successful due to this ability to match regulatory instruments to the features of specific issue areas.

In particular, little reliance has been placed on supranational authority, and the scope for discretionary decisionmaking at an international level has been minimized. Even in the area of radio regulations, which do have a binding character on participants, the use of priority rules and of general principles such as "common use of common frequencies" has substantially curtailed the discretionary power of the International Frequency Registration Board. And excepting the areas such as frequency allotment where common observance was essential to the process's success, decisions have not been formally binding on participants, though in practice they have generally been treated as such.

In short, the historical stability of the international telecommunications regime can be traced to specific features affecting the demand for, and supply of, multilateral cooperation in this industry. In particular:

1. The jointness of supply arising from the monopoly status of each carrier in its home market creates a need for international agreements.
2. The effective provision of international service requires that such agreements be reached with large number of suppliers.
3. Together with the fairly technical nature of these agreements, and the need to revise them in line with changing technologies, this creates scope for significant transactions costs savings from multilateral as against purely bilateral approaches.
4. It has proven possible to organize such multilateral cooperation effectively because monopoly status has conferred significant credibility to participants in the bargaining process: participants shared a common culture and broadly similar objectives; the relatively slow pace of technological change has permitted gradual, negotiated adaptation (notably through standard setting); and the ITU and its subbodies have achieved an unusually close fit between regulatory mechanisms and the features of individual issue areas.

PRESSURES FOR CHANGE

These forces for stability now appear threatened by changes in domestic and international regulatory arrangements. The changes center on the liberalization of entry into the provision of common carriage services, but their effect has been compounded by rapid technological advances.

Changes in the Demand for Multilateral Cooperation

Two fundamental changes appear likely, over the long term, which will affect the demand for multilateral cooperation.

The first of these changes arises from the growing prospect of carriers offering direct end-to-end service, or in other ways minimizing their need for interconnection. As entry into domestic markets is liberalized, foreign carriers may seek to interconnect into the domestic network at the local level rather than at a designated international gateway. Indeed, for the largest corporate users, end-to-end service may be provided, for example, through satellite or digital microwave links.

New technologies are of obvious relevance in this respect. To begin with, satellite and digital microwave technologies appear to reduce the sunk costs a carrier must incur to provide end-to-end service into a foreign market. They consequently increase the "contestability" of telecommunications service both domestically and internationally, further reducing the scope for exclusive joint supply arrangements.

At the same time, the enhanced information- and signal-processing capabilities of digital switching, and of PCM transmission, increase the telecommunications network's flexibility in coping with differing and/or changing formats and protocols. The availability of "black boxes" for protocol and code conversion reduces the need for interface standards to be specified in considerable detail and makes it possible to implement a common service in diverse network contexts.

However, the importance of these developments should not be exaggerated. Despite market liberalization and the availability of new technologies, end-to-end international service is likely to remain a fairly limited phenomenon, primarily an option for the very largest users (though of broader significance in the VAN context). Moreover, inexpensive protocol conversion does not eliminate the advantages of standardization, particularly for smaller users of advanced services. In short, joint supply arrangements are likely to remain the central pattern, but they will be more in the nature of *commercial joint ventures* than of the cooperative structure that was dominant in previous years.

Changes in the Supply of Multilateral Cooperation

The factors altering the demand for multilateral cooperation are also acting on the supply side of the equation. But here their impact appears to be more drastic and immediate. Three trends, each of which makes it increasingly difficult to secure international agreement, stand out.

First, liberalization erodes the bargaining mandate of participants in international negotiations. As the number of common carriers increases, and as the interests of those carriers diverge, the definition and implementation of a national bargaining position becomes more problematic. Moreover, the growing divide between the interests of government representatives, on the one hand, and the (increasingly frequently private) carriers on the other, increases the likelihood that the "soft law" of the ITU will be respected less fully than it once was. These trends are already evident in the United States, the United Kingdom, and, to a lesser extent, Japan.

Secondly, the rapid pace and changing character of technical advance also complicated the negotiation process. The clearest examples can be seen in the area of technical standardization. As technical advance accelerates and comes to depend on technological and scientific bases outside of telecommunications, it becomes more difficult to identify a particular standard as "optimal" in terms of user needs, and current and prospective changes in technology. That standardizing microelectronics-based products requires a finer level of definition (for example, in terms of electrical structure) than was needed for electromechanical or analog technologies, further exacerbating these difficulties. It has therefore become more difficult to both identify the direction technological change will take, which is indispensable if standards are to be set in a dynamic context, and to specify the standards themselves.

The technical difficulties are also compounded by the growing number of actors involved in the standardization process and the conflicting nature of their interests. This is partly a natural consequence of the intersection of the technologies of computers and of communications, which has brought a broad range of suppliers of electronics-based equipment into the telecommunications policy-making process. But it is also a result of the telecommunications equipment industry's response to the regulatory changes of recent years—a response that involves greater independence from the common carriers and an increased reluctance to passively accept the standards these carriers set.

Third and last, it is the change in the carriers themselves which may prove most significant over the long run. As liberalization proceeds, both the engineering confraternity and the ideology of public service give way to a more commercial emphasis. Shared technical objectives become of less concern relative to the competing objectives of the marketplace, a trend the increased scope for end-to-end service can only accentuate. At the same time, the ideological divide between the countries that are liberalizing their telecommunications markets and those that are not inevitably affects the context for multilateral negotiation.

The Overall Outcome

Overall, the factors weakening the basis for multilateralism in telecommunications can be summarized as follows:

1. The prospects for end-to-end service will alter the nature and significance of joint supply arrangements.
2. The greater flexibility of digital technologies reduces the need for detailed multilateral agreements about interfaces and network characteristics.
3. The increasing number of entities involved in providing telecommunications common carriage (including value-added services), and their more arm's-length relation to governments, erode the negotiating mandate of participants in multilateral bargaining.
4. The more rapid pace of technological change, and the digitalization of telecommunications technologies, make it more difficult to set and specify standards.
5. Finally, the increasingly competitive nature of the telecommunications industry is altering its cultural context from an emphasis on shared engineering goals to one based more on commercial values.

The effects of these trends are, of course, far from immediate. They are more in the nature of gradual shifts than of cataclysmic breakdowns. The differing national approaches to liberalization make the process both more complex and more drawnout. Nonetheless, the signs of change are evident.

Technical standardization is perhaps the most relevant area in this respect. The changing technological context, the expanding number of participants, and the growing diversity of their interests have interacted to vastly complicate the standardization process. While it would be inaccurate to say that fewer standards are being set, the following trends are apparent:

1. Standards increasingly lag behind product development, to the point where some standards set at great cost are virtually obsolete by the time they are released (teletext is a case in point).
2. Even when set, standards are formulated in an increasingly loose manner, with a proliferation of options which undermine interconnectability. X25 set the pace in this respect, but similar outcomes appear likely in the definition of the intermediate stages of OSI.
3. As a result of (1) and (2), standards are having a more limited impact on product development than they had in the past; for example, in the evolution of electronic mail.

By no means does this imply international standards are becoming irrelevant; on the contrary, the emerging OSI standards, and even those for 2B + D ISDN, may have a far-reaching impact on carriers and equipment manufacturers. But standardization is no longer the game in town, and new corporate strategies of leap-frogging the standard-setting process are likely to gain in importance.

A second area where the multilateral institutions are under increasing pressure is that of *disputes and settlements*. Bilateral disputes in international communications have been rare; most conflicts involve differing interpretations of CCITT/CCIR regulations, rather than a substantial rejection of those regulations. Indeed, in one famous instance, the senior Secretariat official of CCITT wrote to the Chairman of the FCC to remind him of how a CCITT regulation, which merely had the status of a recommendation, was to be interpreted. But more recently the liberalization of the use and resale of international leased circuits, and the licensing of competitive international carriers, have created new sources of conflict; for example, in charges of traffic diversion, of discrimination in the granting of licenses, or of "whipsawing" with respect to new entrants. These conflicts have not been dealt with through multilateral procedures; rather, they have resulted either in bilateral consultations, as in past conflicts between the United Kingdom and Japan and between the United States and Germany, or through ad hoc multilateral discussion with limited numbers of participants.

These instances of standard setting and disputes settlement highlight the growing gap between the traditional practice of multilateralism in telecommunications and changes underway in the industry structure. It will be a major challenge to adapt multilateral institutions to these trends; for, though multilateral cooperation in telecommunications is both inevitable and desirable, the process will be far less smooth than in the days when the ITU was a "monopolies' club."

Gerard Pogorel is Professor of Economics and Policy Advisor, France Telecom University. He has served as a consultant to OECD, the EEC, and several institutions involved in formulating public policy in France and Europe. His research has focused on communications management and policy, with applications fo the management of technology, transborder data flows, government and business policies in the area of data banks and international communications. He received honors degrees in business administration from the Ecole des Hautes Etudes Commerciales (HEC Paris, 1966) in sociology from the Sorbonne (1970), and holds a Doctorat d'Etat in economics from the Universite de Paris I (1973).

REFERENCES

Keshane, R.O. (1983). The demand for interntional regimes. In S.D. Kramer (Ed.), *International regimes*. Ithaca, NY: Cornell University Press.

Kramer, S.D. (Ed.). (1983). *International regimes*. Ithaca, NY: Cornell University Press.

Chapter 3
Oligopoly in International Telecommunications*

William W. Sharkey

INTRODUCTION

The telecommunications industry is unlike any other industry in one important respect: The fundamental output of the industry is communication, or more broadly, information flows between individuals or among groups of individuals. In order to satisfy any reasonable demands for all such information flows, it is necessary to construct a communications network of great complexity. In principle, this network knows no international boundaries. As the costs of long distance transmission of messages continue to fall, one can expect an ever-increasing demand for communication across international boundaries.

The global communications network is not, however, organized as a natural monopoly. Individual nations, and political jurisdictions within some nations, retain the right to regulate the industry within their boundaries. Even if all political jurisdictions agreed on the proper organization of the industry within their boundaries, there would remain important issues of coordination and control of the total network. This, more or less, represented the status quo prior to the agreement in 1982 between the American Telephone and Telegraph Company and the United States Department of Justice,[1] in which it was agreed that control over long distance communications would be

---

* This chapter represents the author's opinions and not necessarily those of Bell Communications Research, Inc.

separated from control over short haul communications and access to the network.[2] As a result of this agreement there is competition in the United States interexchange communications markets, and it is the policy of the Federal Communications Commission to encourage such competition, and to eventually remove all regulatory restraints in this portion of the network.

The official competition policy in the United States is not the only change in the worldwide status quo in the organization of telecommunications networks. In all countries, technology is advancing at a rapid pace. New technologies, such as fiber optics, offer the potential of a dramatic increase in communication capacity at a reasonable cost. New information-processing technologies offer the prospect of services that have never before been provided. In many respects the industry today resembles the industry nearly a century ago, soon after the invention of the telephone.[3] Together, the impact of changing technologies and the deregulation of certain portions of the global communications network create a new environment for both the managers of telecommunications companies and their regulators or governmental overseers. New problems of coordination and control now arise. Instead of the relatively simple bargaining problems between national monopolies, there is now the potential for complicated strategic interactions among competing firms within a country, which allows competition, and firms outside the country, whose cooperation is necessary in any transnational communication flow.

Economists can contribute to the understanding of these new forms of competition. However, there has so far been relatively little analysis of the problems of deregulation in network industries. The objective of this chapter is to begin to fill this gap. Specifically, I will consider several different models of oligopoly in international telecommunications in which telecommunications firms in two or more countries interact strategically. The goal will be to examine the nature of the equilibria of the resulting noncooperative games, and in particular the potentially undesirable consequences that oligopolistic equilibria may have.

The organization of the chapter will be as follows. Section 2 will consist of an overview of the advantages and disadvantages that might be associated with the growth of competition in telecommunications markets. Section 3 will describe the more technical models of noncooperative competition on some simple international networks. Examples of both leased-line networks and switched services will be considered. In these examples, which assume a constant returns to scale technology, a pure strategy equilibrium can be shown to always exist. That is, a price or quantity choice exists for each firm that maximizes profits, assuming the other firms maintain their chosen strategy. In other networks with two or more firms on one link and prices as the strategic variable, in general only mixed strategy equilibria exist. In these cases each firm has a probability distribution of prices that is optimal against its rivals' strategies, but there is no set of individual prices that satisfies the equilibrium conditions. The nonexistence of pure strategy equilibria is not really surprising when there are fixed costs of production. However, there may also exist only mixed strategy equilibria when marginal and average costs are constant, and when firms compete in different markets. This may happen in a triangular network with competition on only one of the three possible links. It may also happen more generally if firms have a cost advantage in one market but are able to compete effectively in more than one market.

When pure strategy equilibria exist, they are generally inefficient due to insufficient coordination between firms in different countries. These inefficiencies exist even if each country's market is a monopoly. However, in some cases, increased competition in one country has the effect of increasing the equilibrium price in the monopoly market of another country.

AN OVERVIEW OF COMPETITION IN
INTERNATIONAL MARKETS

In the United States prior to the divestiture of AT&T, there was entry by firms in the markets for long distance telecommunications.[4] Today entry into long distance markets continues, entry into local telecommunications markets has begun, and there is the potential for entry into almost all sectors of the industry. In the international arena there are also many possible markets in which competitive entry might occur. International competition might take the form of entry by an affiliate of one nation's carrier into competitive markets of another country. Even if transnational entry does not occur, there are important problems associated with coordination across national boundaries when the policy is procompetitive on one side, and promonopoly on the other side. Finally, the potential for intermodal competition between satellites and terrestrial carrier systems is much greater in international than in domestic markets.

Some have argued that telecommunications markets are rapidly becoming "naturally competitive" (Fowler, Halprin, & Schlichting, 1986; Huber, 1987). The advantages of a competitive marketplace are well known and do not require elaboration here. In the context of a network industry, these advantages include the elimination of cross subsidies that tend to arise in regulated price structures, the incentives for cost minimizing behavior that result from the threat of entry, the incentives for innovation that competitive markets are thought to possess,[5] and the ability of small firms to meet the specialized needs of individual consumers.

The real question, however, is whether workable competition is attainable in an industry such as telecommunications. The argument takes two forms, both related to the rapidly changing technology in the industry. First, advances in both switching and transmission technologies have substantially eroded the traditional arguments for natural monopoly in telecommunications. Second, innovations in the potential uses of the communications network have made it impossible to draw a reasonable boundary between the wholesale service of transporting information and the retail service of providing or enhancing information. Rather than bear the inefficiencies associated with artificial regulatory boundaries, or alternatively, regulatory intervention into largely competitive markets, it is argued that completely unregulated markets would provide to best overall performance.

The factual basis of the first argument is clear. The implications of these changes in transmission and switching appear to work in different directions, however. Technical advances in transmission technologies have occurred at a steady pace for many years since the introduction of coaxial cable and microwave radio, and continuing through the development of fiber optic media. These innovations have lowered the average cost of transmitting a unit of information a given distance, but they have also increased the minimum efficient scale of transmission plant on any given route in the network. That is, innovations in fiber technology do not reduce the average cost of transmission on portions of the network that are optimally served by coaxial cable. As a result the minimum cost network tends to become more "tree-like" as cost reducing innovations in transmission technology proceed.[6] Of course, these tendencies may be counterbalanced in markets in which demand is growing over time. In any case it is true that economies of scale are exhausted on the most dense routes, since it would be prohibitively costly, even if it were feasible, to design a technology which could be fully utilized only on the largest capacity routes in the network.

Advances in digital technologies, and in particular in ISDN (Integrated Service Digital Networks), also have an ambiguous effect. Once a standard set of protocols exists in the public domain, it should be possible for more than one firm to cooperatively provide digital services. Until that time, the creation of ISDN simply raises the fixed costs of serving any collection of nodes.

In this case of switching technologies, the effect of the change is more clearly procompetitive. In any communications network, there is a tradeoff between switching and transmission that must be accounted for in a minimal cost design. Advances in digital technologies have reduced the cost of switching machines overall, and more importantly have made it possible to incorporate advanced technology features into switches of relatively small size. It is likely, therefore, that the network will evolve into one with more end office switches and shorter local loops, where the population density is sufficiently large.[7] When the number of local switches increases, the number of nodes in the overall network increases correspondingly. An increase in the number of nodes generates an exponential increase in the number of possible pairwise connections between nodes. Putting aside the possible economies of coordination and control, the innovations in switching technology appear to be unambiguously procompetitive.

Consider now the innovations in the use of the telecommunications network. Since current generations of telephone switching machines resemble digital computers, it is not surprising that the telecommunications network has the capability to manipulate information as well as to transmit it. The question is whether firms who transmit information should also be allowed to compete with other firms who provide so-called "information services" directly to consumers. The information services market is itself competitive, or more properly, monopolistically competitive by nature. Product differentiation and customized services are essential components of this market.

However, it is possible that transmission firms have a comparative disadvantage in some portions of the information services market due to economies of scope or to their own innovations. If transmission firms are regulated, and particularly if the transmission network is a natural monopoly under the control of a single regulated firm, there are certain to be undesirable incentives for the regulated firm to enter the competitive markets even in the absence of a cost advantage (Brennan, 1987). In a competitive telecommunications market, however, the transmission firms would have no such incentives; they would choose to enter related information markets if and only if there were a cost advantage. Thus, a competitive marketplace could reduce the costs of extensive regulatory accounting constraints whose only objective is to prevent cross subsidy, and at the same time allow firms to enter any markets in which they wish to compete.

I now turn to the arguments that might be made against competition, or competitive entry, into telecommunications markets. These arguments fall into three categories. Competitive markets may be inefficient. They may be unstable. Or they may lead to competitive outcomes that are considered unfair. I will consider each of these possibilities in the remainder of this section. Natural monopoly is the primary argument supporting claims that competitive equilibrium may be inefficient.[8] Natural monopoly in telecommunications may arise from scale economies in transmission, as has already been noted. More importantly, there are substantial economies of coordination that make it more efficient to plan and operate a large multiple link network more efficiently than would be possible with a collection of smaller networks. One example of such an efficiency is the possibility of alternative routing. When demand between two points varies over time, it is possible to overflow unusually large demands from a primary link to a secondary link which has unused capacity. Large networks have more alternative routes, so that a given probability distribution of point-to-point demand can be carried with less overall capacity on a large network than on two or more smaller networks.

Similar economies occur in the planning and expansion of network capacity. If demand is growing over time, it is possible to expand by relatively large increments on selected routes rather than by more frequent and smaller increments on all routes. Finally, a large network is able to take maximum advantage of the scale economies that exist in transmission, even if these are exhausted on the most densely used point-to-point links. For any set of three nodes for which point-to-point traffic exists, it can be shown that when demands are sufficiently small and fixed costs of transmission are positive, the two-link tree network is the minimum cost network. When competitive entry is possible on individual links in the network, it is possible that too many links will be constructed.

Closely related to the technical economies of scale and scope are the economies of coordination in network industries and the economies that result from the internationalization of network externalities (these issues are discussed by Carlton & Klamer, 1983, and Farrell & Solaner, 1986). The need for coordination occurs in virtually all technologically advanced industries. For example, in the computer industry, peripheral devices must be designed to work with each other and with a central processor, both physically through plug-in connec-tions, and electronically with compatible software. In some, but not all cases, competitive markets can achieve a degree of coordination through leadership by a dominant firm, or a bandwagon effect when all firms agree on the same standard. When firms disagree about the proper standard and when technology is rapidly changing, coordina-tion is less likely to be achieved.[9] In network industries, standards are particularly important. Railroads at one time operated on tracks of different gauge, necessitating the costly reloading of freight for shipments on more than one carrier. For a period of time, competitive pressures worked against the agreement on a common standard, as carriers sought to maximize their share of the total traffic (Chandler, 1977).

In telecommunications, protocols are just as necessary. The full establishment of ISDN requires worldwide cooperation of both users and carriers through the CCITT (Consultative Committee on International Telephony and Telegraphy). Because the technology of digital communications continues to evolve rapidly, there will be a need to continually evaluate the existing standards. At some point in the future after a standard has been accepted, it may be desirable to change the standard to take advantage of interim innovations. Even if all parties agree that such a change is worthwhile, however, there may be resistance to change since the benefits of changing a standard are only achieved if most or all parties act in unison. Since the cost to any one firm of organizing a common action may exceed its individual benefit, the old standard may prevail long after it is technically obsolete.

Another aspect of the need for coordination is strategic behavior of competing firms whose interests do not coincide.[10] An example is the sharing of revenue for telephone calls that cross jurisdictional boundaries. If there is one firm on each side of the boundary, the division of revenue can be determined through a bilateral bargaining process. However, once a formula is agreed upon , there may be inefficient incentives to relocate facilities or construct unnecessary new facilities in order to maximize a firm's share of the revenue. If a monopoly firm in one jurisdiction bargains with several competing firms in a different jurisdiction, the competing firms may be forced into a "prisoner's dilemma" in which the incentive to strike an independent bargain compels each to accept a minimal share of the joint revenue.

Closely related to the economies of coordination and standardization, are the economies which result from the internalization of network externalities. The benefit that an individual user obtains from joining a communications network depends on the number or other subscribers with whom he or she can communicate. If competing networks are not universally interconnected, then a new user will prefer to join a large network rather than a small one, although the primary incentive will be to join a network in which there is a community of interest. Firms that control large networks have a higher incentive to attract new subscribers, by charging lower access fees, because the benefits of increased communication possibilities are spread to a larger number of existing subscribers. Even if interconnection is costless, competing networks may refuse to interconnect in order to gain or enhance a competitive advantage.[11]

The second category of possible arguments against competitive telecommunications markets concerns the potential instability of the competitive process. The first, and most straightforward, context in which to describe unstable competition is to determine if something that resembles a traditional competitive equilibrium exists. It is not necessary that all of the technical conditions for existence of competitive equilibrium hold, since these are known to fail in the presence of indivisibilities associated with decreasing average costs. An alternative and more appropriate question is whether there exist "shadow prices," which would guide producers and consumers to reach optimal decisions in a decentralized manner. In the case of a simple triangular network in which scale economies are sufficiently great that only two of the three links are necessary, it can be shown that no such prices exist (Sharkey, 1990). Actual communications networks are much more complicated than the triangular example. However, the example demonstrates that if the minimal cost network is relatively sparse or tree-like, then prices by themselves cannot be relied upon to achieve the necessary coordination among competing firms and their customers.

A second possible source of instability in the competitive process may be examined from the perspective of cooperative game theory. The core of a game represents a set of outcomes that can be achieved by the set of all players, which no subset of players can object to. It is well known that the core contains the competitive equilibrium when the latter exists, but that the core exists in many cases in which there is no competitive equilibrium. The triangular network is one such example. Elsewhere (Granot & Huberman, 1981) it has been shown that core existence can be demonstrated in the class of all "spanning tree" games and some of their extensions. Even though it is possible to find examples of a communications network with a nonexistent core, from this point of view, competition appears to be quite workable.

A final context for determining competitive stability is based upon the properties of noncooperative competition. As noted in the introduction, section 3 is devoted to a study of these issues in some simple examples of competition in international networks. Several of the examples suggest the presence of unstable tendencies due to the nonexistence of pure strategy equilibria.

The final criterion with which to judge competitive markets is the issue of fairness. One unambiguous concept of fairness that has been suggested is that similar individuals should be treated similarly in the marketplace. For example, in a taxation setting, two people with similar incomes and similar characteristics should pay approximately the same taxes. By this standard competitive outcomes in telecommunications markets might have at least the appearance of unfairness, since competition cannot be expected to be equally effective on all parts of a complex network. Densely used routes will attract more firms than sparse routes. Therefore, customers on sparse routes might pay more than customers on dense routes, even if the average cost of production is the same. Furthermore, if competing firms control more than one link in a network, and there are overhead costs that must be recovered, competitive markets will tend to result in low prices on the routes where there is direct competition, and in higher prices on noncompetitive routes.

It is possible that competition on a portion of the network has spillover effects on other portions of the network. The results of section 3 indicate that spillovers exist, but that their effects may be unexpected. In one example, it is shown that increased competition on one link tends to raise the price set by a monopolist on another link, in equilibrium. In another example of a triangular network with competition on one link, there are no prices that constitute a pure strategy equilibrium for monopoly firms on the other two links. Compared to the equilibrium with monopoly on every link, profits of firms on every link fall, but customers do not obtain the full benefits of competitive pricing due to the mixed strategy equilibrium.

NONCOOPERATIVE EQUILIBRIUM IN SIMPLE INTERNATIONAL NETWORKS

Competition on International Leased Line Networks

Because the global telecommunications network includes many separate political jurisdictions, the need may arise for two or more companies in separate jurisdictions or countries to cooperate in the provision of a particular service. International leased or private lines are a particular example. Multinational companies that wish to establish private networks linking branch offices in two or more countries must secure individual pieces of the network from a telecommunications provider in the country in which the given branch office is located.

This section will consider an example of the competition that exists among firms, in two countries, who must cooperatively supply a given service such as a private line network. First consider the case in which there is a single monopoly supplier in each country. It will be assumed that the international service offerings of each firm are unregulated, so that profit maximization is the sole objective of each firm.[12] The firms will be assumed to interact strategically in the choice of the prices p_1 and p_2 that are set in countries 1 and 2, respectively. Each firm will be assumed to have a constant returns to scale technology with constant marginal and average costs equal to c_1 in country i. Let $Q(p)$ = $Q(p_1 + p_2)$ represent the demand function for the international service. The profit function for supplier i, is therefore given by II, $(p_1, p_2) = (p_i - c_i) Q(p_1 + p_2)$. Assume that firms are able to choose any nonnegative price. For any price p_j in country j, country i has a profit maximizing "best response" price p_i, as a function of p_j. A Nash equilibrium of the resulting game consists of a pair of prices $(p^e_1, p^e_2$ such that p^e_i is a best response against p^e_j for $i \neq j$.

As long as the market demand function is reasonably well behaved, it is easy to see that a Nash equilibrium always exists in this example.[13] Suppose, for example, that the demand function crosses the vertical axis at $\tilde{p}$ and that the joint profit function $II(p) = (p - c_1 - c_2) Q(p)$ is concave for $p = p_1 + p_2 \leq \tilde{p}$. It follows that the best response

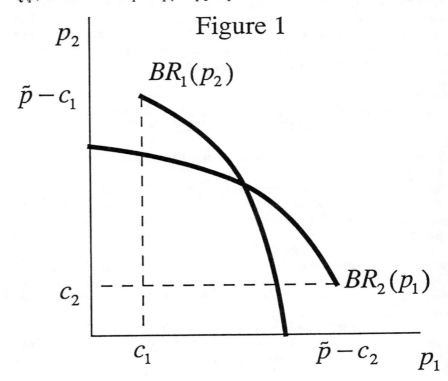

Figure 1

functions are continuous and single valued, and that they necessarily intersect. A typical case is illustrated in Figure 1.

It is not necessarily true that there is a unique equilibrium. For example, the demand and cost functions of Figure 2a generate the reaction functions of Figure 2b for which a continuum of equilibria exist. These conditions might prevail in a market such as international teleconferencing, for there is potentially high value to a very limited number of users. The multiplicity of equilibria is a sign that the simple pricing model does not fully capture the dynamics of competition, since there is a source of conflict regarding the actual equilibrium to use. In a more complicated dynamic game this choice might be made through a bilateral bargaining procedure.

Each of the equilibria is inefficient, in the sense that total profits are less than the joint profit maximum. At any equilibrium point, differentiating the joint profit function and making use of the first

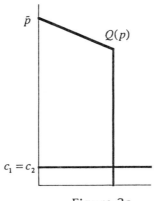

Figure 2a

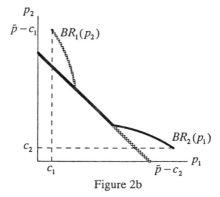

Figure 2b

order conditions which must hold at an equilibrium point leads to the result

$$\frac{\partial(II_1(p_e) + II_2(p^e))}{\partial p_i} = Q(p^e_1 + p^e_2) + (p^e_1 + p^e_2 - c_1 - c_2)Q'(p^e_1 + p^e_2)$$

$$= (p^e_j - c_j)Q'(p^e_1 + p^e_2) < 0.$$

That is, both firms should reduce prices from their equilibrium values in the interests of joint maximization. Of course, any joint maximizing prices (p^*_1, p^*_2) are not equilibrium prices. Neither firm is willing to take account of the additional profits that accrue to the other firm following a price reduction.

Suppose now that competition is allowed in one of the countries. As long as average costs are constant and firms compete only by choosing prices, the number of competitors in the competitive country does not matter, if there are two or more. Thus, suppose that firm 1 represents the monopoly supplier in one country and that firms 2 and 3 represent the competitive suppliers in the other country. All firms compete by choosing prices and the low price supplier in the competitive country will be assumed to serve the entire market. In the event that both competitive suppliers choose the same price, they evenly divide the market. Profit functions are then given by

$$II_1(p_1,p_2,p_3) = (p_1 - c_1)Q(p_1 + Min\{p_2,p_3\})$$

$$II_i(p_1,p_2,p_3) = \begin{cases} 0 & \text{if } p_j < p_i \\ (p_i - c_i)Q(p_1 + p_i) & \text{if } p_i < p_j \\ (p_i - c_i)Q(p_1 + p_i)/2 & \text{if } p_i = p_j \end{cases}$$

Firms in the competitive country behave as ordinary competitors in a Bertrand pricing game. If marginal costs in the competitive country are equal, $c_2 = c_3 = c$, then with suitable restrictions on the demand function, a unique pure strategy equilibrium is given by $p^e_2 = p^e_3 = c$ and

$$p^e_1 = c_1 - \frac{Q(p^e_1 + c)}{Q'(p^e_1 + c)} .$$

It is possible that the equilibrium price in the monopoly country either rises or falls with the introduction of competition in the other country. The result depends on the particular demand function. With linear demand functions, the supplier in one country always raises price in response to a reduction in the price set by the other country. In this case the price reduction brought about by competition is partially offset by a price increase in the monopoly country.

Competition in International Switched Service Markets

International switched services present another set of issues regarding coordination and competition between telecommunications suppliers in different countries. In contrast to private line offerings, which make use of dedicated facilities, switched services can be purchased by any subscriber in the home country and transmitted virtually anywhere in the world. The costs of carrying a given message are therefore shared by at least two suppliers in different countries. The revenue from an international message, however, is collected entirely by the supplier in the originating country. As a result, a set of institutional arrangements have arisen to compensate a supplier in one country for message transmissions which originate and are billed in another country. While the actual arrangements are complex, they involve, in essence, a negotiated accounting rate which is used to compensate the destination country for the costs which it incurs. This rate, which differs from the tariffed rate in either country, is applied to the difference between incoming and outgoing minutes of use during a given time period (Eward, 1985, p. 399).

This practice has led to concern over possible abuses that might arise when competitive entry occurs in one country, but not in the other. Depending upon whether the monopoly country was a net originator or receiver of a particular kind of service, the supplier in that country would have the incentive to set either a low or a high accounting rate. If there were several competing suppliers in the other country, it would be possible for the monopoly country to effectively impose its desired rate by selectively directing services to the competitive supplier offering the most favorable terms. This practice has been described as *whipsawing*. The straightforward remedy for this potential abuse is for the government in the competitive country to act as the agent of the suppliers in the negotiation of the accounting rate. It will be assumed that the government in the competitive country accepts this responsibility.

Taking these institutional assumptions as a starting point, this section will describe the nature of the outcomes which can be expected when firms in two countries interact in the choice of prices for an international switched service. Initially, assume that there is only one supplier in each country. Let $Q_i(p_i)$ represent the demand function for traffic which originates and is billed in country i. Let p^a represent the negotiated accounting price, which is assumed to be determined independently of the setting of prices in either country. As in the previous section, it will be assumed that marginal and average costs are constant and equal to c_i in country i.

Profit functions are therefore given by

$$\Pi_i(p_1, p_2) = p_i \, Q_i \, (p_i) - c_i \, [Q_1(p_1) + Q_2(p_2)] - p^a[Q_i(p_i) - Q_j(p_j)]$$
$$= (p^a - c_i) \, Q_j(p_j) + (p_i - c_i - p^a) \, Q_i(p_i)$$

From the second equation in the profit function, it is clear that, while profits depend upon prices in each country, there is no room for meaningful strategic interaction. Each supplier has a dominating strategy that consists of setting price equal to the price p_i^e which maximizes $(p_i - c_i - p^a) \, Q_i(p_i)$, assuming that demand functions are such that a maximum exists. This strategy is a best response to any price p_j that might be set by the other country. Thus, each firm sets a price, which would be a profit maximizing price if the true marginal costs were $c_i + p^a$. If marginal costs are equal in each country and the accounting price is set equal to this common value, the equilibrium prices also maximize the joint profits. If the accounting rate exceeds the marginal cost of both suppliers, then, as in the previous section, the partial derivatives of the joint profit function are negative at the equilibrium prices, and so a price reduction by each supplier would be mutually beneficial.

The introduction of competition in one country does not change the equilibrium price chosen in the monopoly country, since p_i^e was shown to be a dominating strategy. If country 1 is the monopoly country, and two or more firms in country 2 compete as Bertrand competitors, with identical marginal costs, it is easily demonstrated that the unique equilibrium price in the competitive country is given by

$$p_1^e = c_l + p^a - \frac{(p^a - c_l)q_1(p_1^e)}{Q_2(p_2^e)}$$

If $p^a > c_i$ then necessarily $p_2^e < c_i + p^a$. If in addition Q_2 is small relative to Q_1 it is possible that $p_2^e < c_i$.

Competition in a Market with Fixed Costs*

One aspect of competition in a network industry is the possibility of entry into new markets by firms who are established in other markets. An example is the airline industry, as planes can be easily switched from one city pair route to another. This form of competition has been described as *hit-and-run entry,* and it has been argued that, under some conditions, the potential competition of this form is

---

* This section, and the following one, describe in summary form results that appear elsewhere (Sharkey, 1987).

sufficient to lead to "competitive" outcomes even if there is room for only one active carrier on a given route (Baumol, Panzer, & Willig, 1982). Markets in which hit-and-run entry is possible are known as *perfectly contestable markets.*

Most telecommunications markets do not satisfy the contestability conditions due to the required investments in right of way, which are required for terrestrial transmission facilities. International telecommunications markets, however, may satisfy the contestability conditions. Transmission by satellite makes it possible for a carrier to switch instantly from one route to another, as long as there is sufficient capacity. Another example is the potential competition between international record carriers and voice carriers. At one time the technologies of hard copy transmission and voice transmission were sufficiently different that each kind of carrier was restricted to its own market. Newer technologies, such as packet-switching networks, are being adopted by both kinds of carrier. Thus, the same facilities can be used to enter each other's markets.

This section will consider a model of hit-and-run entry when there are positive, but possibly small, fixed costs associated with entry. These may be due to the need to advertise a firm's intention to compete. The fixed costs may also be due to foregone profits in an alternative market that must be temporarily abandoned in order to compete in a new market. Production may require physical plant, which embodies large fixed costs that are "sunk" costs only to the extent that the capital is unavailable for other uses. The degree to which the fixed costs are sunk costs is therefore related to the length of the period during which a commitment is necessary in order to effectively compete in a given market. This time interval may depend on the responsiveness of consumers, the complexity of the product or service, and so on. In any case, the interpretation will be that a fixed cost equal to f must be incurred if a firm chooses to compete, but can be avoided if the firm chooses not to compete. There will be two firms who can potentially serve a given market. If either or both of the firms choose to enter the market, competition will be in terms of prices. If both firms are in the market at the same time, then the firm quoting the lowest price serves the entire market, and the firm that loses the market pays the fixed cost but does not receive any revenue. In the event of a tie, it will initially be assumed that both firms share the market equally.

In order to represent the market as a game, it is necessary to describe the exact sequence of moves, and the payoffs to each player at the end of every possible sequence. It is also necessary to specify the information available to each player at each point at which a decision or move must be made. There are two possible representations, depending upon the information that is available to each player at the time a pricing decision must be made. In each case the two players simultaneously choose whether or not to enter the market, not knowing the choice of the other player. Then the player or players in the market choose a price, without knowing the choice of the rival player. The game forms differ only in whether or not each player can observe the entry decision by the rival before choosing a price.

Suppose first that the entry decision is observed before prices are chosen. This game is easily solved by a backward induction argument.[14] If both firms decide to enter the market, they will compete in prices according to the standard model of Betrand price competition. Prices are forced down to marginal cost, and the net profit of each firm is equal to $-f$. If only one firm is in the market, it is free to choose the monopoly price, p^m, knowing that the other firm has already chosen not to enter. If neither firm chooses to enter, they both earn net profit equal to 0. It is easily demonstrated that there are two pure strategy equilibria corresponding to the entry by exactly one firm. In both cases, price in the market remains at the monopoly price. This result holds for any value of fixed cost $f > 0$. Therefore, potential competition, or hit and run entry, is of no value in disciplining a market which is accurately described by this game form.

It is interesting to observe that for this game, a regulated minimum price would improve market performance. Suppose that neither firm is allowed to charge a price less than p^{min} in the second stage game after entry decisions have been made. Then if both firms choose to enter, the unique equilibrium requires both firms to choose p^{min}. If net profits of each firm at p^{min} are greater than zero, then p^{min} is the unique equilibrium strategy for the entire game. If p^{min} is sufficiently small, profits of each firm will be close to zero in this equilibrium, and the market price will close to the minimum possible price.

The more interesting case is the one in which firms must make a decision to enter or not, and then choose a price if entry was chosen, all without observing any of the decisions of the rival firm. In this game, it is convenient to use a different tie-breaking rule in the event of equal prices. Suppose that one firm, designated the "incumbent," serves the entire market in this case.[15] The strategy sets for each player consist of the sets $S_1 = \{out, p_i\}$ where p_i represents the strategy "enter the market and choose price p_i."

It is easy to see that a pure strategy equilibrium does not exist for this game. If both firms choose to not enter the market, then both would like to enter at the monopoly price p^m. If both firms choose to enter the market, then the high price firm, or the nonincumbent in case of a tie, would prefer to to choose {*out*} or to choose a lower price. If only one firm chooses to enter at a price $p_i < p^m$ that firm would prefer to raise its price to p^m. If there is one firm in the market charging a monopoly price, the outside firm would prefer to enter at a slightly lower price.

The nonexistence of a pure strategy equilibrium indicates that neither firm is able to choose an equilibrium price, taking any particular price of the rival firm as given. Thus there is a fundamental uncertainty on the part of each firm about the exact price that will be chosen by the rival firm in equilibrium. This uncertainty is described by a mixed strategy equilibrium, which specifies a probability distribution of strategies for each firm. As in a pure strategy equilibrium, neither firm would wish to alter its probability distribution, given the equilibrium probability distribution of the rival.

In this example there are two mixed strategy equilibria. In the asymmetric equilibrium, firm 1, the incumbent, always chooses to enter the market and chooses a price in the interval $[p^f, p^m]$. p^f represents the zero profit price, net of fixed costs, and p^m represents the monopoly price. Firm 1 chooses the monopoly price with positive probability, which depends on the size of the fixed costs f. For all prices less than p^m the probability distribution function $F_1(p)$ is continuous, so that there are no mass points. In equilibrium, firm 2, the rival, chooses to stay out of the market with positive probability (equal to the probability that firm 1 chooses p^m) and to choose prices from the

This example is consistent with the assumptions necessary for a perfectly contestable market, except for the existence of a positive fixed cost f. If f is small, the probability that the incumbent firm chooses the monopoly price, and the probability that the rival firm chooses to stay outside of the market is also small. Similarly the cumulative distribution functions $F_1(p)$ and $F_2(p)$ converge to the pure strategy choices $p_1 = p_2 = p^f$, as f approaches zero. In this way the equilibrium in this model confirms the prediction of the contestable market hypothesis, which is that potential entry is sufficient to force the market price to the zero profit point. However, if fixed costs are founded away from zero, the zero profit p^f is never chosen with positive probability by either firm, and although both firms continue to earn zero expected profits, any price up to and including the monopoly price can be expected in the market.

Figure 3 illustrates the probability distribution functions for the incumbent player, with various values of fixed costs, and a market characterized by a linear demand function and constant marginal cost

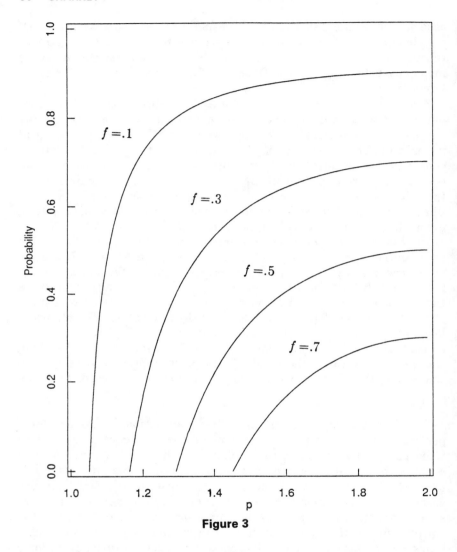

Figure 3

of production equal to 1. In this market, maximum profits equal to 1 are attained at a price of 2. The zero profit price p^f depends on the size of the fixed costs f. For all prices p between p^f and 2, the probability, $F_{(p)}$ that the nonincumbent chooses a price less than or equal to p is shown. The function F_i is discontinuous at $p = 2$, and the size of this discontinuity represents the probability that the incumbent chooses the monopoly price (and also the probability that the non-incumbent chooses to not enter the market). Thus, for small fixed costs, the probability of choosing a price far from their zero profit price is small.

For large fixed costs, the probability that the incumbent chooses the monopoly price, and the probability that the nonincumbent chooses to not enter, becomes large. This equilibrium therefore resembles the equilibria in the two-stage game analyzed previously. It is also true, in this example, that the conditional probabilities of choosing a price less than or equal to p, given that entry occurs and that the monopoly price is not chosen, are the same for both players.

In the case of moderate to large fixed costs, both equilibria also have a disturbing property, that is characteristic of some but not all, mixed strategy equilibria. In equilibrium, the incumbent firm and the nonincumbent firm both expect to receive zero profits, on average, if the other firm uses its equilibrium strategy. However, both firms could earn zero profits with certainty by choosing a certain pure strategy, even if the other firm does not use its equilibrium strategy. The incumbent can do so by choosing $p_1 = p'$, and both can do so by choosing to remain out of the market. These strategies are clearly not in equilibrium. The incumbent would prefer to charge any price $p_1 > p'$. However, if the incumbent behaves as a Stackleberg leader, then it is possible to choose a mixed strategy that will earn positive profits, and for which the best response of the non-incumbent is to remain outside of the market. Any mixed strategy F for which $F(p) > F_1(p)$ for all $p \in [p', p^m]$ will have this property. There is no comparable leadership advantage for the nonincumbent. Therefore, it is plausible to argue that the incumbent can earn positive profits by acting as a mixed strategy Stackleberg leader.

The implications of the two models described in this section are straightforward. When firms compete in a single market using prices and entry decision as strategic variables, the outcomes depend critically on the timing of moves and the magnitude of the fixed costs that can be avoided by choosing not to compete. If the entry decision can be observed before prices are chosen, then the only (subgame perfect) equilibria consist of one firm choosing to enter the market at a monopoly price, and the other firm choosing not to compete. If the entry decision the pricing decision are made simultaneously, then there is a unique equilibrium, and the outcome is more competitive. If fixed costs are small then this equilibrium may be indistinguishable from the contestable market prediction. However, if fixed costs are large, the market equilibrium is less satisfactory. Although both firms earn zero profits in equilibrium, the equilibrium depends on mixed strategies on the part of both players. Prices higher than minimum average cost are set in every realization of the probabilistic mixed strategy. In this example, there is an additional problem due to the slight asymmetry involving the definition of incumbency. The safe strategies do just as well for each firm as the equilibrium strategies, but the incumbent can earn positive profits by acting as a Stackleberg leader.

Competition Between Foreign and Domestic Suppliers

The previous section considered the equilibria in a market in which a prospective entrant was required to bear a fixed cost before competing. This section will also consider competition between suppliers in different markets. However, instead of a fixed cost, it will be assumed that each market is supplied by a constant marginal cost technology. The suppliers in each market supply an output or service that is identical in every respect, except for location or other characteristic that defines the market. It will be possible for a supplier in one market to compete for customers in another market, but each supplier will be assumed to have an advantage in its own market. This advantage will take the form of a cost differential on each unit of output that is sold.

There are a number of cases in which this form of competition is reasonable. One obvious example, which has received some attention in the literature, is spatial competition.[17] When two firms supply a product for which transportation costs must be incurred in reaching final consumers, location is an important competitive advantage. Every firm can compete for the customers of every other firm, but each firm has a local monopoly due to the lower cost of supplying nearby customers. If products are differentiated in quality or attribute, the spatial model is also appropriate, since firms must choose a location in characteristics space.

In the telecommunications industry there are other examples of potential competition across market boundaries. A communications network generally has many different possible paths linking a given pair of points. If individual links in the network are owned by different suppliers, it is possible for two firms to compete for the same point to point traffic. Each carrier will have an advantage in serving some of the point to point markets. Consider a triangular network linking three different countries, or within a country with each link owned by a different supplier. Suppose that one link is highly competitive, while the other two are controlled by a single supplier. Each of the monopoly suppliers is able to compete for the other link's traffic by using the competitive link as a partner. However, there is a symmetric cost advantage for each carrier in its own market if the cost of using the competitive link is greater than zero.

In addition to the literal locational or network examples, there are more general instances of cross market competition in the telecommunications industry. Technology which is well suited to one kind of communications traffic may be adaptable, at a reasonable cost, to a different kind of traffic. International record carriers and international voice carriers might compete in this manner. New information-processing technologies such as videotext are also examples of this form of competition. While similar in technology, different kinds of data services require specialized knowledge of the market, which confers a cost advantage on the primary supplier.

This section will investigate the equilibria in a model in which two firms in different markets compete in the above manner. It will be assumed that the firms have constant marginal cost technologies. Each firm can compete for customers in the other market but there is a cost penalty of $c > 0$ for each unit sold outside the firm's own market. Competition is in terms of prices. The supplier quoting the lowest price, including the penalty c, supplies the entire output in either market. In the event of a tie, that is, $p_i = p_j + c$, it will be assumed that each firm serves only its own market.

In this example, there may exist a pure strategy equilibrium, if the cost advantage is sufficiently large. A pure strategy equilibrium can exist only if each supplier serves its own market, and at least one of the suppliers charges a monopoly price. Each firm can guarantee positive profits by choosing a price equal to c. Thus, no firm will allow its rival to undercut its price in equilibrium. But if (p^e_1, p^e_2) is an equilibrium pair, the low-price firm will always prefer to raise its price a small amount, unless it is already at the monopoly price. Therefore, if a pure strategy, equilibirum exists, it is unique and can be characterized by prices (p^e_1, p^e_2) such that firm i sets a monopoly price, $p^e_i = p^m_i$, and $p^e_i < p^e_j < p^e_i + c$. The low-price firm sets a monopoly price. The other firm sets a price at which neither firm wishes to capture the other market. If the cost advantage c is large, then it is more likely that both firms will set a monopoly price.

If c is sufficiently small, but positive, then no pure strategy equilibrium can exist. Since $|p^e_j - p^e_i| < c$ at any candidate for equilibrium, it follows that at least one firm would prefer to reduce its price and capture both markets. Whenever a pure strategy equilibrium fails to exist, there is a unique mixed strategy equilibrium. This equilibrium has a particularly simple and intuitive form. Firm i chooses prices from an interval $[p^l_i, p^h_i]$. It can be demonstrated that $p^h_i - p^l_i \leq 2c$ and that $p^h_i - p^l_i < 2c$ only if $p^l_i = p^m_i$. Furthermore, $p^l_i \leq p^l_j + c \leq p^h_i$. At a mixed strategy equilibrium, each player receives the same expected payoff at each of the prices that could be used in equilibrium, given the equilibrium distribution of prices of the opposing player. Therefore, the distribution functions $F_i(p_i)$ and $F_j(p_j)$ must be chosen to equalize the expected profit of the opposing player over the relevant interval. If firm i chooses the price $p^l_j + c$ it is certain that neither player will underprice the other, given the above inequalities. Therefore, the expected profit of player i is positive and is equal to the profit of serving the home market at the price $p_j^i + c$.

If market i is strictly larger than market j then $p_i^i > p_j^i$. If market i grows in size, so that the profit function Π_{ii} shifts up at every price, p_i^i unambiguously increases. p_j^i may either increase or decrease, but it is certain that the profits of firm j increase.

These results suggest that a small country can be a more effective competitor to a large foreign supplier than a country of comparable size, assuming that suppliers in each country are freely allowed to enter each other's territory. The reason is that small markets allow only small profits in equilibrium. The firm in the larger market must therefore charge prices that are sufficiently low that entry is unattractive. These results hold for both pure and mixed strategy equilibria. If the markets in two countries are comparable in size, firms in each market earn higher expected profits than in the asymmetric case. Of course the price interval in the mixed strategy equilibrium must be chosen low enough relative to c, so that undercutting of prices is not a profitable activity.

CONCLUSIONS

The objective of this chapter has been to describe the nature of competition in markets like telecommunications which have been traditionally organized as regulated monopolies or public enterprises. In the largely nontechnical section 2, a broad survey of known results was attempted. One of the implications of that survey is that relatively little is actually known about the kind of outcomes that can be expected as more and more countries allow competitive entry into certain telecommunications markets. These markets are by no means perfectly competitive, but they may not be natural monopolies either, in most countries, due to changing technologies and overall growth in the markets.

Section 3 represents an attempt to describe the oligopolistic equilibria that can be predicted in simple markets, which have some of the characteristics of actual telecommunications markets. Sections 3.1 and 3.2 were concerned with inefficiencies in international competition for leased line and switched service markets. In the private line market, these inefficiencies are inevitable, unless there are binding agreements not to use equilibrium pricing strategies, due to the failure to coordinate pricing decisions. In switched service markets, the inefficiency arises only if the negotiated accounting rate is set at too high a level above marginal costs. It was pointed out, however, that a country with a large net inflow of traffic has an incentive to bargain for a high accounting rate.

Sections 3.3 and 3.4 were concerned primarily with the mixed-strategy equilibria that arise when firms in one market compete with firms in another market. Mixed-strategy equilibria arise when there is either a fixed cost of entry or a cost advantage of serving the home market. As these costs go to zero, the equilibria in both cases converge to the pure strategy, zero profit, Betrand equilibria. If it is reasonable to suppose that the costs are significant, one should expect that competition of this type would be fundamentally unstable. The instability or unpredictability of competitive outcomes is not necessarily a bad thing. One must examine the alternatives. If the alternatives are monopoly conditions in each market, then competition unambiguously lowers prices and enhances consumer welfare. If the alternatives are regulated or state-owned monopoly, then no definite conclusions can be drawn at this level of generality. Even though the profits of firms are limited by competition, the mixed-strategy equilibria involve the use of prices higher than would be necessary to attain these profit levels. In the fixed cost example all prices up to the monopoly price can be chosen by either firm. In the example of the cost advantage, the prices are confined to a definite interval, whose size depends on the size of the advantage.

REFERENCES

Baumol, W.J., Panzer, J.C., & Willig, R.D., (1982). *Contestable markets and theory of industry structure.* New York: Harcout, Brace, Jovanovich.

Brennan, T.J. (1987). *Cross-subsidization and discrimination by regulated monopolists.* Discussion Paper EAG 87-2, Economic Analysis Group, U.S. Department of Justice.

Brock, G.W. (1981). *The telecommunications industry: The dynamics of market structure.* Cambridge, MA: Harvard University Press.

Carlton, D.W., & Klamer, J.M. (1983). the need for coordination among firms, with special reference to network industries. *University of Chicago Law Review, 50,* 446–465.

Chandler, A.D., Jr. (1977). *The visible hand: The managerial revolution in America business.* Cambridge, MA: Harvard University Press.

d'Aspremont, C., Gabszewicz, J.J., & Thisse, J.F. (1979). On Hotelling's 'stability in competition' *Econometrica, 47,* 1145–1150.

Eward, R. (1985). *The deregulation of international telecommunications.* Dedham, MA: Artech House.

Farrell, J., & Solaner, G, (1986). *Competition, compatibility and standards: The economics of horses, penguins and lemmings* (Working Paper 8610). Berkeley, CA: Department of Economics, University of California.

Fowler, M.S., Halprin A., & Schlichting, J.D. (1986). 'Back to the Future': A model for telecommunications. *Federal Communications Law Journal, 38,* 145–200.

Gal-Or, E. (1982). Hotelling's spatial competition as a model of sales. *Economics Letters, 9,* 1–6.

Granot, D., & Huberman G. (1981). Minimum Cost Spanning Tree Games. *Mathematical Programming, 21,* 1–18.

Huber, P.W. (1987). *The geodesic network: 1987 report on competition in the telephone industry.* Washington, DC: U.S. Government Printing Office.

Hotelling, H. (1929). Stability in competition. *Economic Journal, 34,* 41–57.

Sharkey, W.W. (1990). Cores of games with fixed costs and shared facilities. *International Economic Review, 30,* 245–262.

Sharkey, W.W. (1987). Models of competitive telecommunications networks. *Annales des Télécommunications, 42,* 620–628.

ENDNOTES

[1] U.S. vs AT&T, U.S. District Court for the District of Columbia, Civil Action No. 74–1698.

[2] The divestiture of AT&T resulted in the creation of seven regional companies to own and manage the 22 former Bell Operating Companies. The territory of each operating company was divided into one or more Local Access and Transport Areas (LATAs), which defined the boundaries between local communications and long distance communications. At the time of divestiture, it was thought that inter-LATA toll markets would be open to competition between AT&T and new entrants, while intra-LATA toll and local access would remain regulated monopolies. Since the divestiture, some states have allowed competition in intra-LATA toll. There has also been competition in local access markets, particularly from large users.

[3] In the United States, the first patent for the telephone was granted to Alexander Graham Bell on March 3, 1876. In 1893, when the Bell patents expired, the industry was opened to competition at the local level, although the Bell companies retained a monopoly in long distance communications. Before the Communications Act of 1934 established the era of regulated monopoly, AT&T had the potential to enter markets outside of the traditional telephone industry, such as radio broadcasting and sound motion pictures.

[4] There was successful entry into the markets for terminal equipment even earlier. Today equipment markets seems to be highly competitive. However, this chapter will not be specifically concerned with equipment manufacturing or retailing.

[5] Both the theoretical and empirical support for this point are ambiguous, however.

[6] The minimal cost network is a (spanning) tree if there is only one possible path between every pair of nodes. If all of the costs involved in transporting messages were fixed costs, then the minimum cost network is necessarily a tree.

[7] This argument is made by Huber (1987). Since the local loop does not make use of shared capacity to a significant extent, there are relatively few innovations in transmission which are likely to counterbalance the reductions in switching costs.

[8] Whether or not the telecommunications network in any given country is a natural monopoly is an empirical question. In any case, for obvious political reasons, the worldwide network cannot usefully be considered a natural monopoly. The intention of this chapter will be to disregard the traditional arguments for natural monopoly in network industries, so as to focus more closely on the properties of competitive markets. Therefore, the case for natural monopoly will only be sketched at this point.

[9] The competing formats in videocassette recorders is an example.

[10]Section 3 contains several examples of strategic interaction on simple networks. In most of the examples, the noncooperative equilibrium is inefficient to the firms or their customers, and in some cases both.

[11] In the early years of this century, competing local telephone companies in the United States typically refused to interconnect, and AT&T for a time refused to provide long distance service to nonaffiliated companies. Brock (1981) documents the growth of the industry from the invention of the telephone up to the time of the divestiture of AT&T.

[12] The firms need not pursue profit maximization as an overall objective. However, if there is a budget constraint, or a welfare objective other than profit maximization overall, it is assumed that profits from the international market are sought in order to subsidize domestic markets.

[13] In this example there always exists an equilibrium in "pure strategies" as defined above. In some of the examples to be considered later, pure strategy equilibria do not exist. However, there will always exist at least one equilibrium in "mixed strategies" in which players are allowed to choose a probability mixture of the pure strategy choices and payoffs are in terms of expected profits.

[14] Equilibria which can be solved in this way are known as *subgame perfect* equilibria.

[15] This assumption is natural for telecommunications markets that were at one time served by regulated or public monopolies, which are later challenged by potential entrants. It will be shown that, in equilibrium, ties cannot occur with positive probability. Every equilibrium of the asymmetric game can also be shown to be an equilibrium of the symmetric game in which the market is shared equally when prices are equal. In the latter game there there is one additional equilibrium.

[16] There is also a symmetric equilibrium in which both firms use the equilibrium strategy of the rival firm. In a symmetric version of the example, with no advantage of incumbency, there are two asymmetric and one symmetric equilibria.

[17] The original contribution is due to Hotelling (1929). d'Aspremont, Gabszewicz, and Thisse (1979) pointed out an error in Hotelling's analysis and observed that a pure strategy equilibrium need not exist in a model of spatial competition. Gal-Or (1982) computed the mixed-strategy equilibria in the standard Hotelling model. This section generalizes these results to essentially arbitrary demand functions.

Chapter 4
Financial Agreements for Jointly Provided International Services*

Robert E. Dansby
Thomas R. Luciano

INTRODUCTION

The purpose of this chapter is to discuss changes in the market for international voice telecommunications that are having substantial influence on pricing and settlements policies. Traditional international monopoly markets are evolving into competitive ones. In response to customer needs, vendors that once offered a single class of service have begun to offer multiple services with several pricing options. These market-driven changes in the international telecommunications market imply that service providers and regulatory authorities must re-assess their policies regarding accounting rates. The view that prices should conform to accounting rates must be replaced by the philosophy that accounting rates must reflect the underlying cost structure. The view that accounting rates are somewhat static must be replaced by a willingness to change accounting rates in response to relevant market factors. These considerations lead us to focus on specific options whose implementation would improve the structure of accounting rates.

* Dansby is Division Manager of Regulatory Economics and Pricing Theory at Bellcore, and Luciano is District Manager of International Settlements at AT&T. The initial draft of this chapter was written while both authors were employed by AT&T. The views and opinions expressed herein are those of the authors and do not necessarily reflect either Bellcore or AT&T policy.

59

International accounting rate practices are discussed in the first section. In the next section properties of efficient and incentive compatible settlement rates are derived. Practical impediments to the implementation of efficient accounting rates are discussed in the section after that, and suggestions are made for a "reasoned" movement toward incentive compatible and efficient accounting rates. The latter two sections also give insights regarding the implementation of time of day collection and accounting rates. The final section gives a summary of principle conclusions.

INTERNATIONAL ACCOUNTING RATE PRACTICES

Since international calls use jointly owned equipment and facilities of at least two countries, some equitable methods must be negotiated to compensate the partners fairly for the value each adds to the partnership. International service is provisioned on a partnership basis between two administrations. Each shares the risk and provides half the investment. But because revenue from jointly provided service may not be billed in equal shares by the administrations, a form of revenue sharing through an accounting rate process has been established. Accounting rates can serve this role to the extent that they result in a fair two-way division of revenue between the partners. The United States is represented in accounting agreements with over 200 countries. Responsibility for transmission of U.S. telecommunications traffic resides with private voice and record carriers. Each of these has its own arrangements for settling international traffic, although the FCC's Uniform Settlement Rates Policy on parallel routes constrains the freedom of the International Record Carriers (IRCs) to reach separate accounting rates with their correspondents without obtaining an explicit waiver from the Federal Communications Commission. In general, the policy requires an "equal division" of the accounting rate between the U.S. carrier and the foreign administration. It also specifies that each carrier must use the same accounting rates for like services on parallel routes. Although some competition has emerged for voice traffic from the U.S. to other international points, the FCC has determined that the Uniform Settlements Rates Policy also applies to voice carriers.

For every minute of calling, an administration or carrier collects a charge from its customers called the *collection rate*. The sum of all charges to its customers is called *total billed revenue* (TBR). While most of this revenue comes from domestic originating international calls (i.e., *sent paid* messages), additional monies are derived from calls which are *received collect*. The accounting rate is a mutually negotiated value for a minute of calling between two countries, to be divided equally between the parties. If two countries have equal collection charges, the accounting rate would normally be set at the same level. In general, the collection rate of the respective countries are not equal. In such cases an accounting rate is usually chosen which falls somewhere between the two collection charges.

By convention and by international agreement the settlement rate, which equals one-half the accounting rate, denotes one correspondent's share of revenue for a predetermined measure of usage, generally a minute. A correspondent's retained revenue equals collected revenue minus net settlements, which in turn is defined by the relationship:

$$(\text{Collection rate minus Settlement rate}) * (\text{Outbound Minutes})$$
$$\text{Plus}$$
$$(\text{Settlement rate}) * (\text{Inbound minutes}).$$

This represents a correspondent's share of the two-way traffic revenue stream that results from the joint provision of international telephone service. The net financial impact on an administration of the settlements process is determined by the accounting rate and the ratio of outbound to inbound traffic. Obviously, these factors and their rates of growth are very important in the bilateral negotiation of the terms and conditions of international joint agreements. The accounting rate is the critical component of these agreements. Its value is determined bilaterally by assessing the key variables in provisioning two-way service, i.e., price, two-way traffic flows, costs, growth rates, volumes, diversification, transit considerations, and competitive alternatives.

EFFICIENT AND INCENTIVE COMPATIBLE ACCOUNTING RATES

In order to better serve customer needs, it is important that international carriers implement market driven pricing strategies. This applies both to domestic and international collection rates as well as international accounting rates. Many considerations are involved in the determination of appropriate market driven prices. We focus on two fundamental considerations that influence the character of market-driven accounting rates: (a) incentive compatibility and (b) marginal-cost-based prices. Incentive compatibility refers to the principle that both parties to an international interlinking agreement should find the terms and conditions of such agreements "satisfactory." The negotiation process should allow both parties to influence the final terms and conditions in such a way that both parties (a) have an incentive to adhere to the terms of the joint agreement without need for monitoring, and (b) are better off when the joint agreement is implemented. The economic properties of such accounting rates are discussed in the following section.

Marginal-cost-based prices (or incremental cost pricing) have been recognized in the public utility industry as the preferred pricing philosophy. In the international arena, the application of this philosophy means that collection rates must reflect underlying costs, and accounting rates should parallel collection rates. The structure of international traffic patterns implies that both collection rates and accounting rates should embody a peak/off-peak price structure. Aspects of a peak load structure for international rates are also discussed below.

Bilateral Contracts for International Services

In this section we analyze a bilateral model of international accounting rate negotiation which embodies elements of noncooperative and cooperative strategic decision making. The results discussed in this section summarize the principle results, as applied to international telecommunications agreements, of Dansby (1987).*

Basic Assumptions of Model

We assume that each international carrier chooses its collection rates independently. Accounting rates are jointly negotiated in discussions between two international carriers. We assume there are two firms, which respectively face demand curves $Q_i(p_i)$, $i = 1,2$. The firms are further distinguished by differences in their production technologies. In order to supply international calls to its domestic customers, the domestic carrier must use its own facilities and must rely on its foreign correspondent to employ its production facilities to complete each international call.

Suppose each international carrier knows the overall demand Q_i for its domestic originating calls. However, each firm is uncertain of the proportion, a_i, of calls with a foreign destination. Thus, each firm is uncertain about the level of demand that will require use of its

---

* This paper is a general economic analysis of incentive compatible joint production contracts.

facilities and the production facilities of its foreign correspondent. We assume that firms know the distribution of (a_1, a_2); the joint distribution of these random parameters is $f(a_1, a_2)$. Firm i observes the parameter a_i but does not observe realizations of the parameter $a_j, j \neq i$. It is also assumed that neither firm can observe the other's aggregate demand. This structure is a fair representation of the international telecommunications demand environment.

Firm i's cost of production is denoted C_i. We assume that C_i has three arguments. The first is the total quantity, Q_{ii}, of domestic calls, calls that originate and terminate in country i. The second is the quantity, Q_{ij}, of outbound traffic, international calls that originate in country i and terminate in country j. The third is the quantity of inbound traffic, international calls originating in country j and terminating in country i; Q_{ji}. Thus the cost function for firm i is:

$$C_i(Q_{ii}, Q_{ij}, Q_{ji}) =$$
Cost (Domestic Orig. Calls, Outbound Calls, Inbound Calls).

The total output produced, and the total production cost incurred by each firm, will depend on the arrangements made to gain access to facilities needed to complete international calls. The focus of this discussion is the use of negotiated production agreements as a mechanism for consummating joint production. If the firms do not enter into a joint production agreement and have access only to their own domestic production facilities, then each will only be able to accommodate $(1-a_i)$ percent of its total demand. Hence, in the absence of a joint production agreement, the firms will earn profits given by

$$\pi_i = [(1)-(a_i)P_iQ_i] - [C_i((1-a_i)Q_i,0,0)].$$

In this case firm i's optimal pricing strategy is a contingent price schedule, which maximizes profit in each state a_i:

$$P_i^*(a_i) = [C_i(1-a_i)Q_i,0,0) / Q_{ii}] * [E_i / (E_i-1)]$$

where E_i is the price elasticity of demand.

If firm i implements its optimal contingent price schedule, then its profits will be a nonincreasing function of a_i. If the demand Q_i is perfectly elastic, the optimal profits are unaffected by changes in the proportion of international calls. If the market is not purely competitive, then optimal profits will decrease as the proportion of international calls increase. Therefore, firm i has greater incentive to secure access to the correspondent's facilities as realizations of high values of a_i become more likely.

Though realizations of a_j do not directly affect the profits π_i^* of firm i, absent a joint production agreement, a_j does influence firm i's incentive to enter into a joint agreement. If Q_j is not perfectly elastic, then firm j suffers declining profits as a_j increases. Thus, firm j's optimal profit using the contingent price schedule and only its own production facilities will be small if large values of a_j are realized. To this extent a_j affects firm i's incentive to enter a joint production agreement; firm i will be in a stronger bargaining position if large values of a_j are more likely.

Moreover, the bargaining power of an administration is influenced by the ratio of its outbound to domestic traffic. The incentives of international carriers to enter a joint production agreement are better understood by an examination of their profits in that regime. Let π_i denote the profits of firm i when it operates under a joint agreement. The joint production agreement is a contract specifying that each carrier makes an irrevocable commitment to cooperate in the joint completion of international calls that originate (terminate) in the respective countries. The joint production agreement provides that firm i will supply facilities and service to complete inbound calls, Q_{ji}, and will gain access to its correspondent's facilities and service to complete Q_{ij} of its outbound international calls. The joint production agreement also establishes a set of accounting/settlement rates. Without loss of generality, we let T_i denote firm i's net payments. The net payments of firm i are assumed to depend on the level of outbound and inbound calls, i.e., $T_i = T_i(Q_{ij}, Q_{ji})$. If firm i's collection rate is P_i then profits from its international operations will be

$$\pi_i = P_i Q_i(P_i) - C_i(Q_{ii}, Q_{ij} Q_{ji}) - T_i(Q_{ij}, Q_{ji})$$

when the joint production agreement is operative.

Contract Negotiation

The firms have an interest in negotiating the terms of the joint production agreement so as to be incentive compatible. The process by which contract terms are negotiated must reflect each firm's independent discretion in the choice of their respective collection rates. Therefore, we assume the negotiation process has two stages. In the first stage each firm independently selects an optimal contingent price schedule assuming a given value of its potential correspondent's outbound calls. This calculation yields an optimal payoff function and price reaction function for each specification of the contract's terms. In the second stage, this data is used as the basis for bargaining on contract terms.

Thus, if the market demand for firm i is perfectly elastic, its optimal contingent pricing schedule would set its collection rate equal to the marginal cost of producing its own output, plus the marginal net payments made under the joint production agreement. Price would be set above marginal total cost if demand is not perfectly elastic. The deviation of price from marginal total cost is influenced by the proportion of inbound to outbound calls. More precisely, the optimal collection rate P_i^* equals the elasticity factor $E_i / (E_i - 1)$ times: (a) the marginal cost of total domestic originating calls, plus (b) the proportion of outbound calls times the marginal net cost of international calls.

Optimal collection rates are intrinsically related to, and dependent on, marginal (incremental) accounting rates. When the optimal contingent prices P_i^* are substituted into the profit functions π_i, we obtain, for each firm, a function that describes its "best" payoff if the contract terms are T_i. The best response payoff functions are the basis for negotiation in the second stage. Each firm enters this second stage knowing the greatest profits, π_i^*, it can achieve for various inbound and outbound call levels and for any proposed net payment schedule. Negotiations in the second stage will result in the specification of a net payment schedule, T_i.

Bilateral Accounting Rates

A general characterization of the incentive compatible net payment schedule is that the marginal settlement rate for outbound calls, plus the marginal settlement rate for inbound calls, must be equal to the marginal cost of firm j's outbound calls minus the marginal cost of firm i's outbound calls. This relationship arises because optimal accounting rates impact optimal collection rates, which in turn are based on marginal cost. Hence, if the marginal cost of the joint output Q_{ij} is constant for both firms, then the joint production agreement is incentive compatible if and only if the net payment (settlement) schedule is given by

$$T_i(Q_{ij}, Q_{ji}) = \{[\partial C_j / \partial Q_{ji}]^* Q_{ji}\} - \{[\partial C_i / \partial Q_{ij}]^* Q_{ij}\}.$$

When incentive compatible accounting rates are employed, collection rates will have the least deviation from marginal production cost and will be efficient. Another important property of incentive compatible net payment schedules is that there exists an incentive compatible joint production agreement only if the total marginal cost of outbound calls is invariant to changes in the level of inbound calls. Hence, incentive compatible contract terms are always achievable if both firms have strictly linear cost functions. However, incentive-compatible joint production agreements may not exist if both firms have production technologies that exhibit economies of scope or weak production complementaries in the joint production of inbound and outbound calls.

A Basic Model of Peak Load Prices for the Overseas Market

This section discusses a generalization of the Boiteux-Steiner Model of Peak Load Pricing, which incorporates the principal aspects of the overseas telecommunications market. This is a summary of results in Dansby (1983). The principal considerations relevant to developing peak load prices for the overseas market may be summarized as follows:

1. Capacity decisions regarding certain components of the overseas network are made exogenous to the domestic pricing process, and several types of capacity, with different cost characteristics, are used to provide service;
2. Prices may have an asymmetric impact on domestic and foreign originating demands;
3. Revenues must be divided according to a separations formula that affects pricing incentives; and
4. Profits from the service must satisfy regulatory constraints.

The traditional peak load pricing literature provides guidance concerning some of these considerations, but not all. Consequently, Dansby (1983) generalized the traditional peak load models in order to prescribe optimal peak load prices for the overseas market. This section describes the simplest model that incorporates these considerations and analyzes their impact on the optimal peak load prices. The simplest model is one of bilateral trade between two regions. In this basic model, we first examine the impact of foreign demands and the settlements process on optimal peak load prices.

Suppose that q_j and q_j^f are respectively the U.S. originating and foreign originating demands in period j between the U.S. and the foreign region. Let P_j and P_j^f respectively denote the marginal price per call in period j for calls between the U.S. and the foreign region. It is assumed that q_j and q_j^f depend on P_j and P_j^f. However, in keeping with the Boiteux-Steiner framework, the cross elasticities of demand q_j and Q_j^f with respect to prices in other periods are assumed to equal zero.

For a single bilateral market, with two pricing periods, the public utility's profit from trade with a foreign correspondent during the two periods is

$$\pi = [P_1 - b]q_1 + [P_2 - b]q_2 - b[q_1{}^f + q_2{}^f]$$
$$- [T][(q_1 + q_2) - (q_1{}^f + q_2{}^f)] - BK.$$

Here we assume that the settlement rate for calls to the foreign region is a uniform rate T. Thus, the quantity $[T][(q_1 + q_2) - (q_1{}^f + q_2{}^f)]$ is the net settlement that must be paid to the communication concern of the foreign region, since $[T][q_1{}^f + q_2{}^f]$ is received from the region and $[T][q_1 + q_2]$ must be paid to them. The domestic public utility incurs an operating cost $b[q_1{}^f + q_2{}^f]$ when serving the foreign originating demands. It is assumed that B is the marginal capital (capacity) cost of the domestic public utility; B includes the marginal cost of both cable and switching capacity, since these facilities are assumed to be expanded in fixed proportion. Any costs associated with the transmission of overseas calls through the domestic network are assumed to be included in the marginal operating cost.

The optimal peak load prices and capacity of the overseas carrier are assumed to maximize welfare, which equals profit plus consumer surplus subject to a constraint that demand not exceed capacity. Using standard methods, it is found that the optimal peak load prices and capacity are characterized by:

$$P_1^* = [b + B + T] + \{[b + B\text{-}T]*[(\partial q_1{}^f/\partial P_1) / (\partial q_1/\partial P_1)]\};$$
$$P_2^* = [b + T] + \{[b\text{-}T]*[(\partial q_2{}^f/\partial P_2) / (\partial q_2/\partial P_2)]\}; \text{ and}$$
$$K^* = q_1 (P_1^*, P_2) + q_2^f(P_1, P_2^*)$$

where period 1 is taken to be the peak period.

These results show that the optimal peak period price depends on marginal operating and capacity cost but also on the accounting rate and the relative elasticities of foreign and domestic originating demands, i.e., the ratio R_j of $\partial q_j{}^f/\partial P_j$ to $\partial q_j/\partial P_j$. This ratio appears in the pricing formula because it gauges the impact of a price change on total traffic in a particular period. A price increase will cause total usage in a period to: (a) decrease if the ratio is greater than minus one; (b) remain unchanged, though the percentage of foreign originating demand increases, if the ratio equals minus one; and (c) increase if the ratio is less than minus one. Therefore, the ratio R_j reflects the adjustments in prices that must be made in response to foreign originating demands. The optimal peak and off-peak prices depend in the same way on the accounting rate; i.e., both prices are functions of $[T] (1 - R_j)$, $j = 1,2$. This quantity may be viewed as the price adjustment induced by the settlements process. Hence, a lower accounting rate: (a) leads to lower optimal collection rates if $R_j < 1$, (b) leads to higher optimal collection rates if $R_j > 1$, and (c) has no impact on the optimal collection rates if $R_j = 1$. In the case being considered, the incentive compatible accounting rate would equal: (a) marginal operating cost in the off-peak period, and (b) marginal operating plus marginal capacity cost in the peak period.

If marginal production costs are constant, then incentive-compatible accounting rates will have a peak/off-peak structure, and the associated peak/off-peak collection rates will be efficient in the Boiteux Steiner sense. Consequently, when settlement rates are not incentive compatible, the optimal peak and off-peak prices may be significantly different from the Boiteux-Steiner prices. The optimal prices for this simple bilateral trade model are equal to the Boiteux-Steiner prices if and only if $T + [b+B-T]R_1 = 0$ in the peak period and $T + [b\text{-}T]R_2 = 0$ *in the off-peak period; this implies that the prices are equal only if* $b/(b+B) = (R_2-1)/(R_1-1)$. However, the optimal capacity level satisfies the Boiteux-Steiner rule that capacity be equal to demand in the peak period.

To illustrate the potential magnitude of the price differences, we consider some special cases. Suppose that any U.S. price change has no effect on total usage in either period, i.e., $R_j = -1$ for $j=1,2$. Then the optimal peak and off-peak prices are, respectively, $P_1^* = T$ and $P_2^* = T$. Hence, if prices do not affect total inbound plus outbound usage, even though price increases may reduce U.S. originating demands in each period, the optimal pricing strategy is to charge the accounting rate. If the foreign originating demands are unaffected by U.S. prices, then the optimal peak and off-peak prices equal the Boiteux-Steiner prices plus the accounting rate; i.e., if $R_j = 0, j=1,2$, then $P_1^* = (b+B)+T$ and $P_2^* = b+T$. If the foreign originating demands respond in exactly the same way to U.S. price changes as U.S. originating demands, then the optimal prices are exactly twice the Boiteux-Steiner prices; i.e., if $R_j = 1, j=1,2$, then $P_1^* = 2(b+B)$ and $P_2^* = 2b$.

The optimal prices may also be stated in terms of the ratio r_j of foreign originating to domestic originating demand in each period, if the ratio of foreign to domestic demand in period j is invariant to the price level. This would be consistent with the widely discussed view that "every domestic originating call begets a certain number of foreign originating calls." Consequently, if the "every call begets a call" hypothesis is empirically true, then the optimal pricing rules are

$$P_1^* = [(b+B) * (1+r_1)] + [T * (1-r_1)]$$
$$P_2^* = [b * (1+r_2)] + [T * (1-r_2)].$$

An important implication of these results is that if $T > b+B$, then the optimal peak and off-peak prices increase as the fraction of foreign to domestic demand decreases. This again emphasizes the need for incentive compatible accounting rates and collection rates which have the "correct" economic relationship.

ACCOUNTING RATE POLICY IMPLICATIONS

This section provides insights regarding implementation strategies that achieve some efficiency gains while balancing concerns about disruptions in the cash flows of correspondents. To understand the financial aspects of telephone message accounting, one must consider the following elements, country by country:

1. the level of the collection charges to the customer (called *collection rates*);
2. the level of the accounting charges established between telephone administrations (called *accounting rates* and/or *surcharges*);
3. the units of time chosen to record and account for the calling volumes (expressed in seconds, minutes, or pulses);
4. the total calling volume of telephone traffic, in each direction, between administrations (expressed in messages and/or minutes);
5. the rates of exchange between national currencies or the medium of exchange used in settlements (called *exchange rates*); and
6. the costs involved in the establishment and maintenance of telephone service (such as circuit and switching costs, access charges, or operator handling expenses).

The interaction among these elements determines the revenue available for settlement.

Some aspects of the efficient/incentive compatible settlement rate structures discussed above may not be practical to implement in the short run. For example, the FCC's Uniform Settlements Policy for Parallel International Communications Routes (CC Docket No. 85-204) requires "all carriers providing the same service to the same foreign point to have the same accounting, settlement, and division of tolls arrangements with the foreign administration." Our examination of efficient settlement schedules has shown that: (a) collection and accounting rates should be based on marginal cost, and (b) accounting rates should reflect the structure of collection rates.

Consequently, it may be efficient and incentive compatible for two U.S. carriers to have different accounting rates with a foreign correspondent if the U.S. carriers have different cost structures. The desire to promote competition would in fact be consistent with the implementation of different settlement rates if the firms have different costs. In the long run, as competitive pressures drive out high-cost providers, all firms might be expected to have similar costs. But certainly this could not be expected in the short run. As a result of these considerations, we conclude that current regulations of the FCC and of foreign administrations may limit the ability of international carriers to adopt fully efficient and incentive-compatible collection and accounting-rate structures. It is important, therefore, that international carriers identify pricing strategies that improve the status quo while continuing to move toward market-driven price structures.

Various international carriers have begun to implement time-of-day collection rate structures. The results in previous sections indicate that efficiency requires that a time of day structure also be implemented for accounting rates. Since time-of-day accounting rates will depend on traffic patterns, it is clear that these may differ among carrier pairs. This is appropriate, since settlement rates should reflect the underlying marginal costs incurred by parties to the joint agreement. Implementation of incentive compatible settlement rate structures may require departures from status quo accounting-rate practices. Typically, the settlement rates for partners to a joint agreement are identical. That is, the settlement rates applied to inbound and outbound calls are the same. Incentive compatibility may require that different settlement rates be applied to inbound and outbound calls, respectively. The extent of any differential treatment will depend on the relative marginal costs of the partners. Perhaps even more problematic is the fact that incentive compatible settlement rates themselves may change as the levels of inbound and outbound traffic changes. This will occur if the cost functions of the partners exhibit increasing returns to scale. Finally, existing settlement rates generate levels of revenue for correspondents that foreign PTTs may be reluctant to give up.

Toward Implementation

Some of these impediments to changes in the structure of settlement rates may require enactment of FCC and Foreign Administration policy changes. However, some movement toward incentive compatible and efficient settlement rates can be achieved within the current regulatory framework. The accounting rate level, and structure, need to evolve to match the new, more competitive, environment. Without a change, accounting rates could retard the development of efficient, low-cost international telecommunications.

Accounting rates were initially established as a revenue sharing mechanism; the accounting rate level was set at a level approximately equal to the collection rate that each administration charged. The initial flat rate structure of the accounting rate was consistent with the flat rate collection rate structure that administrations initially used for international services. The relationship of the accounting rate to the underlying unit cost of provisioning international service was closely aligned when the initial accounting rate levels were set. For a monopoly environment, this philosophy was appropriate and equitable and insured a financial commitment by both partners. The following principles are useful guides in today's more competitive environment:

* Establish accounting rate levels that reflect the character of the underlying cost of provisioning the international;
* Establish accounting rate levels and structures that create financial incentives for both partners to stimulate and grow their respective markets profitably; and
* Establish accounting rates that provide fair compensation to the partner terminating the imbalance of traffic.

Establish Accounting Rates Based on Underlying Costs

As collection rates decline, it is necessary that accounting rates be adjusted in order to maintain the efficiency of pricing relationships in the international market. Efficiency in the market can only be attained if collection rates and accounting rates bear the correct economic relationship. The nature of these relationships were discussed in Section 3. Optimal collection and accounting rates were shown to be dependent on marginal production costs, and the ratio of foreign to domestic originating demands in a particular period.

The downward adjustment of collection rates in response to declines in the cost of providing international service dictates that accounting rates also be reduced if the market is to remain efficient. When accounting rates are set equal to the efficient collection rates, the most profitable arrangement is to then set efficient collection rates, irrespective of the ratio of inbound to outbound traffic. However, when accounting rates are not equal to the efficient collection rates, the ratio of inbound to outbound traffic has a substantial influence on the most profitable collection rate. If the ratio of inbound to outbound traffic is less than one, i.e., $r < 1$, then the accounting rate should be reduced as the collection rate declines. If $r > 1$ then the accounting rate should be increased as the collection rate declines. In any bilateral market, the ratio of inbound to outbound traffic will be greater than one for one partner and less than one for the other partner, the only exception being the case of balanced traffic. Consequently, the implementation of more efficient accounting and collection rates creates significant tradeoffs in the division of cash flows associated with international telecommunications.

If one administration responds to lower facility costs by reducing collection rates, and the other does not, then a greater two-way traffic imbalance between the two administrations is likely. The failure of administrations to negotiate lower accounting rates as facility costs decline is a national issue. If one administration refuses to reduce the accounting rate to reflect changes in costs, it can effectively impose significant disincentives for the other administration to reduce their collection rates.

Matching Accounting Rates with Collection Rate Structures

Historically, accounting rates implemented revenue sharing by establishing an accounting rate that was typically the average of the collection rates charged by two cooperating international carriers. Those initial collection rates were also flat rate, and not time-of-day sensitive. As time-of-day rates were introduced in the domestic collection rate plans of each international carrier, these rate structures were also applied to international tariffs. The savings that accrued to each carrier from lower facility costs and greater network efficiencies were the basis for lower collection rates. However, in most cases the accounting rate agreements were not changed to reflect the time-of-day nature of the collection rates. The time-of-day collection rate structures have proven to be effective pricing strategies that moved traffic away from peak periods and stimulated off-peak call volumes. The flat rate nature of accounting rates may create disincentives to promote outbound traffic growth. As an example, the U.S.–Japan market has a flat accounting rate of $1.17 in each pricing period. The revenue margin (defined as the difference between the collection and accounting rate) varies across periods; this is due in part to the flat accounting rate. The off-peak revenue margins are negative. In contrast, the U.S. to U.K. market has a time-of-day accounting rate structure of $1.06 peak and $.76 off-peak. The revenue margin in the U.S./U.K. market is $0.26 in the off-peak period.

Moving the accounting rate to a time-of-day structure should be the preferred accounting rate structure where collection rates are time-of-day sensitive. This is in keeping with a revenue sharing concept that would reflect lower accounting rates where lower collection rates are deemed appropriate. The principle that should be followed is that the accounting rate should parallel the structure of the collection rate. Implementation of both lower accounting rates and time-of-day structure are the most appropriate steps for aligning the financial arrangements between partners.

Recognize the Need for Transition

Another factor that weighs heavily in the decision to move to more efficient financial arrangements is the impact of reducing the net settlement amount. For a two-way traffic stream that is relatively balanced, moving to a peak/off-peak structure results in small net changes in the net settlement. As the traffic stream becomes heavily imbalanced (i.e., one partner generating more than 60% of the two-way traffic), a change in the accounting rate to time-of-day will significantly change the net settlement. In a growing traffic stream this impact can be mitigated by recognizing the need to make a gradual transition to the appropriate structure and establish several interim rate steps over a two or three year horizon to reach the end objective. Moving away from the conventional application of a 50/50 flat rate accounting-rate structure should also be considered, if it can achieve a more market oriented financial structure. One accounting-rate structure recently agreed to in the U.S. was a growth-based accounting-rate structure. This has a two-tier accounting-rate structure. The current accounting-rate level would be maintained for traffic that does not exceed historical levels in a test year. Traffic greater than test-year demand levels, from either administration, would be settled at the lower accounting rate. This approach would achieve settlement stability and provide incentives for both partners to stimulate additional traffic.

SUMMARY

In summary, accounting rate levels and structure have significant influence on collection rate strategies of international telecommunications carriers and foreign administrations. The evolving nature of the international telecommunications market suggests that fundamental changes in FCC policies affecting collection and accounting rates need to be examined. Based on this analysis, we recommend that the actions under consideration should include:

- A general lowering of accounting rate levels to reflect the lower unit cost in provisioning international services.
- Developing accounting-rate structures that match the collection rate structure of the two-way market; and
- Recognize the transitional problems of achieving an efficient settlement structure by adopting, where necessary, nonconventional financial arrangements that provide incentive for both partners to grow and stimulate two-way traffic.

REFERENCES

Dansby, R.E. (1983). *Peak load pricing of overseas telecommunications* (Bell Laboratories Working Paper #263). Murray Hill: Bell Labs.
Dansby, R.E. (1987). *Negotiated production agreements* (Working Paper). Unpublished.

Chapter 5
Reconciling Competition and Monopoly in the Supply of International Telecommunications Services: A U.S. Perspective*

Evan Kwerel

INTRODUCTION

In recent years the United States has been pursuing a policy of promoting competition in common carrier telecommunications. The greatest changes have occurred in the domestic market, with the most dramatic of these represented by AT&T's divestiture of its local operating companies on January 1, 1984. The international market has been changing as well. Until 1984, AT&T was the only company providing international message telephone service (IMTS). Now MCI International (MCII) and U.S. Sprint have entered the market and additional carriers are legally free to enter. Private, facility-based competition is emerging as well. The PTAT-1 fiber-optic cable is in

* Portions of this chapter were adapted from Kwerel (1984). The opinions and conclusions expressed here are those of the author and do not necessarily reflect the policies or views of the Federal Communications Commission or any other organization or individual. I wish to thank Tom Spavins for helpful comments and suggestions; Peyton Wynns and Ken Stanley for germane data; and Michele Harding for able editorial assistance.

service between New York and London, and the Federal Communications Commission (FCC) has granted a Cable Landing License to Pacific Telecom Cable for a private fiber optic cable between the United States and Japan.

A strong case can be made for deregulating the domestic interexchange market.[1] The argument is premised on the assumption that the government will assure all interexchange carriers cost-based access to local exchange facilities. Competition is not expected to replace regulation in preventing local exchange carriers from exploiting their market power. In the international market, however, the U.S. government does not have such regulatory authority over similar bottlenecks. The position of foreign telecommunications authorities (relative to U.S. carriers who wish to interconnect) is analogous to that of U.S. local exchange carriers (relative to interexchange carriers), except that foreign telecommunications authorities are not subject to the jurisdiction of any U.S. governmental body. If promoting competition in the international market is to be in the U.S. interest, some mechanism must be developed to prevent foreign telecommunications authorities from using such competition to extract undue concessions from U.S. international carriers.

The remainder of the chapter is organized as follows: The second section provides background information on the international telecommunications market. The third section makes the general theoretical argument that there are no benefits to be had from promoting competition for a single component of a product when another essential component is supplied by a monopolist. In the case at hand, the product is international telecommunications and the monopolized component is access to foreign countries. The fourth section considers the implications of relaxing some of the simplifying assumptions used in the third section. The fifth section examines FCC policies designed to address the problem raised in the third section and considers long-term strategies to move towards cost-based pricing of international telecommunications. The final section provides a summary and conclusions.

BACKGROUND

All countries exercise control over international access to their domestic telecommunications networks by requiring an operating agreement of any carrier who wishes to establish a communications link from abroad. Operating agreements specify the type of service to be provided and the terms for sharing revenues between carriers.

Most governments generally delegate the responsibility for the provision of all telecommunications and postal services to a single government agency or public corporation, the administration of posts, telegraph, and telephones (PTTs). Japan and the United Kingdom have recently privatized their telecommunications agencies and are introducing limited competition. While these are positive developments, they do not signify the end of bottlenecks in these countries. In Japan Kokusai Denshin Denwa (KDD) and its competitor will continue to depend on NTT for local distribution. In the UK, Mercury has the right to terminate calls itself, but it is still highly dependent on British Telecom (BT) for local distribution. The significance of these local bottlenecks depends in large part on the terms on which these new international carriers can obtain access to the local networks. Furthermore, the fact that only a single competitor is being allowed to enter these markets may limit the effectiveness of competition in bringing price down to cost.

In the United States, international telecommunications is provided by the private sector, but statutes and regulations have traditionally limited competition by restricting firms to specific segments of the market. For example, a 1943 amendment to the Communications Act prohibited Western Union from providing international service. Western Union divested its international services and accepted this restriction in exchange for the right to acquire its only competitor in the provision of domestic service. Another artificial barrier was created by the 1964 FCC decision to forbid AT&T from providing international record (data, telex, telegraph) service. This restriction protected the international record carriers (IRCs) from competition by AT&T.[2] In recent years Congress and the Commission have been reversing such anticompetitive policies. In 1982 the FCC eliminated the regulatory segmentation of the voice and record markets, allowing AT&T to enter the record market and the IRCs to enter the voice market (US FCC, 1982). In 1981 Congress enacted the Record Carrier Competition Act of 1981. This allowed Western Union to re-enter the international record market and facilitated the entry of the IRCs into the domestic record market (U.S. Code, 1981).

In the voice market, local exchange carriers (LECs) control access to local networks. All interexchange voice carriers pay the same "access charges" to local exchange carriers for calls originating or terminating on a LEC's facilities. The access charges are the same whether a call is domestic or international. The FCC strictly regulates access charges and has been striving to assure that they are cost based.

AT&T is still the predominant supplier of international message telephone service (IMTS), but MCI International and U.S. Sprint now offer service to a significant number of foreign countries. Given that competition in the IMTS market only began in 1984, it is not surprising that AT&T still carries most of the traffic. In 1985 (the most recent year for which data are available), AT&T carried 98.5% of all IMTS minutes and earned 99.1% of the revenues for all IMTS traffic (excluding Canada and Mexico) originating or terminating in the Continental US (see Table 1). AT&T's market share was several points smaller, however, in certain important markets such as the UK.

Table 2 compares AT&T's international message telephone service minutes and revenue with its total interstate (domestic plus international) switched minutes and revenue. In 1985, 7% of AT&T's interstate switched minutes were international. The overseas market, which is the international market excluding Canada and Mexico, comprised 4.2% of AT&T's business when measured in the same way.

Table 1. Market Shares International Message Telephone Service Originating and Terminating in the Continental United States* 1985 (Minutes and Revenues in Millions)

| | ALL OVERSEAS POINTS** | | | | | |
| | Outbound | | Inbound | | Total | |
	Minutes	Revenues	Minutes	Revenues	Minutes	Revenues
AT&T	2,136.0	760.7	1,217.6	996.4	3,353.6	1,757.1
	98.3%	99.0%	98.9%	99.2%	98.5%	99.1%
MCII	29.4	6.6	11.9	7.3	41.3	13.9
	1.4%	0.9%	1.0%	0.7%	1.2%	0.8%
US Sprint	8.4	0.7	2.0	1.1	10.4	1.8
	0.4%	0.1	0.2%	0.1%	0.3%	0.1%
Total	2,173.8	768.0	1,231.5	1,004.8	3,405.3	1,772.8

| | UNITED KINGDOM | | | | | |
| | Outbound | | Inbound | | Total | |
	Minutes	Revenues	Minutes	Revenues	Minutes	Revenues
AT&T	283.2	179.0	281.9	135.5	565.1	314.5
	94.6%	95.1%	96.7%	96.9%	95.7%	95.9%
MCII	11.1	7.0	7.9	3.7	19.0	10.7
	3.7%	3.7%	2.7%	2.6%	3.2%	3.3%
US Sprint	5.0	2.2	1.6	0.7	6.6	2.9
	1.7%	1.2%	0.5%	0.5%	1.1%	0.9%
Total	299.3	188.2	291.4	139.9	590.7	328.1

*The table was derived from data contained in US FCC (1987, Section 1, Tables 4, 6, and 8). Revenue is "net revenue" after settlements, that is, tariff revenue plus settlements received from PTTs minus settlements paid to PTTs.

**Overseas points exclude Canada, Mexico, Alaska, Hawaii, Puerto Rico, U.S. Virgin Islands and Guam.

International message telephone service accounted for nearly 10% of AT&T's switched revenue, and overseas revenue comprised 7.3% of all switched revenue. These revenues are net of international "settlements," and apply only to switched services, e.g. IMIS, telex, and telegraph. That is, they represent the revenues AT&T retained after making all payments to foreign correspondents for terminating messages abroad and collecting all receipts from foreign correspondents for terminating messages in the U.S. For private leased channel services, the total charge for renting a private line is the sum of the charges established by the PTT and the U.S. carrier. For switched services, however, only the carrier originating the call collects revenues from a customer. The price the originating carrier charges for switched services is known as the *collection rate* or tariff rate. Since

Table 2.   AT&T Interstate Switched Service   1985

	Minutes (millions)	Revenues ($ millions)	Revenues/Minutes ($/minute)
INTERNATIONAL			
Overseas IMTS*			
Outbound	2,136.0	760.7	0.36
Inbound	1,217.6	996.4	0.82
Subtotal	3,353.6	1,757.1	0.52
Canada**			
Outbound	832.9	189.3	0.23
Inbound	845.4	177.5	0.21
Subtotal	1,678.3	366.8	0.22
Mexico			
Outbound	336.1	105.2	0.31
Inbound	170.0	54.0	0.32
Subtotal	506.1	159.2	0.31
Total International	5,538.0	2,283.1	0.41
ALL SWITCHED SERVICES***	79,327.0	24,122.2	0.30
PERCENTAGE OF ALL SWITCHED			
Overseas Share	4.2%	7.3%	
International Share	7.0%	9.5%	

*Overseas data are derived from US FCC (1987, Section 1, Table 4). Overseas IMTS excludes traffic with Canada, Mexico, Alaska, Hawaii, Puerto Rico, U.S. Virgin Islands, and Guam.

**Data for Canada and Mexico are from AT&T (letter from Ray M. Robinson to Ken Stanley of the FCC, May 8, 1987).

***Revenues for "all switched services" are from AT&T ("FDC Report for the 12 Month Period Ended 12/31/85, Schedule 1A"). Minutes for "all switched services" are from AT&T (letter from D. J. Culkin to A. Halprin, Chief of the Common Carrier Bureau, FCC, November 24, 1986).

international communications are provided using facilities owned by both the originating and terminating carriers, some mechanism is generally needed for the originating carrier to compensate the terminating carrier for the use of the latter's facilities. The settlements process is designed to do just that.

The *accounting rate* is a single, negotiated rate carriers use in dividing revenues instead of the collection rate, which varies depending on which end originates a call. The accounting rate, and the terms for dividing it, determine the price each carrier must pay the other to terminate messages. For example, if the accounting rate were $1.00 per minute and it were divided 50–50, the U.S. carrier would have to pay the PTT $.50 for each minute of calls originating in the U.S., and similarly, the PTT would have to pay the U.S. carrier $.50 per minute for calls originating abroad.

Accounting rates are denominated in U.S. dollars, Special Drawing Rights (SDRs), which are a weighted average of international currencies, or Gold Francs (GFs).Changes in the value of SDRs and GFs relative to the dollar affect the dollar amount of settlements denominated in these currencies.

The FCC requires an equal division of the accounting rate between a U.S. carrier and its foreign correspondent, so that a U.S. carrier pays the same price for access to a given foreign PTT that it charges the PTT for access here.[3] The settlements process, including this regulatory requirement, will be discussed in greater detail later in the chapter. Given the uniform price for access, a carrier whose outbound minutes exceed its inbound minutes will make net settlements payments to its corresponding foreign carrier.

Table 2 also presents data on revenues, payouts, and receipts per minute of traffic. Table 2 shows revenue per minute for 1985. Several interesting comparisons can be made. First, AT&T's international revenue per minute exceeds that of all switched services combined, $.41 per minute vs. $.30 per minute. This explains the fact that the international share of revenues is larger than its share of minutes. Second, it is the overseas revenue per minute of $.52 that makes the international average so high. The $.31 revenue per minute for Mexico is about the same as the average for all switched services, and the $.22 revenue per minute for Canada is below that average. Although one would expect it to be more costly to provide overseas service than domestic service, or service to neighboring countries, it is not obvious that cost differences account for the magnitude of these differences in revenue per minute. Finally, there is a large disparity between outbound and inbound revenue per minute for overseas traffic, but not for Canadian and Mexican traffic. For overseas traffic, AT&T earned $.82 per inbound minute but only $.36 per outbound minute. This difference can take on special significance for new entrants such as MCII and U.S. Sprint. Table 1 shows that they have been more successful in generating outbound traffic than in convincing foreign correspondents to send valuable return traffic.

The difference in per minute revenue for outbound traffic and inbound can be explained in terms of the difference between the level of the collection rate and the accounting rate. When the accounting rate exceeds the collection rate, inbound minutes are more valuable than outbound, because the carrier receives half the accounting rate on inbound minutes and retains less than half the accounting rate on outbound minutes. It would keep just half the accounting rate on outbound traffic if the collection rate equaled the accounting rate, but since it is less, the carrier retains less than half the accounting rate.

Foreign receipts per inbound minute of telephone service—the average price foreign PTTs paid AT&T for terminating calls in the United States—also fell during the period 1980 to 1985. One might ask why foreign receipts per inbound minute are not the same as foreign payouts per outbound minute, given that, on a country-by-country basis, the price AT&T pays for terminating its calls abroad is the same price it charges PTTs for terminating foreign calls here. The answer is that what holds true country by country need not hold true for the average, given that the price of access varies across countries. A second question is why foreign receipts per inbound minute fell by more than foreign payouts per outbound minute. This could reflect either changes in the distribution of outbound and inbound minutes across countries with different prices of access or changes in the price of access across countries with different ratios of outbound to inbound minutes. For example, an increase in the number of inbound minutes from a country with a lower than average price of access would lower the foreign receipts per inbound minute without affecting foreign payouts per outbound minute.

A THEORETICAL MODEL OF PROMOTING
COMPETITION PIECEMEAL

This section makes the theoretical argument that promoting competition among U.S. firms may only shift profits abroad, because foreign PTTs have a monopoly on access to their domestic networks. Competition for a component of an international telecommunications service will tend to drive the price of *that component* down to cost. But the price of the *total* service may remain the same if some other essential component of the total service is controlled by a monopolist. In this case, PTTs have a monopoly on access and appear quite willing to exercise their market power in order to provide revenues to subsidize domestic telephone and postal rates. This conclusion raises questions about the wisdom of deregulating U.S. providers of international telecommunication services without taking into account the possible reactions of foreign telecommunications authorities.

Promoting competition among firms supplying the U.S. component of international telecommunications services is analogous to promoting competition among manufacturers of hammer handles when the manufacture of hammer heads is controlled by a monopolist. Handles and heads are used in fixed proportions in the production of hammers. Each hammer requires exactly one head. Likewise, each minute of international telephone conversation requires 1 minute of access to a foreign telephone network. Suppose, initially, that government regulation limits the right to manufacture hammer handles to a single firm. It would be in the interest of the two firms in this "bilateral monopoly" to collude with each other so that the total price of hammers would be at the level that would maximize the profits of an integrated monopoly manufacturer of hammers. Now suppose the government eliminates the regulatory barrier to manufacturing handles, and there are no significant economies of scale in the production of handles. Competition will drive the price of handles to the marginal cost of production but will not benefit the consumer of hammers, because the head monopolist will raise the price of heads to keep the price of hammers at the monopoly level. "Any monopoly profits to be earned from controlling the manufacture of hammers could be captured by control of one essential component of hammers, such as the heads" (Posner, 1971, p. 31).

The same reasoning suggests that, if the FCC succeeded in creating perfect competition among U.S. international carriers, users would still pay monopoly rates but all the monopoly profits would be captured by the PTTs. Under these circumstances, a PTT could acquire access to the U.S. domestic network at cost but could set the fees for access to its network at monopoly levels. Foreign callers would pay high rates because the PTTs would be setting the charges for calls originating abroad, and U.S. callers would pay high rates because U.S. carriers would need to set high rates to cover the high cost of access to foreign networks.

QUALIFICATIONS

The foregoing analysis was simplified in several respects. It assumed that, absent free entry, U.S. and foreign suppliers would collude to maximize joint profits, that the final product is a homogeneous good, that U.S. firms minimize the cost of producing a given output, and that

PTTs would choose to exploit competition among U.S. firms. The discussion also did not take account of the FCC's international settlements policy, which is designed to prevent a PTT from playing competing U.S. carriers off against one another. Under these simplifying assumptions, introducing competition would have no effect on economic efficiency; it would only alter the distribution of profits: Under bilateral monopoly, profits are divided between the U.S. firm and the PTT. Under pure competition among U.S. firms, all the economic profits would be shifted to the PTT. The final output price and quantity produced would be the same under either market structure given that these assumptions hold. Whether these conclusions still hold if the simplifying assumptions are altered will now be considered.

Competition May Increase Economic Efficiency

Competition may lower output prices. The first qualification is that competition among U.S. suppliers of international telecommunications may benefit U.S. consumers if the U.S. carrier and the PTT were not maximizing their joint profits prior to the introduction of competition. If the U.S. carrier and the PTT did not successfully collude, each might set such a high price for its component of the service that the sum of the prices of each component would be above the level that would maximize the profit of a single supplier of the total service. In this case, competition would reduce the price consumers pay for end-to-end service to the level that would maximize the profit of a single supplier of the total service. That is, the reduction in the price of the component for which competition was introduced would not be fully offset by an increase in the price of the component that continued to be monopolized.[4] While competition under these circumstances would make U.S. users of international telecommunications better off, it would also make U.S. suppliers of such services worse off. The reduction in profits to U.S. firms may or may not be greater than the benefits to U.S. consumers. Economic efficiency, however, would increase since prices would be lower and total world profits would be greater.

This qualification may be more germane to introducing competition in the supply of international circuits than in international common carrier service. U.S. international carriers and PTTs cannot provide international communications without mutual cooperation, and therefore, collusion is a very likely outcome. In contrast, Comsat and Intelsat are not essential to the provision of telephone and record service. U.S. carriers and PTTs have the option of using their own underseas cables. Since cooperation with Comsat/Intelsat is not essential, collusion is a less likely outcome. The desire of carriers to build TAT-8 and TAT-9 despite apparently large amounts of excess satellite capacity, suggests that the carriers and Comsat are not acting like an integrated monopolist. Thus introducing competition with Comsat/Intelsat may reduce the price consumers pay for end-to-end international service. With vigorous competition for this input, the price for end-to-end service would be likely to fall to the level charged by a fully integrated monopolist. It should be noted that the same benefits could be achieved by allowing carriers to own and operate international satellites. If carriers could own these facilities, they would face the true cost of using satellite circuits as opposed to the marked-up price charged by Comsat/Intelsat. In this case as well, the price of end-to-end service would fall to that charged by a fully integrated monopolist.

Competition may increase product diversity. The second qualification is that introducing competition for components of a telecommunication service may increase welfare by increasing product diversity. For example, allowing competitive entry into the provision of earth stations may allow certain customers to obtain a design better suited to their needs. The vertical integration literature can be used to analyze this issue, if one is willing to assume that a single U.S. carrier (or a small number of U.S. carriers acting as a cartel) would collude with PTTs to price the final service at approximately the level that would be set by a fully integrated monopolist. Perry and Groff (1983) conclude that a vertically integrated monopolist will generally provide too little product diversity, and that economic efficiency is generally greater under monopolistic competition (see Dixit, 1981; Perry & Groff, 1983). That is, product diversity is greater when the final product is supplied by a monopolistically competitive industry that buys an input from a monopolist than when the input monopolist vertically integrates and becomes the sole supplier of the final product.

Dixit (1981), however, using a slightly different theoretical model of monopolistic competition, concludes that product diversity would be excessive under monopolistic competition and that welfare would be higher under a vertically integrated monopolist. Thus the theoretical literature offers no unambiguous conclusion about whether the increase in product diversity resulting from introducing competition is desirable.

Competition may reduce production costs. The third qualification is that introducing competition among U.S. firms could reduce production costs. This would ultimately benefit U.S. users to the extent that PTTs do not offset these savings by increasing their charges for access. A regulated monopoly may not cost minimize, because rate base regulation may distort its incentives or because the absence of pressure from competitors may permit managerial slack (see Auerch & Johnson, 1962; Liebenstein, 1966). For example, some have claimed that Comsat has not been providing earth station services in the least costly manner (see USFCC, 1984). They argue that for many users small specialized earth stations would be less costly than Comsat's huge general purpose earth stations. It should be noted that the distortion induced by rate base regulation could be corrected by ending such regulation and substituting unregulated competition, an unregulated monopoly, or price cap regulation.

PTTs May Choose Not to Exploit Competition Among U.S. Firms.

The fourth qualification is that the foreign correspondents might not fully exploit the opportunity to profit from increased competition among U.S. firms. Since foreign telecommunications entities are either government agencies, public corporations, or government-regulated private corporations, it may not be appropriate to assume that they will act like unregulated profit maximizing monopolists in setting the terms for access to their local exchange. Examining the historical record of PTT behavior may be helpful in addressing this issue. It should be noted, however, that history may give only limited guidance in this rapidly changing areas as more countries adopt new pro-competitive telecommunications policies.

The conventional wisdom is that PTTs set high telecommunications rates to provide revenues to subsidize their postal services (see U.S. General Accounting Office [USGAO], 1983, p. 15). Table 3 shows that, in March 1981, the international telephone rates to the U.S. exceeded those from the U.S. for 15 out of the 17 European countries listed in the table. The average dialed call charge per additional minute during peak hours was $2.66 to the U.S. and $1.99 from the U.S. The average rate from Europe exceeded the rate from the U.S. by 34%. The same general conclusion holds when comparing weighted averages, where each country's tariff is weighted by its share of total minutes. Weighted in this way, the average tariff to the U.S. was $2.37, and from the U.S. $1.87. The weighted average is lower, because the rates to and from the U.K. are lower than for the Continent, and Britain had over a third of the traffic to and from the seventeen countries in the table. The weighted average tariff to the U.S. exceed the tariff from the U.S. by 27%.

**Table 3. International Dialed Call Charges Peak Hours Cost Per
Additional Minute 1981**

Country	TARIFF TO U.S.*	TARIFF FROM U.S.**	PERCENTAGE DIFFERENCE IN TARIFFS	% OF TOTAL MINUTES TO U.S.***	% OF TOTAL MINUTES FROM U.S.
Austria	$2.73	$2.05	33.3%	1.0%	1.1%
Belgium	$3.50	$2.05	70.9%	2.6%	2.6%
Denmark	$2.89	$2.05	41.1%	1.0%	1.1%
Finland	$2.43	$2.05	18.7%	0.4%	0.4%
France	$2.44	$2.05	19.0%	10.0%	8.8%
German FR	$3.51	$2.05	71.1%	15.4%	22.4%
Greece	$1.78	$2.05	−13.3%	5.2%	3.5%
Ireland	$1.79	$1.55	15.5%	1.6%	2.0%
Italy	$1.92	$2.05	−6.3%	8.1%	8.2%
Luxembourg	$3.29	$2.05	60.2%	0.2%	0.2%
Netherlands	$2.81	$2.05	36.8%	4.6%	3.5%
Norway	$3.53	$2.05	72.3%	1.8%	1.4%
Portugal	$2.48	$2.05	20.9%	0.6%	0.9%
Spain	$3.27	$2.05	59.3%	2.6%	2.8%
Sweden	$2.36	$2.05	15.0%	3.2%	2.1%
Switzerland	$2.81	$2.05	36.8%	4.0%	4.4%
UK	$1.78	$1.55	14.7%	37.7%	34.6%
				100%	100%
AVERAGE	$2.66	$1.99	33.8%		
WTD. AV.****	$2.37	$1.87	26.7%		

*Tariffs in effect March 1981 (Tarifica, 1981).

**Tariff in effect February 8, 1981, to July 15, 1981. From June 6, 1980, to February 7, 1981, the rate was $2.10 to Continental Europe and $1.60 to U.K. and Ireland. On July 16, 1981, the tariff was cut 35%, reducing the rate to $1.35 for direct dialed calls to Continental Europe and $1.00 to U.K. and Ireland.

***In 1981 there were 365 million minutes to the U.S. from the listed countries and 469 million minutes from the U.S. to these countries (USFCC, 1981 edition, Table 15).

****Each country's tariff is weighted by its share of total minutes for the listed countries.

It is worth noting that there was a significant amount of variation across countries in the tariff to the U.S. For example, the rate from Germany to the U.S. exceeded the rate in the reverse direction by 71%, while the rate from the UK to the U.S. exceeded the rate in the reverse direction by only 15%. Given that the cost of providing a translantic call is unlikely to vary greatly across European countries, this variation in tariffs suggests that countries differ in the degree to which they have chosen to exercise their market power.

Tariffs from Europe to the U.S. have continued to exceed those in the reverse direction. This is illustrated in Table 4, which shows rates

Table 4.   International Dialed Call Charges Peak Hours Cost Per
Additional Minute* 1986

Country	TARIFF TO U.S.	TARIFF FROM U.S.		
		AT&T	MCII	US Sprint
France	$1.39	1.09	1.03	0.96
German FR	$1.98	1.09	-----	-----
Switzerland	$2.43	1.09	1.03	-----
U.K.	$0.94	0.99	0.94	0.87

*Tariffs in effect January 1986. Tariffs from the U.S. are those filed with the FCC by AT&T, MCI, and U.S. Sprint. Tariffs to the U.S. are from Center for Communications Management (1986). The exchange rates used to convert the foreign tariffs are from U.S. Council of Economic Advisers (1987), Table B–105.

for January 1986 for four European countries including the tariffs from the US of MCII and U.S. Sprint as well as AT&T. Tariffs to the U.S. exceeded those from the U.S. for three of the four countries. The one exception was the UK, and that was only for AT&T's rates. MCII's rate was the same as the rate from the UK to the U.S., and U.S. Sprint's rate was lower.

The persistence of rates of return above competition levels would be strong evidence that PTTs are exercising their monopoly power. There are no direct data on the PTTs' rates of return on overseas telephone service, but an inference can be drawn from the fact that AT&T has found overseas telephone service highly profitable. In 1979, AT&T's rate of return (the ratio of net operating earnings to investment) was 36.5% for overseas MTS service.[5] Under the reasonable assumption that the cost of providing service is approximately the same in both directions, one need only show that the revenues of the overseas telecommunications authorities exceeded those of AT&T in order to conclude that these overseas correspondents were on average earning a substantial rate of return on overseas telephone service.

Foreign revenues would exceed those of U.S. carriers even if the collection rate were the same in both directions, as long as there is a net outflow of minutes from the U.S. abroad and the U.S. kept less than half its per-minute earnings on outbound traffic. With the same collection rate, each side would earn the same revenues as long as inbound minutes equaled outbound—tariff revenues would be the same, and net settlement payments would be zero. Now suppose outbound minutes exceed inbound. Each side would need to retain half the total revenues, provided that the U.S. carrier paid out exactly half the revenue it earned on those excess minutes, that is, if the accounting rate equaled the collection rate and the accounting rate was split

50/50. But if the U.S. carrier paid out more than half it earned on each excess minutes, then it would retain less than half the total revenues.[6] This was the case, since AT&T's foreign payouts per outbound minute consistently exceeded retained tariff revenue. Since foreign collection rates tend to exceed those in the U.S., this would make the U.S. share of total revenues even smaller.

An examination of past incidents in which PTTs have used competition among U.S. carriers to increase their share of revenues provides further insight into the likely reaction by PTTs to increased competition among U.S. firms providing international telecommunications services. In June 1982, Nordtel, an association of the PTTs of Denmark, Finland, Iceland, Norway, and Sweden, sent identical letters to seven U.S. international service carriers (USISCs). The letters requested that the firms submit bids for providing new data services between the U.S. and the countries represented by Nordtel. The bids were to include the terms for dividing revenues between the USISC and the PTT. Nordtel proposed to award operating agreements to one or a limited number of carriers, based on the competing bids. Shortly after the Nordtel letters were sent, the PTTs of the Benelux countries (Belgium, Netherlands, and Luxembourg) made a similar proposal to the same USISCs (U.S. Office of Management and Budget, 1982). The Nordtel and Benelux proposals are examples of PTTs attempting to increase their monopoly profits by forcing USISCs to compete for operating agreements. The PTTs were unsuccessful in this particular effort because of a strong negative reaction by the FCC and the State Department.[7] In 1985 British Telecom International (BTI) and the European Conference of Postal and Telecommunications Administrations (CEPT) apparently attempted to lower telex rates unilaterally, in order to reduce their net settlement payments to U.S. carriers. The FCC was able to prevent this attempt as well.

The foregoing discussion suggests that at least certain PTTs may attempt to exploit the opportunity for greater profits created by increased competition among U.S. firms. This conclusion, however, appears inconsistent with the fact that foreign countries have been reluctant to grant multiple operating agreements for international switch voice service. Granting additional operating agreements would appear to strengthen the bargaining position of a PTT vis-á-vis U.S. carriers.

There are a number of possible explanations for the PTTs' lack of enthusiasm about granting multiple operating agreements. Interconnecting with additional carriers (as opposed to having carriers bid for an exclusive agreement) imposes immediate costs on a PTT. The PTT must install additional facilities and incur ongoing recordkeepng and other administrative costs. Yet the benefits to the PTT are neither certain nor immediate.

There are two reasons why PTTs may see little near-term prospect for successfully exploiting competition in the voice market. First, they may expect AT&T to retain a predominant market share for the foreseeable future. If this were the case, which is likely, AT&T would be in a position to defend itself against PTTs. A threat to terminate AT&T's operating agreement unless AT&T agreed to a higher accounting rate would not be credible. AT&T would know that the PTTs are as dependent on its traffic as it is on theirs. It would be some time before the new U.S. entrants would be able to fill the gap left by AT&T. AT&T's size also gives it the ability to respond to lesser threats. It can use its pricing and advertising policies to affect the amount of its outbound traffic going to a PTT. Even a 5% reduction in AT&T's traffic could be significant to a PTT. Finally, AT&T's size may enable it to influence the regulatory and political process in the U.S. Thus, an adverse action taken against AT&T might quickly result in the U.S. government pressuring a foreign government to restrain its PTT.

Second, the FCC's international settlements policy may limit a PTT's ability to successfully *whipsaw* U.S. carriers. The constraints embodied in this policy may be particularly effective in the voice market because the net flow of voice traffic is outbound from the U.S. The FCC's antiwhipsawing policies will be discussed in the next section.[8] PTTs may also fear reaction from other parts of the U.S. Government if they allowed multiple entry and then tried to exercise their market power. PTTs may not want to take this chance given the high profits they appear to be earning.

Another possible benefit of competition from a PTT's perspective is that the new entrants would stimulate traffic from the U.S. to the PTT. To attract customers, the new entrants would be likely to underprice AT&T, and AT&T would be likely to at least partially meet their price reductions. The level of new traffic stimulated by the price reductions would depend on the price elasticity of demand, which PTTs have traditionally viewed as relatively low. Moreover, it is not obvious that stimulating such traffic would necessarily be in the long-run interest of the PTT. While additional traffic terminating at the PTT would increase the total settlement payments to the PTT at the current accounting rate, it could reduce the total profits available to split between U.S. and foreign carriers, if the collection rates prevailing before the introduction of competition were at the joint profit maximizing level.

In addition to the costs of interconnection and the lack of immediate certain benefits, there are two more possible explanations for the initial reluctance of PTTs to grant multiple operating agreements. First, the long-term working relationship between PTTs and AT&T may have lead PTTs to identify with AT&T's interests, over the interests of potential entrants. Second, many PTTs are philosophically opposed to competition. In their view the primary outcome of competition will be higher costs. Even if competition increased their share of the net benefits from competition, they might oppose it, because they believe competition is inefficient from a global perspective.

Current FCC Policies May be Adequate to Prevent PTTs From Exercising Their Market Power

The fifth qualification is that the analysis failed to take into account the FCC's policy of requiring U.S. international carriers to obtain its approval of the terms of their operating agreements. This policy, traditionally known as the *uniform settlements policy,* and recently renamed the *international settlements policy* (ISP) has its origins over 50 years ago.[9] The policy has focused on preventing PTTs from playing one U.S. carrier against another to the detriment of U.S. carriers and ratepayers. Such practices are often referred to as *whipsawing.*

To prevent whipsawing, the Commission has required that all operating agreements must: (a) provide for an equal division of the accounting rate between the U.S. carrier and the foreign PTT, and (b) specify the same accounting rates and settlement rates (the rates for converting currencies in settling accounts) for the same services on parallel routes (USFCC, 1980).

In January 1986 the commission extended the scope of the international settlements policy when it concluded that the policy applies to indirect transit traffic as well as to traffic routed directly, and to voice and enhanced services. The Report and Order also made clear that every change in an operating agreement is subject to Commission review. Thus a simultaneous request by all carriers to change the terms of their operating agreements is subject to review, even if the new agreements would be the same for all carriers (USFCC, 1986).

The remainder of this section analyzes the effects of the requirements specified by the international settlements policy. These requirements potentially constrain PTTs in two ways. First, they limit the range of possible divisions of available revenue. Secondly, they limit a PTT's ability to change the current terms for dividing revenues. These will be discussed in turn.

A PTT's share of revenue earned on switched international services may be limited by the equal division requirement. The effect of the requirement depends on the direction of the net flow of traffic. When the net traffic flow is into the U.S. (as it is for record traffic), the best a PTT can do, given the equal division requirement, is to set a zero accounting rate and thus make no payments to U.S. carriers. Without the requirement, the accounting rate could be divided so that a PTT could receive net payments from U.S. carriers even though the net traffic flow was into the U.S. However, we observe no zero accounting rates for record service, so the equal division requirement appears not to have been a binding limit on the foreign share of record revenues.[10]

When the net traffic flow is out of the U.S., as with international MTS, the equal-sharing requirement cannot limit a PTT's share of total revenue unless accounting rates affect the volume of traffic.[11] If traffic volume is independent of accounting rates, the PTT can extract any share of total revenue from U.S. carriers by demanding a sufficiently high accounting rate.

If, however, an increase in the accounting rate induces U.S. carriers to raise their collection rates, which in turn reduces traffic originating from the U.S., the equal division requirement may limit a PTT's potential revenue share. If the PTT found the volume of outbound traffic falling as it increased the accounting rate, a higher accounting rate would no longer translate into a greater share of a fixed level of revenues. In attempting to increase its *share* of the profits, it might find the total revenues and profits shrinking, since, at a sufficiently high accounting rate, U.S. carriers would be charging above the profit maximizing level of a joint monopolist. Moreover, the net flow of traffic might reverse from outbound to inbound as the accounting rate rose. With such a reversal, a high accounting rate would now imply high net settlements by a PTT to the U.S. carriers, just the opposite of what the PTT intended. Without the equal division requirement, a PTT facing perfectly competitive U.S. carriers could impose a division of the accounting rate, so that U.S. carriers would receive only marginal cost for terminating the PTT's traffic, while they would pay the PTT a much higher fee, one set to maximize the monopoly PTT's profits, for terminating their messages. But with the equal sharing requirement, the PTT cannot do this.

The second major effect of the international settlements policy is to limit a PTT's ability to change the terms of operating agreements. The two major instruments PTTs can use to win concessions from U.S. carriers are its power to grant or deny operating agreements, and its control over the distribution of return traffic. The equal division and uniformity requirements embodied in the international settlements policy are most effective in limiting the use of the second instrument.

In the record market, the uniformity requirement plays an important role in limiting a PTT's ability to use its control of return traffic to change the terms of operating agreements. When the balance of traffic is inbound to the U.S., as it is in the record market, PTTs are making net settlement payments to U.S. carriers and would benefit from a reduction in the accounting rate. Absent the requirement that all carriers have the same accounting rate, a PTT could threaten to reduce the share of return traffic to carriers who refuse to accept a lower accounting rate, and increase the share to those who do. This is of immediate benefit both to the PTT, whose cost of terminating messages is reduced, and to those carriers for whom the increased volume of return traffic more than offsets the loss from the reduction in the accounting rate. Typically, it is a new entrant with minimal return traffic, who is the most willing to accept the reduced accounting rate. Since such a carrier's outbound traffic exceeds its inbound, it would benefit from a reduction in the accounting rate even if it were not allocated an increased share of the return traffic. The carriers whose return traffic was reduced would then be likely to agree to a reduction in their accounting rates rather than face a further reduction in return traffic. The uniformity requirement is intended to prevent PTTs from playing carriers off against each other in this way.

In the voice market, the uniformity requirement may be unnecessary to prevent such whipsawing, given that the equal division requirement remains in place. With a net flow of traffic to the PTT and the equal division requirement, the PTT would want an increase in the accounting rate.[12] The PTT could threaten to reduce the share of return traffic to carriers who refuse to increase their accounting rate, and increase the share to those who accept a higher rate. The initial carriers to accept such an offer could benefit if the increased share of return traffic were large enough to offset the loss from the higher accounting rate. However, the PTT could be temporarily worse off, since it would be reallocating return traffic from carriers with lower charges for terminating messages to ones with higher charges. The PTT would not face this dilemma if the accounting rate could be divided unequally. In that case it could reallocate traffic to carriers who would terminate return traffic at a lower rate, while continuing to pay the PTT the same rate for traffic it terminated.

FCC regulations reflect the fact that the uniformity requirement is less important in the voice market than in the record market, and have established a more streamlined procedure for waivers in the voice market. There is a 21-day semiautomatic grant procedure for unopposed waiver requests to establish nonuniform accounting rates for voice service and a 60-day semiautomatic grant procedure for record service waivers (USFCC, 1987).

The other tool a PTT can use to change the terms of operating agreements is its ability to grant or deny operating agreements. The uniformity and equal division requirements of the ISP are not sufficient to prevent PTTs from using this instrument to change the status quo, even when the net flow of traffic is outbound from the U.S. If a PTT wants a greater share of the international communications revenues, it can do so despite the ISP requirements by threatening to terminate the operating agreements of those carriers who refuse to accept its new terms. With competition among U.S. carriers, at least one carrier would accept the new terms as long as the terms provide positive profits. In the case of net outbound traffic, these new terms would specify higher accounting rates.

A PTT forcing U.S. record carriers to simultaneously change their accounting rate agreements is not merely a theoretical possibility. For example, in 1975, TRT, a small U.S. international record carrier, negotiated a reduced accounting rate with the British PTT. The new rate was $1.75 per minute, while the prevailing accounting rate for telex traffic between the U.S. and the UK was $2.25 per minute (USFCC, 1977). A lower rate would have favored the UK if the rate were applied to all carriers, because the UK was sending four million more telex minutes to the U.S. than it was receiving from the U.S. The Commission rejected the new accounting rate because if it were allowed to go into effect the Commission reasoned that the UK could whipsaw the other carriers into accepting the unfavorable rate. Despite the Commission's rejection of TRT's accounting rate, the UK was eventually able to get the other carriers (ITT Worldcom, RCA, and WUI) to accept a lower accounting rate by threatening them with termination of their telex operating agreements (Povich, 1980, p.8). The modification of the ISP in January 1987 was designed to deal with such a contingency. As noted above, the *Report and Order* states that any change in accounting rates is subject to Commission review, even if all carriers agree to make the same change.

It should be noted that the usefulness of a policy which tends to preserve the status quo depends on the desirability of that status quo. For example, in the voice market, one may presume that AT&T, as the sole U.S. international carrier until 1984, was in a strong position to bargain for settlements rates that served U.S. interests. Thus preserving these terms of trade as additional firms enter the voice market may be a reasonable short run policy. But rejecting all changes is not a sensible long-run policy. There is no reason to believe that all the current accounting rates are optimal or would remain so as circumstances change. The FCC needs to know which proposed changes it should approve, and which it should reject. This issue will be discussed in the section on policy.

Summary of Qualifications

The essence of the first three qualifications is that competition may increase economic efficiency. With a "bigger pie" the U.S. may gain even if its share of the pie shrinks. But it is also quite possible that competition may so reduce the U.S. share of the pie that the U.S. ends up with less. In particular it was found that: (a) Competition would lower the price of international communications to U.S. consumers if, prior to its introduction, U.S. and foreign suppliers had failed to cooperate and had set prices for their components above the level that would maximize their joint profits. In this case, free entry into all services supplied by U.S. firms would unambiguously increase efficiency, but U.S. firms would see their profits shifted abroad. (b) If telecommunication services are not homogenous products, introducing competition would increase product diversity. Efficiency would increase only if the increase in product diversity is not excessive. (c) Eliminating rate-base regulation and removing regulatory barriers to entry may induce firms to reduce their production costs. Rate base regulation could be removed, however, without allowing free entry.

The fourth and fifth qualifications concerned the behavior of PTTs and the FCC. Specifically, it was argued that: (d) PTTs may choose not to use increased competition among U.S. firms to increase their share of the international telecommunications profits. The high tariffs PTTs have traditionally charged, and the attempt by the Nordtel and Benelux PTTs to extract monopoly rents from U.S. firms, suggest, however, that at least some PTTs would be likely to exploit the opportunity for greater profits created by increased competition among U.S. firms. (e) The FCC international settlements policy reduces but does not eliminate the PTTs' ability to exercise their market power.

The fact that firms such as MCI wish to enter international MTS market is not inconsistent with the view that PTTs would be able to capture the benefits from competition if the FCC did not enforce the international settlements policy. The new U.S. entrants may believe that vigorous enforcement of the ISP will prevent PTTs from exploiting competition among them. Alternatively, the new entrants may believe that the FCC will not take countermeasures, but that profits are large enough to make entering the market worthwhile as long as the PTTs take some time to respond. In any case, the fact that firms wish to enter does not necessarily imply that total U.S. benefits will increase, because these new entrants do not take into account the lost profits of the incumbent firm, AT&T.

POLICY

It has been argued above that promoting competition among U.S. providers of international telecommunications services without taking account of the resulting loss of market power of these U.S. firms vis-á-vis PTTs is not a desirable option. There are two major alternatives to this course. The first would be to limit provision of international telecommunications to a single provider. Under this arrangement the structure of U.S. provision of international services would be similar to that abroad, except that the single U.S. firm need not be a government entity. The U.S. has soundly rejected this option. The second alternative would be to promote competition among U.S. firms but assure that the benefits are not undermined by the exercise of market power abroad. This alternative entails appropriately enforcing the FCC's international settlements policy, and a continued effort by the U.S. to promote competitive telecommunications policies throughout the world. The remainder of the chapter will discuss this second option, focusing on how the FCC should implement the international settlements policy.

Implementing the International Settlements Policy

Policy objectives: Efficiency vs. equity. If the only concern is maximizing global economic efficiency, we should aim for setting the price of access at marginal cost. This could result in deviating from the 50/50 split of the accounting rate to the extent that the cost of access differed at each terminating end. To achieve the efficiency benefits of such a price structure would also require that the remaining components of international service be priced efficiently. This would be the case if international services were fully competitive and the price of access to U.S. local exchanges continues to be appropriately regulated. Under such an industry structure, reducing accounting rates to marginal cost would result in lower prices for end users and expanded industry output.

The goal of promoting cost-based telecommunications prices for U.S. users may conflict with the desire to achieve an equitable division of profits between U.S. international carriers and foreign PTTs for jointly provided international service. First, consider a uniform reduction in telex accounting rates. There is more inbound telex traffic to the U.S. than outbound traffic. Because of the 50/50 division of the accounting rate, this means that PTTs make net settlements payments to U.S. record carriers. Given the current traffic patterns, a reduction in the accounting rate would reduce the net settlement payments to U.S. record carriers. But it might also reduce the price *competitive* U.S. carriers would charge U.S. users, since it would reduce the marginal cost of terminating calls.

Second, suppose a new entrant in the telex market wants a waiver for a lower accounting rate.[13] It proposes to set a lower collection rate than the incumbents. In contrast to the previous case, in which the reduction in collection rates is speculative, here it is certain that at least initially, some U.S. customers will have lower rates. The long-run consequences of granting such a waiver request are likely to be the same as granting a uniform reduction in accounting rates. New entrants in the telex market have two possible reasons to seek a lower accounting rate. First, they generally have more outbound traffic than inbound traffic so that a reduction in the accounting rate would benefit them given current traffic patterns. Second, the PTT may agree to allocate an increased share of the return traffic to the new entrant. This will benefit the new entrant since the return traffic is highly profitable even at a reduced accounting rate. This arrangement is also in the PTT's interest since it will reduce the PTT's settlement payments on the traffic reallocated and give the PTT leverage to induce the established carriers to agree to the lower accounting rate (by making credible the threat to send them even less return traffic if they refuse to accept the lower rate).

Third, consider the case of a waiver from the uniform accounting rate requirement in the voice market. Suppose that, in order to get an operating agreement from a PTT, a new entrant must offer a higher accounting rate than AT&T is paying. If it enters, it will charge less than AT&T in order to attract customers. Entry may also induce AT&T to reduce its prices. Thus in the short run, FCC approval of the waiver will benefit consumers. On the other hand, the entry will shift some profits from AT&T to foreign PTTs. This will be true to the extent that entry shifts outbound traffic from AT&T to the new entrant and the new entrant pays the foreign PTT more than it had received from AT&T. But, unlike the record market, there is little danger that permitting such a waiver will enable a PTT to whipsaw the incumbent carriers into accepting less advantageous accounting rates. (See earlier section.)

When the Commission is weighing efficiency benefits (price cuts) with distributional losses (shifting revenues to PTTs), it may also wish to consider the "demonstration effect" on foreign governments of the relative weight it places on efficiency. Placing greater weight on moving prices to cost may put the U.S. on the high moral ground in negotiating with foreign governments for cost-based international telecommunications.

One case in which there is no conflict between reducing prices that U.S. consumers pay and increasing the share of revenues going to U.S. carriers is that of a uniform reduction in the accounting rate in the voice market. A reduction in the accounting rate for all U.S. carriers would both shift revenues to U.S. carriers from PTTs and likely reduce prices for U.S. customers.

Bargaining power of U.S. carriers. The need for FCC intervention in the setting of accounting rates depends on the bargaining power of U.S. carriers relative to PTTs. If U.S. carriers have sufficient bargaining power, there may be little benefit to FCC intervention, and under certain circumstances such intervention could be counterproductive. This is likely to be the case in the voice market as long as AT&T maintains its strong market position. It could also be true in the record market if record carriers act collusively in bargaining with PTTs over accounting rates.

Currently, U.S. international carriers are not perfectly competitive, and at least AT&T has sufficient market power to view accounting rates as outcomes of bilateral negotiations with PTTs. When the accounting rate is arrived at in this way, carriers are not likely to treat it as the marginal cost of terminating messages. It is not in the interest of bilateral monopolists to bargain over only the accounting rate and then let each party choose its collection rate, taking the accounting rate as fixed. This would likely result in both sides setting collection rates above the joint profit maximizing level, and thus have less total profits to share between them (see footnote 4). Instead, bilateral monopolists are more likely to determine the joint profit maximizing collection rates and treat the accounting rate as a mechanism to divide that joint profit. Or they might bargain simultaneously over both the accounting rate and the amount of traffic each carrier will deliver. To maximize the profits available for division between the parties, the PTT would want U.S. carriers to deliver more traffic (and hence charge less) than they would if they took the accounting rate as a fixed per-minute price of terminating traffic.

If the FCC or any other governmental body were to impose accounting rates on such bilateral monopolists, the monopolists would be likely to treat the rates as the marginal cost of terminating traffic and wish to charge higher collection rates than if the same accounting rates had been the outcome of a bargaining process. Thus if the current accounting rates were exogenously imposed, AT&T would have the incentive to set collection rates above the present levels. Even with lower accounting rates (or termination charges), such bilateral monopolists might wish to charge more than the current prices, if these lower accounting rates were externally imposed. This analysis suggests that

FCC intervention in setting accounting rates in the voice market could be counterproductive as long as AT&T is able to bargain on an equal basis with PTTs. It could result in higher collection rates, yet it would be unlikely to achieve a more favorable distribution of revenues between the U.S. and abroad. It might even lead to lower profits for AT&T by inducing PTTs to raise their collection rates, thereby reducing the flow of traffic to the U.S. And under traditional rate-of-return regulation, this could compel the Commission to permit AT&T to implement its desired rate increases.

As competition grows, AT&T's bargaining power will decline and there will be a greater potential benefit to FCC involvement in the setting of accounting rates. The above analysis suggests the need to continue regulating AT&T's collection rates during the transition to full competition. As Haring and Kwerel (1987) argue, the best way to do this would be through price caps, based on cost factors not under the control of the firm. To the extent that accounting rates are taken out of AT&T's control, it would be required to pass on reductions in these costs. But as long as accounting rates are the outcome of bargaining between AT&T and PTTs, AT&T should be allowed to keep a portion of the savings it realizes through negotiating more favorable rates, and by the same measure should not be able to pass on the full cost of increases in accounting rates. The analysis also suggests that, to the extent that government regulation supplants private bilateral negotiation on accounting rates, the government must also concern itself with foreign collection rates. It would make sense for the U.S. government negotiating with foreign governments over new international access arrangements to negotiate for reductions in international collection rates at the same time the reduction in international access costs are adopted.

Predicting the consequences of changes in accounting rates. Even if U.S. carriers were perfectly competitive, it may be difficult to predict the effect of changes in accounting rates on prices paid by U.S. consumers. The answer may depend on how PTTs allocate return traffic among competing U.S. carriers and on the direction of net traffic flow.

For example, in a competitive international telex market one would expect that reducing the accounting rate would reduce the prices of telex messages originating in the U.S. But this is not always the case. If each minute of outbound traffic generates more than 1 minute of return traffic, U.S. carriers could in effect receive a subsidy for each minute they originate. Traffic might be linked in this way because PTTs allocate return traffic in proportion to traffic they receive from each U.S. carrier, or because responses to messages are directed via the carrier of the originator of the message because that is the only telex service to which the originator subscribes. In this case a reduction in the accounting rate would reduce the subsidy (per minute of outbound traffic), and thus lead to an *increase* in the collection rate.

Long-Term Strategy to Move Towards Cost-Based Access

To maximize the benefits from competition among U.S. international carriers, the U.S. and its foreign correspondents should develop a long-term strategy to move towards cost-based access to domestic networks. Ideally, foreign countries would adopt a telecommunications policy that parallels U.S. policy—full facility-based competition for international and domestic interexchange services and cost-based access to local exchanges.

The U.S. cannot assume, however, that its example and exhortations will be sufficient to convince foreign governments to liberalize their international communications policies. As competition increases among U.S. international carriers, it may be appropriate for the U.S. to take more positive steps to move towards cost-based access. These steps could be of the form of greater FCC involvement in the setting of accounting rates or it might be of the form of promoting market rules that would be likely to result in movement towards cost-based international access.

An example of market rules which might promote cost-based access would be to require the unbundling of the international components of facilities from the domestic components, and permit international carriers to terminate traffic on foreign domestic networks on the same terms as domestic users. The usefulness of this approach would depend on the degree to which domestic tariffs are cost-based. It might also require renegotiating various International Telegraph and Telephone Consultative Committee (CCITT) multilateral telecommunications agreements that the U.S. has signed.

The unbundling might be achieved by permitting carriers to purchase "whole" cable circuits (*indefeasible rights of use*—IRUs), and purchase or lease whole satellite circuits. Currently, corresponding carriers each purchase or lease "half circuits." Under this agreement, every circuit is jointly owned by the corresponding carriers. With such joint ownership, it is natural that part of the accounting rate is intended to compensate the terminating carrier for the use of its share of the international facilities. Under a whole circuit arrangement such compensation would generally not be necessary. A carrier would own or lease the entire international component of the circuit it uses to originate calls. Carriers would purchase or lease circuits based on the level of traffic they expected to originate. (Some mechanism would still be needed to allow use of the correspondents circuits when traffic flows exceed ownership in one direction but not the other.) The price of whole circuits would be cost based, because carriers would be able to purchase cable circuits at cost at the time a cable is built. That is, cable costs are paid in proportion to capacity shares.

Preventing discrimination between international and domestic traffic would require departing from the current settlements arrangements. Under this approach international carriers would be charged domestic rates from certain designated gateways. A major issue this approach raises is the treatment of private lines. Few foreign countries (if any) allow sharing and resale of private line services. But this approach would allow just that for private lines employed by international carriers. For example, this would be true of the private lines to the designated gateways. At sufficient traffic volumes international carriers could find their costs below domestic toll costs on certain routes. This would give them an incentive to carry such domestic traffic on their leased lines. PTTs who do not favor domestic competition would presumably not wish to create such an opportunity. Thus the entire approach is likely to be adopted only in countries that also wish to liberalize their domestic telecommunications policies.

This same general approach could be applied to international private line service. Telecommunications carriers or private users would be able to purchase whole circuits in international facilities. The domestic portion of the private line rates would be at domestic rates.

It is worth emphasizing that such antidiscrimination provisions would not prevent countries from monopoly pricing of telecommunications. But it would require them to treat international carriers seeking access on the same basis as domestic customers. Since countries are likely to be more concerned about domestic customers than customers seeking access from foreign countries, this constraint would be likely to result in a closer correspondence between cost and the price *competitive* U.S. carriers pay to terminate messages.

There is a second important caveat. It raises troubling questions about how to make the transition from the current situation to a long-run ideal. As discussed above, greater FCC involvement in establishing accounting rates may not be beneficial if U.S. carriers possess sufficient bargaining power to negotiate on equal terms with PTTs. In that case, imposing accounting rates on carriers could raise collections rates, reduce profits, and reduce economic efficiency. If the U.S. government becomes more actively involved in establishing the cost of terminating messages during the transition to full competition, it must also concern itself with the collection rates of carriers with market power including PTTs. It is not enough for the FCC to replace carriers in bargaining over accounting rates (or other forms of termination charges). If it does this, the U.S. government may also need to negotiate with PTTs over collection rates, filling a role played by U.S. carriers prior to the rise in competition.

SUMMARY AND CONCLUSIONS

Increased competition among U.S. suppliers of international telecommunications services could result in a reduction in the U.S.'s share of the benefits from such services unless the U.S. government takes appropriate action.

The proposed model of piecemeal competition is predicated on the assumption that the FCC permits free entry into the U.S. segment of international telecommunications but plays no role in establishing the terms of the operating agreements U.S. firms negotiate with foreign PTTs. In this theoretical model, promoting competition among U.S. suppliers of international telecommunications may do nothing more than shift profits abroad. Competition for a component of an international telecommunications service will tend to drive the price of *that component* down to cost. But the price of the *total* service may remain the same if some other essential component of the service is controlled by a monopolist. The PTTs have a monopoly on access and may be willing to exercise their market power in order to provide revenues to subsidize domestic telephone and postal rates.

The FCC's international settlements policy provides a useful framework to assure that the benefits of international telecommunications are shared equitably between the U.S. and foreign countries. The requirement that accounting rates be divided equally appears to constrain the maximum share of total revenues accruing to either correspondent. This requirement, in conjunction with the requirement that all U.S. carriers have the same accounting rates for similar service on parallel routes, also limits the ability of PTTs to change the current terms for dividing revenues. Without these requirements, PTTs could use their control over return traffic to gain concessions from competing U.S. carriers in the telex market and other markets where there is a net flow of traffic inbound to the U.S.

Unfortunately, establishing "market rules," such as the equal division and uniformity requirements, is not sufficient to assure that accounting rates are in the country's interest. The FCC must often make case by case judgments in implementing its international settlements policy. It must be able to balance the benefits of reducing prices for U.S. consumers with the cost of shifting revenues from established U.S. carriers to PTTs. For example, in the telex market a reduction in the accounting rate might reduce the rate end users pay, but also transfer revenue from U.S. carriers to PTTs.

The Commission must also tailor its policy to particular market circumstances. Even if U.S. record carriers act competitively, a reduction in the accounting rate might lead to a rise in the collection rate, if PTTs tend to allocate return traffic in proportion to the amount of traffic originated by individual U.S. carriers. In this case, a reduction in the accounting rate would be unambiguously detrimental to the U.S.

One of the most important market circumstances is the degree of competition among U.S. carriers. When competition is weak, as in the voice market, FCC intervention may be unnecessary or even counterproductive. At present, AT&T has sufficient strength to bargain as an equal with PTTs. The degree of competition in the record market is ambiguous and requires further examination. As competition grows, so does the need for government involvement in regulating accounting rates. The FCC should not, however, limit itself to overseeing accounting rates. During the transition to competition it should continue to regulate AT&T's international collection rates, but it should do so using price caps, not rate of return regulation.

This would give the FCC greater leverage in dealing with PTTs, since it would maintain the FCC's influence over the volume of traffic originating in the U.S. Continuing regulation of collection rates will also prevent collection rates from rising if AT&T begins to view the accounting rate as the marginal cost of terminating messages and not merely as a device for dividing revenues.

Can competition among U.S. carriers be reconciled with PTT monopolies? The FCC's international settlements policy can only partially achieve this end. For the U.S. to fully benefit from competition among U.S. international carriers, foreign countries must themselves decide to liberalize their telecommunications policies. Only with cost-based access to local networks will competition among carriers linking these networks ensure efficient end-to-end prices.

Will this come to pass? Perhaps as countries see themselves losing businesses to countries that have liberalized, they will reconsider their policies. Or, perhaps in their efforts to protect PTT revenues and employment, they will not. But those countries that cling to their traditional ways will be the losers as the countries that see the rewards of efficient pricing forge bilateral agreements and move ahead in this information age.

REFERENCES

Averch, H., & Johnson, L. (1962). Behavior of the firm under regulatory constraint. *American Economic Review, 52,* 1053–1069.

Center for Communications Management. (1986). *1986 Eurodata Foundation yearbook.* Ramsey, NJ: Eurodata Foundation.

Cornell, N., Kelly, D., & Greenhalgh, P. (1980). *Social objectives and competition in common carrier communications: Incompatible or inseparable?* (Working Paper No. 1). Washington, DC: U.S. Federal Communication Commission, Office of Plans and Policy.

Dixit, A. (1982). *Vertical integration in a monopolistically competitive industry.* Princeton, NJ: Woodrow Wilson School, Princeton University.

Haring, J., & Kwerel, E. (1987). *Competitive policy in the post-equal access market* (Working Paper No. 22). Washington, DC: U.S. Federal Communications Commission, Office of Plans and Policy.

Kelley, D. (1982). *Deregulation after divestiture: The effect of the AT&T settlement on competition* (Working Paper No. 8). Washington, DC: U.S. Federal Communications Commission, Office of Plans and Policy.

Kwerel, E. (1984). *Promoting competition piecemeal in international telecommunications* (Working Paper No. 13). Washington, DC: U.S. Federal Communications Commission, Office of Plans and Policy.

Leibenstein, H. (1966). Allocative efficiency vs. X-efficiency. *American Economic Review, 56,* 392–415.

Pearce, A. (1983). International telecommunications service industry: On the verge of massive structural change as competition and deregulation threaten the status quo. *Telcom Insider, 3,* 5–6.

Perry, M., & Groff, R. (1983). *Forward integration by a monopolist into a monopolistically competitive industry* (Bell Laboratories Economic Discussion Paper No. 271). Murray Hill: Bell Labs.

Posner, R. (1971, Spring). Taxation by regulation. *Bell Journal of Ecomomics,* pp. 22–50.

Povich, L. (1980). *Considerations in revising procedures for requiring operating agreements and influencing settlements with foreign correspondence.* Washington, DC: U.S. Federal Communications Commission, Common Carrier Bureau, Memorandum.

Schmalensee, R. (1973). A note on the theory of vertical integration. *Journal of Political Economy, 81,* 442–449.

Tarifica (1981). Western Europe telecommunications informations service, manual. London: Logica UK Limited.

U.S. Code 47, Section 222. (1981). *Containing the General and Permanent Laws of the United States.* Washington, DC: U.S. Government Printing Office.

U.S. Council of Economic Advisers. (1987). *Economic report of the president.* Washington, DC: U.S. Government Printing Office.

U.S. Department of Commerce, National Telecommunications and Information Administration. (1987). *NTIA regulatory alternatives report.* Washington, DC: Author.

U.S. Federal Communications Commission. (1936). Mackay Radio and Telegraph Co. *FCC Reports, 2,* 592.

U.S. Federal Communications Commission. (1964). TAT-4 decision. *FCC Reports, 37,* 1151.

U.S. Federal Communications Commission. (1980). Uniform settlements rates. *FCC Reports, 84* (2nd ed.), 121.

U.S. Federal Communications Commission. (1982). TAT-4 Revisited. *FCC Reports, 92* (2nd ed.), 641.

U.S. Federal Communications Commission. (1984). Earth station ownership. *FCC Reports, 97* (2nd ed.), 444.

U.S. Federal Communications Commission. (1986). Uniform settlements policy. *Report and Order,* FCC 86–30; Federal Register 51, 4736.

U.S. Federal Communications Commission. (1987). Uniform settlements policy. *Order on Reconsideration,* FCC 87–61; Federal Register 52, 8453.

U.S. Federal Communications Commission. (1981). *Statistics of communications common carriers.* Washington, DC: U.S. Government Printing Office.

U.S. Federal Communications Commission. (1987). *International communications traffic data report for 1985.* Washington, DC: Industry Analysis Division, Common Carrier Bureau.

U.S. General Accounting Office. (1983). *FCC needs to monitor a changing international telecommunication market.* Washington, DC: U.S. Government Printing Office.

U.S. Office of Management and Budget. (1982). *Issue paper on the NORDTEL and Benelux proposals.* Washington, DC: Author.

Warren-Boulton, F. (1974). Vertical control with variable proportions. *Journal of Political Economy, 82,* 783–804.

Westfield, F. (1981). Vertical integration: Does product price rise or fall? *American Economic Review, 71,* 334–346.

ENDNOTES

[1] See Cornell, Kelly, and Greenbalgh (1980); Kelly (1982); U.S. Department of Commerce (1987). See also Haring and Kwerel (1987), who propose a streamlined form of regulation to limit AT&T's ability to exercise whatever market power it may still possess.

[2] U.S. Federal Communications Commission (USFCC) (1964). The major international record carriers include ITT World Communications Inc., RCA Global Communications Inc., Western Union International, FTC Communications Inc., and TRT Telecommunications Corp. None has more than a 30% market share.

[3] Some people speak of access as beginning at the midpoint of jointly owned international cables or at international satellites, whose circuits are leased on a "half-circuit" basis.

[4] This qualification can be illustrated in terms of the preceding hammer example. It can be shown that output is lower and the total price higher when each firm maximizes its profits taking the other's price as given (i.e., acts as is postulated in a "Cournot" model of oligopoly pricing) instead of colluding to

maximize joint profits. Suppose that the two firms failed to appreciate their mutual interdependence, and that the handle maker set his price taking the price of heads as fixed, and the head maker did the same taking the price of handles as fixed. The head maker would see customers as willing to pay a price for heads equal to the maximum amount these customers would pay for hammers minus the price of handles. Analogously, the handle maker would see his derived demand as the market demand for hammers minus the price of heads. The head maker firm acting as a monopolist would choose an output so that $MR - P_j = MC_i$, where MR is the marginal revenue associated with hammers, P_j is the price of handles and MC_i is the marginal cost of heads. The price he would wish to charge would be the price on his derived demand curve associated with this output. This price would exceed marginal cost. That is $P_i > MC_i$. Analogous conditions would hold for the handle maker. At the Cournot equilibrium each firm must be producing the same number of units of output and charging the profit maximizing price given the price the other firm is charging. In contrast the condition for maximizing joint profits is $MR = MC_i + MC_j$. The output which satisfies these conditions must be greater than the output satisfying the Cournot conditions since under the Cournot solution $MR = MC_i + P_j > MC_i + MC_j$, and the marginal revenue curve must cut the marginal cost curves from above at a profit-maximizing solution.

[5] USGAO (1983, p.7). 1979 was the last year AT&T was required to separately report its rate of return on overseas MTS. Overseas service (as opposed to international service) is generally defined as service between the lower 48 states and the rest of the world excluding Canada and Mexico. Under this definition Alaska, Hawaii, Puerto Rico, the Virgin Islands, and Guam are considered overseas points. Excluding Alaska, Hawaii, Puerto Rico, the Virgin Islands, and Guam (as was done in Tables 2 and 3) would almost surely have increased the reported rate of return. The basis for this conclusion is that both retained tariff revenue per outbound minute and foreign receipts per inbound minute were greater when these points were excluded, and the average cost per minute of serving these points is unlikely to be below that of the average for serving other overseas points. For example, in 1982 the retained tariff revenue per outbound minute was $.37 when these points were excluded and $.30 when included, and foreign receipts per inbound minute was $.95 excluding these points and $.62 including them.

[6] The condition that revenue on inbound minutes exceeds retained revenue on outbound minutes is equivalent to the accounting rate exceeding the collection rate. Thus if the collection rate is the same in both countries, the country with the net outflow of traffic will keep the smaller share of the total revenue if the accounting rate exceeds the collection rate. This can be shown mathematically. Let C = collection rate, A = accounting rate, M_u = minutes outbound from the U.S., M_f = minutes outbound from a foreign country (i.e., U.S. inbound minutes). Then U.S. net revenue is given by $C M_u - .5A M_u + .5M_f = C M_u - .5A(M_u - M_f)$. Likewise, foreign net revenue is given by $C M_f + .5A(M_u - M_f)$. The U.S. net revenue is less than the foreign net revenue if $C M_u - .5A(M_u - M_f) < C M_f + .5A(M_u - M_f)$, or if $C(M_u - M_f) - A(M_u - M_f) < 0$, which is equivalent to $(C - A)(M_u - M_f) < 0$. This is true if either $A < C$ and $M_u > M_f$ or $C > A$ and $M_u < M_f$. That is, the U.S. net revenues will be less than

the foreign net revenues if either the accounting rate exceeds the collection rate and U.S. outbound minutes exceed inbound minutes, or the collection rate exceeds the accounting rate and U.S. outbound minutes are less than inbound.

[7] *See* Pearce (1983) for a discussion of the actions taken by the FCC and State Department.

[8] The fact that PTTs were reluctant to grant multiple operating agreements does not imply that the FCC policies to prevent whipsawing are unnecessary. Without such a FCC policy, whipsawing might be more likely to succeed and PTTs might have seen competition among U.S. carriers as creating an opportunity for increasing their share of the benefits of international telecommunications.

[9] USFCC (1936). The policy was renamed in Implementation and Scope of the International Settlements Policy for Parallel International Communications Routes, Order on Reconsiderations, CC Docket No. 85–204. (USFCC, 1987).

[10] There is one minor exception to the broad statement that there are no cases of a zero accounting rate. Western Union International has a sender keep all arrangement with Canada and Mexico. This arrangement, however, is a result of network design and not market power of the Canadians or Mexicans. Apparently the arrangement evolved because there is no inexpensive way to monitor the messages going to and from these countries, given the way WUI's network is set up.

[11] Accounting rates would not affect traffic volume if they did not affect the pricing decisions of the carriers, or if demand were highly inelastic. Pricing decisions might be unaffected if the accounting rate is arrived at through a bargaining process between a PTT and a single U.S. carrier or a group of U.S. carriers acting as a cartel. In this case the U.S. carriers might view the accounting rate as distributional device and not as the marginal cost of terminating traffic.

[12] This assumes that raising the accounting rate does not significantly reduce the flow of traffic to the PTT.

[13] In the case of telex services the Commission has never granted a waiver request for a deviation from a uniform accounting rate.

Chapter 6
Industrial Organization for the Telecommunications Sector: Main Scenarios

Jacques Arlandis

There are certainly several ways of understanding the "regulation" of an industrial sector. If the public actor is focused on, the way it sets the economic rules will be stressed. If the industrial system is focused on, the question will be how such an almost cybernetic system functions. If the relationships between the industrial actors are focused on, the question becomes where economic added value comes from and how they are shared by these actors. The latter has been chosen in our analysis.

In this perspective, an unoriginal although necessary remark should be made: The overall added value of the telecommunications sector in 1989 (the revenue was about 330 billion dollars*) is produced and shared from a relation between the power struggle among actors and the market structure. However, this relation is hard to grasp. Compared with the past (from the 1950s through the 1970s) designating the parameters of this relation is no longer easy. Faced with such a prosody, no less than three main vectors are needed to define the issue:

- technological innovation due to increasing research and development expenditures;
- the gap between consumer demand and the wide range of supply;
- the rising number of industrial actors in a position to have their say.

---

* All figures and statistics are IDATE estimates.

Today's priority, not only for the economic partners but also for the exegetes that we are, is to organize this uncertainty.

The regulation of an industrial sector, that is the way added value is produced and shared, is easier to perceive when it is identified with one market (or a small number of markets). Up until the early 1980s, this was true of the telecommunications sector.

Before deregulation, an oliogopolistic structure was imposed on the equipment market by the monopolistic supply of telecommunications services. As the entire telecommunications market was interdependent, the demand for services could not play a well-defined part. The value added partition rules were set beforehand by the public network operators' efforts to minimize their transaction costs with the few industrial partners. This partition never went further than the national boundaries inside which the public monopoly was legitimized.

From this prospect, deregulation is only the end of this pattern; it is the public announcement that the old distribution rule is no longer suitable. It suits neither the public nor the private partners, since it does not enable them to optimize the use of their own resources.

Nowadays, almost everyone agrees that the real deregulatory challenge resides in the capacity to make up a new set of rules—whether accepted or imposed—defining how the overall added value should be shared.

Why did deregulation not impose its own clear set of rules? Actually, the reasons were rather trivial: the system was becoming more complex; the industry had started creating new types of externalities (new demands to share the profits with outsiders); and economic activities were going international. It is easy enough then, to understand why a consensus has become too hard to reach. New coalitions are always coming up, causing a systematic resetting of the rules that seemed to have been emerging. At this point, the motion launched deregulation into an apparently everlasting struggle.

The Japanese understood this long before their American counterparts. Their political authorities chose an economic deregulation which left the industry as the defenders of Japanese interests. This is clearly a pragmatic approach to the regulation issue.

So, complexity and uncertainty are almost equivalent definitions of the relation referred to earlier when describing the partition of the added value produced by the telecommunications sector.

At this point, I would like to shift to a different attitude, and prefer explanatory diagrams to rhetoric, tools to words: "Draw me your concept," as the Little Prince would have said on today's telecom planet.

COMPLEXITY, UNCERTAINTY, AND VALUE-ADDED PARTITION: A THREE-LAYER MODEL

In 1989, the overall telecommunications market was estimated at 330 billion dollars. This added value was partitioned as follows:

1. equipment production,
2. network operation,
3. telecommunications services.

Up until the late 1970s, the partition of this added value troubled little water. But the 1990s will probably be a decisive turn in the evolution of this partition. The partition is becoming more and more conflictual because:

1. Although limited-business and household communications expenditures, investment or consumption expenditures, cannot rise two-fold from one decade to another, the market growth rate is unpredictable;
2. Industrial structures, that is, the nature of the markets and the number of actors involved, are not stabilized. This is partially due to regulation, but also to the burden of technological variable and actor strategies which, in a way, amplify this destabilization.

Figure 1 represents these evolutions.

It is necessary to examine the specificity of the rules that control the partition of added value. The first step will be to apply the conventional concepts of industrial economics to the telecommunications sector.

Subject to an implicit agreement up until the 1980s, the partition of

Uncertain growth rate		Changing market structure
New needs		
Multiservices	SERVICE SUPPLY	Deregulation
Multinetworks	NETWORKS OPERATION	New entrants
Multiproducts	EQUIPMENT	Agreements and alliances
New technologies		

Figure 1.

economies of scale between those who manufacture technological equipment of subsystems and those who integrate and organize networks is now being transformed because of constraints due to research and development efforts and due to the fall of natural monopolies (see Figure 2).

The partition of economies of scope which define the conditions of valorization for a pool of services "using" the same type of infrastructure is also becoming a central and challenging issue. Today, technoeconomic conditions in the telecommunications sector open the door to several "arrangements": a dedicated network that optimizes one service only; a network that optimizes one category of services; a service optimized by the opportunistic use of different networks; or a universal or integrated services network optimized by the opportunistic management of all its present and future services. No exact science can guide us in the choice between so many options. Only the intelligence of industrial actors and the justification (if not too late) of a technoeconomic choice based on profit making or strategic criteria can help.

The partition of the value of use is an even newer issue. It is based on the analysis of the role which telecommunications play and will play in the economic activity of the other industrial sectors. Telecommunications are increasingly present in economic activities; they are present in the production phase during which telecommunications and technologies cooperate to improve productivity. They are also present in the transaction phase, where telecommunications networks are used more frequently as the means for market organization. Telecommunications are even present in the products themselves, with the trend to "computerize" market production.

Hence the value of telecommunications is clearly increasing, giving the telecommunications sector a reason to claim "higher fees" for their services. However, users can also argue that they are responsible for the value of use.

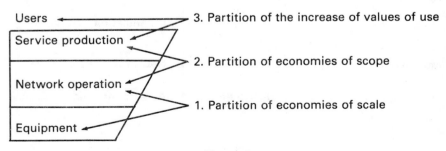

Figure 2.

As said before, a universal rule cannot be used to arbitrate between the internalization and externalization of the value of use. On the other hand, the arbitration will be subject to changes of equilibrium during the years to come. For, although the "distance from supply," that is, user understanding of network and telecom services, is diminishing (it's almost nonexistent in banking) and is still important in many industries. For the moment, this diversity should save the partition of added value from being overpowered by a line of force.

Here again, considering the production and distribution of added value, the economic analysis of the telecom sector remains rather vague.

Nevertheless, it is possible to anticipate how added value will be partitioned in the future by examining the different pressure to which the system is subjected. The following scenario defines a consistent system of parameters. This definition may seem cursory to some, but it leads to a more analytical reflection in order to articulate three categories of parameters: economic (amount of added value, partition, etc.), structural (market structure, concentration of supply, etc.), and behavioral (competitive and cooperative strategies, etc.). Each scenario is designated by a name, a mnemonic chosen from everyday telecommunication jargon, whose definition has already been the subject of many discussions. Our objective is certainly not to contribute to this confusing situation, but to clarify it some by choosing a different angle so as to attribute a "value" to expressions such as ISDN, VAS, VAN, etc.

Four scenarios will reflect the four major levels of the partition of added value. In the first, the ISDN scenario, the largest part of the added value goes to the industrialists. Equipment is economically the determining factor. Industrialists now realize this, although they were slow to adopt the ISDN concept.

The second scenario refers to the notion of value added networks (VAN). In a value added network, all the economic partners accept the idea that networks are essential—and even strategic—for the production of added value. So the network operators are in a good position to "reap" the benefits.

In the VAS scenario, services become the system's strategic point. The commercial valorization of services conditions the breakdown of the overall added value produced by the sector. Thus, computer services and other service providers are in a good position to turn the advantages of their strategic position into economic benefits.

Finally, the private networks configuration should not be ignored. Here, users internalize their telecommunications activities as much as possible. This strategy is based on the existence of private networks, which do not necessarily have a discriminant management.

What counts in this system is how private networks are controlled: cooperative; exclusively private with possible third party use; private with several joint-ventures; or virtual private networks on public networks. Concerning the partition of added value, a scenario such as this one obviously tends to be beneficial for the consumers, and to a lesser extent, for industrialists who, opportunistically but not strategically, may make some profit out of it.

These brief scenarios are analytical grids to interpret what is at stake in a sector more so than predictive tools meant to measure the exact breakdown of added value. They also reflect the logic involved in regulation more than the way they are applied. Although roughly superposable on the former, the model used in the second part of this analysis is slightly different.

METHODS FOR THE PARTITION OF ADDED VALUE AND TRANSACTION COSTS: A FIVE-LAYER MODEL

Uncertainty and complexity are the two terms of reference in the argument developed in the first part of this analysis. The apparently simple three-layer model that I had chosen seemed helpful in grasping the logic behind the partition of added value in the telecommunications sector. This simplification appeared eloquent enough in so far as it enabled a biunivocal relationship between markets and actors. In this perspective, it is clear that the nature of the actors determined the nature of the markets for a long time.

Today, this is no longer exact. Affected by deregulation (directly in the U.S. and France), "technologics," and economics (relationships between the telecommunications sector and other sectors), the system has been reorganized. The actors are no longer the total masters of the game. Structural evolution obeys its own logic and the three-layer model becomes insufficient.

In fact, the partition of added value reflects the arbitration on the sector, and four markets seem to be emerging in today's telecom landscape:

1. communications services,
2. network services,
3. telecommunications functions,
4. technologies.

Basically, this is called market typology, with each type or category corresponding to a variable number of segments (the difference between a market and a marketplace). It should now be easier to grasp the complexity of the problem and it has even become possible to illustrate this with a diagram (see Figure 3).

This diagram allows us to seize the system's complexity, multiplying markets, logic (from applications to technologies) and actors (per level, on each market).

This five-layer model should be a first step toward a better understanding of this complexity. But the second major term of our analysis—uncertainty—remains unexplained. The first part of the analysis dealt with this aspect in an almost anecdotal way, touching upon market growth rate, new technologies, networks, services, and uses. The discussion now becomes much more precise. The true culprit of today's uncertainty in the telecommunications sector is the possibility for actors to "reorganize" their relationships and change a situation in view of optimizing their share of the added value. Techno-economic evolution has supplied them with the opportunity to "recuperate" this added value on four markets instead of two.

However, uncertainty can also be perceived on another level. We know, and this was made even clearer by Williamson (1975), that there are basically two ways of breaking down added value: markets, of course, but also *hierarchies,* the integration of industrial relationships in the well-defined boundaries.

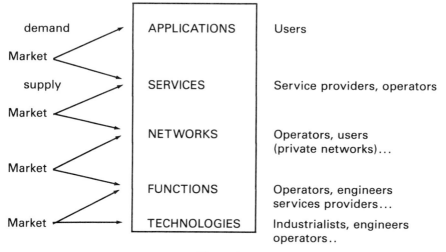

Figure 3.

The diagram of a generic matrix which associates five layers with two forms of industrial organization can illustrate this uncertainty (see Figure 4).

Given this perspective, the earlier definition of a scenario becomes important, since it enables the characterization of the logic-dominating actor strategy as well as a better comprehension of how the rules are set: Choices made between markets and hierarchies at each level of the telecommunications system will lead to very important practical repercussions.

Since each combination gives rise to a new coherence, there are far more scenarios this time. Conversely, the four scenarios presented before should become a subset of these possibilities. This exercise, although of a formal nature, is rich in concrete information.

The future of the ISDN scenario depends on the hierarchic relationships including technologies, functions, networks, and services (see Figure 5).

There is only one market: services (value-added services). This suggests it would be a fairly rigid system, with a serious bottleneck when it comes to the partition of added value.

Figure 6 is an open scenario: Economic relationships between actors can be polarized on three market levels. Nevertheless, the telecommunications services remain by definition the determinant factor in this scenario.

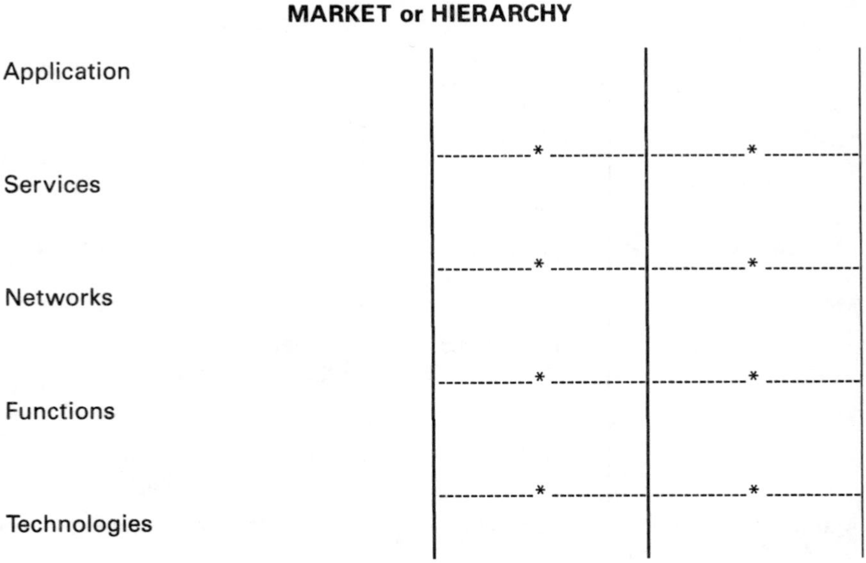

MARKET or HIERARCHY

Figure 4.

1. ISDN scenario

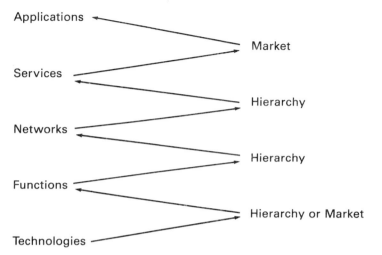

Figure 5.

2. VAS scenario

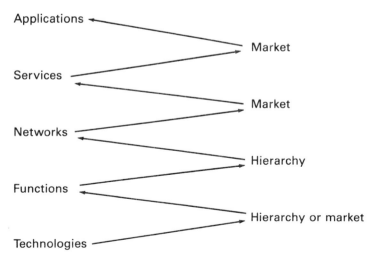

Figure 6.

3. VAN scenario

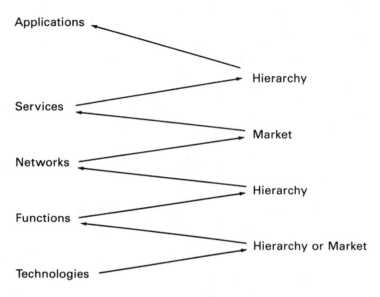

Figure 7.

In this third scenario (Figure 7), the system focusses on the network: market downstream, hierarchies upstream. As for industrial relationships, the aim is to try to control this level.

The scenario (Figure 8), in which consumers "integrate" (internalize) the biggest share of added value, can only work if a real market based on functions is created (Centrex, for instance), and if public and private networks are transparent (ONA/ONP).

However, this type of analysis does not give a satisfactory answer to one fundamental question: What makes actors choose between defining their industrial relationships in a market context or in a hierarchical context? Williamson helps solve this problem, or at least ask the right question, by explaining why transaction costs are an essential factor.

Transaction costs are all the costs connected with the transfer of property rights. In other words, they are the costs, often unseen, which make transaction possible: The acceptance, or certification, of a telecommunications terminal costs something, and this "something" must be located in order to control certain market-related industrial relationships which may develop.

4. Private networks scenario

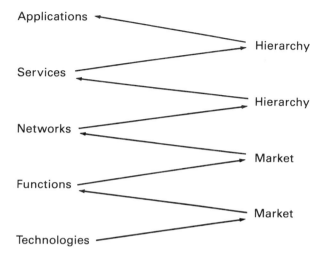

Figure 8.

Minimizing transaction costs has always been an objective common to industrial actors and customers. In a system that increases the ways an inter-actor equilibrium can be reached and authorizes a growing number of actors, this preoccupation has become of major importance. The stakes for transaction costs are shifted from the periphery to the center. Their perception becomes a key element of success or failure.

This is the direction which will be taken, since today's telecommunications sector possess all the "virtues" of a system in which the mastering of transaction costs has become essential. However, this statement is a profession of faith more than an actual demonstration.

Although a reasoned intuition, it does merit a far more analytical argument. These three questions need to be answered:

- Where are the transaction costs located?
- Who is in charge of estimating them?
- Who will accept the cost for them?

These basic questions were already brought up during discussion about deregulation in France. Answering these questions will probably take some time. But before then, industrial actors will become aware that today's strategic orientation should be in increasing their market power—that is, their capacity to impose a choice between markets and hierarchies—while minimizing their transaction costs.

REFERENCE

Williamson, O.E. (1975). *Markets and hierarchies*. New York: Free Press.

Chapter 7
Competition, Concentration, and Competitiveness of the European Manufacturing Industry

Godefroy Dang Nguyen

It is a widely held opinion that the European telecommunications industry is too fragmented, due to regulation and the protection of "national champion." This chapter tries to investigate the consequences of this protection on the competitiveness of European firms, in particular the way they conduct R&D in the essential public-switching market. It then becomes apparent how the opening of national markets caused by deregulation may impinge on the competitiveness of the European manufacturing industry.

First, a description of the telecommunications manufacturing industry is made, which shows a clear stability of structures over time. Then second sourcing, a common practice by carriers to improve the competitive supply of equipment, is examined. The impact of second sourcing is shown. Finally, an estimation is made of potential benefits from alliances or mergers. A distinction is made between the end 1970s period, when alliances had a large potential benefit, and 1980s period, when the benefits from partnership are more limited. In conclusion, some indications are put forward on the limits of our model.

THE TELECOMMUNICATIONS MANUFACTURING INDUSTRY

The Situation in 1985

In 1985, the market for telecommunication equipment reached $79 billion. Although not comparable to the telecommunications service market (more than $200 billion), it has a strategic importance for the major manufacturers: AT&T, Alcatel, Siemens, NEC, Ericsson, etc. The geographical structure of the demand is shown in Table 1.

The public switching systems account for 40% of the total market by 1990, with an annual growth rate of only 1.8%. The central importance of public switching in the telecommunications equipment market is due to many factors, including the impact on network architectures and long-standing relationships between the seller and the buyer. With deregulation and technological progress, however, this relationship will be loosened.

The main suppliers of central exchanges in 1984 are shown in Table 2.

That telecommunications manufacturing is too fragmented was a well-admitted opinion in the mid 1980s. The European Commission, in particular, had claimed that the amortization of a current central exchange generation over a life time of 10 years required a market share of 7%. Therefore, by 1990, many experts expected 5 major suppliers to remain in the market, instead of the 10 that existed at the time.

Table 1.   Telecommunications Equipment (million $)

	1983	1984	1985
North America	$23,361	24,964	27,014
Europe	22, 625	21,945	21,967
Far East	11,433	11,383	11,637
Soviet Union	6,000*	6,400*	6,750*
Pacific area	3,275	2,848	3,870
Middle East	3,487	3,230	3,349
Latin America	2,549	2,595	2,963
Africa	1,963	1,852	1,670

Source: Golschmann (1986)
*Estimation.

Table 2.   Telecommunications Manufacturing Industry in 1969 and 1984. ($ million)

1969		1984	
1) Western Electric	4,000	1) AT&T	11,300
2) ITT	820	2) ITT	4,381
3) Siemens	700	3) Siemens	3,600
4) GTE	590	4) Northern Telecom	3,318
5) Ericsson	480	5) Ericsson	3,268
6) Northern Electric	300	6) Alcatel-Thomson	2,794
7) NEC	260	7) NEC	2,564
8) Plessey	192	8) GTE	2,496
9) AEG	190	9) Plessey	807
10) Philips	150		
11) CGE	136		

The simple arithmetic mixes two different things, products and firms. Current figures for R&D expenditures ($600 million for development, and $100 million per year for adapting the system to different national networks and new functionalities such as ISDN) clearly lead to a concentration of the supply, particularly in Europe. But this does not necessarily lead to mergers. Several firms have joined their efforts to develop a public exchange: GEC, Plessey, and STC for System X, GTE, and Italtel for the Italian UT/10-3. Conversely some firms have merged but still offer two lines of products: Alcatel NV produces Alcatel's E 10/MT and ITT's System 12.

In general, alliances are unstable, while mergers sooner or later lead to product rationalization. But in the medium term, the structure of the supply is not necessarily given by the number of suppliers: in fact, oligopolization and concentration is parallel to the major customers, the carriers, opening the market. Carriers tend to buy from at least two sources, and the Swiss or Italian PTTs even have three suppliers. But this market opening is not as large as one could claim.

The U.S. market has been the most open since AT&T's divestiture, and this confirms that deregulation has an impact on the opening of carriers purchases. In the U.S. case, this has benefitted Northern Telecom for the central exchange segment. According to Northern Business Information in 1985, the Canadian manufacturer succeeded in selling as many public and private exchanges as AT&T. This became possible as a result of the earlier digitization of the Canadian network and the similarity of U.S. and Canadian network features.[1]

The European network operators have also tried to open their purchasing procedure, while preparing themselves for deregulation.

The Bundespost opened to second sourcing in 1981, but the second manufacturer, SEL, has long been present in Germany, and this firm is accustomed to working in cooperation with Siemens, its main competitor. One could say that the situation evolved from a recognized cartel to a more competitive duopoly. In the UK, Ericsson has become a second source to British Telecom, to swap their national champion (GEC/Plessy and Alcatel, respectively) as second sources. In the British case also, two sources of the former generation of exchanges, the analog TXE2 and TXE4 already existed; hence, second sourcing is not a novelty. In France, Ericsson recently bought the French second source, CGCT, after a strong competition with Siemens and AT&T. But second sourcing had also been introduced in 1975–76, when Thomson supplied Ericsson's CP 400 and ITT's Metaconta to the French PTT, in addition to Alcatel's E 10.

Although the "duopolization" of the major public switching markets is not as impressive as is sometimes claimed, it is nonetheless present. The major difference is that the second is now a true "foreigner" (Ericsson in the UK, the Netherlands and France, Alcatel in Germany), while in the past, the second source was a national company, or a long established subsidiary of a multinational, which behaved as a local manufacturer.

Additionally, the telecom manufacturing industry evolves along "long cycles," making its structure more stable than often perceived.

The Manufacturing Industry in the 1960s

At that time, national markets were more protected than now; the share of world trade was less than 10% of world production, compared to 15% more recently. Also, public switching was not yet digital. However the industry structure was not very different, as we see from the comparison of Table 2.

In the public switching segment this similarity also holds while the breakthroughs of Alcatel, Ericsson, and Northern Telecom are noticeable: These three companies have been innovators in the transition from analogue to digital technology, and this explains their breakthrough. The stagnation of other manufacturers' production is explained by the investment cycles of their main customer: NTT's program culminated in 1974, while this happened in France in 1982 only.

Long-Term Determination of Market Structure

Although the market structure of the public switching segment has not evolved radically since the 1960s, current technology may lead to major changes, with the lifetime reduction of market positions evolving more quickly; for example, the implementation of the ISDN in European networks requires the adaptation of existing exchanges, with new development costs. The issue is thus the following: Could the firms have anticipated this market evolution (concentration and increased competition)? Has the national market protection prevented the firm's adaptation? Will deregulation and the practice of second sourcing in Europe lead to a better competitiveness? We will try to answer these questions in the remainder of this chapter.

THE EUROPEAN INDUSTRY: MARKET POWER AND CONCENTRATION

Purchasing Policies of the Main European PTTs

With digital exchanges, the purchasing policy of European PTTs has evolved. In Germany, after the expiration of Siemens' patent life for the EMD electromechanical exchange, the Bundespost redesigned its purchasing policy. From 1975 onwards public tenders have been set up each year, which are limited to the four German suppliers (Siemens, De Tewe, SEL, Telefonbau): An incentive mechanism gives an increase in market share of 2% to the best offer each year. Since 1979, after having discarded Philips' PRX, the Bundespost has competitively selected two new digital exchanges, Siemens' EWSD and SEL's System 12. Now, the two systems compete annually.

In Italy, the purchasing policy of SIP, the Italian main carrier, is biased since it is owned by STET, the State holding company which also owns Italy's major manufacturer, Italtel. According to Pontarollo (1983), SIP writes a "Memorandum" in which the amount of orders and prices are defined. The latter are determined from investigations into manufacturer costs. Pontarollo claims that prices are aligned with the most expensive proposal, since it is generally the one of Italtel. Digitization has led to the delivery of three systems to SIP: Ericsson's AXE, Alcatel's System 12, and Italtel's UT 10/3 Proteo.

In the UK, the privatization of British Telecom was followed by a change of the relationship of BT with the "Ring" of suppliers. In March 1985 the "System Y" of Ericsson was selected as a second source, with the first shippings at the end of 1986. The aim of BT is to bring the share of System Y to 25–30% of its orders at the beginning of the 1990s. In France, the merger of telecom activities of Alcatel and Thomson in 1983-1984 upset France Telecom's purchasing policy. The latter has strived for competition between suppliers since 1976, and suddenly faced a monopoly, Alcatel-Thomson. The arrival of Matra/ Ericsson as second source has enabled France Telecom to restore the competition between suppliers.

On the whole, the European PTTs have taken the opportunity of digitization to redesign their purchasing policy. The aim is now to focus on functional compatibility between different systems, and to put pressure on prices, through a yearly competitive bidding between several (generally two) recognized bidders.

The Competitive Behavior of Firms

It is generally admitted that manufacturers benefit from "rents" in their protected markets where prices and margins are higher than in the world market. According to an OECD study (1983), the prices of equipment in Europe were 20% to 30% higher than in the U.S. On the other hand, carriers are eager to reduce these margins: With the introduction of a second source, some incentives for competition are set up, with limited results.

First, as in the case of Italtel and SIP, or Bell Canada and Northern Telecom, vertical integration between a supplier and the customer leads to internal transfers: some lucrative market segments (telephone services) pay for risky projects (R&D in public switching). Second, the customer is in most cases a monopoly and can pass the burden of excessive prices to the end user, the telephone subscribers; it can thus put a mild pressure on pricing behavior by the suppliers. Third, industrial policy considerations are still present that require supporting national champions. In any case, it is not yet proven that the "rents" mentioned above are socially wasteful, since they permit the financing of R&D. Several theoretical papers have shown that in some cases, monopoly rents may be more efficiently employed as R&D subsidies (see, in particular, Dasgupta & Stiglitz, 1980).

A Theoretical Model

Consider a carrier who buys a quantity q of equipment from 2 suppliers. In order to stimulate competition, he organizes public tenders between them each year. The final price is the lowest proposal and market shares are function of the proposals. Mathematically

$$p = Inf(p1, p2)$$
$$q1 = f(p1, p2)$$
$$q2 = q - q1$$

where $p1$ is the price of the first bidder, $p2$ the other proposal, $q1$ and $q2$ the market shares. The strategy of the firms is to maximize their profits. A usual solution to this problem is the concept of Nash equilibrium. It can be shown (see Appendix 1), that, in case of repeated tenders (each year), and, provided market share do not change very much, collusion between the suppliers may be the outcome. This is a variation on the well known "prisoner's dilemma" problem, where the fear of retaliation leads to cooperative behavior (see Axelrod, 1984).

We can expect that suppliers will propose the highest price that the customer is ready to pay (Pareto optimal Nash equilibrium). So what is the purpose of the second source?

First, the incumbent has its market share reduced, even if its profit rate remains the same. It has to export if it wants to maintain its benefits. Second, a second source with a different technology may provide a better information to the buyer, and this will lower its maximum acceptable price. Third, in the medium term, production capacities will be better adjusted to demand evolution, particularly when fixed costs are high.

To summarize, the margin of the manufacturers, and the capability to finance R&D with profits earned from their protected markets, will be computed from the maximum acceptable price, p^*, that the buyer is ready to pay.

Market Power and the Financing of R&D

We assume that R&D costs for the next generation of public exchanges is $\$K$ billion, with K near to 1. The manufacturers will use the margin derived from their market power to finance this R&D. We suppose that the costs are linear, and fixed costs are mainly R&D costs:

$$c_i(q) = K_i + a_i^* q_i$$

We suppose that all manufacturers have the same R&D costs, $K_i = K$. Let p^* be the maximum acceptable price. A carrier will successfully introduce a second source, if it can pay for a fair share of R&D costs to this second source. Typically, if m is the proportion of its orders compared to world orders, it will pay mK to its suppliers. Then for a second source with a marginal cost a_i and market share q_i:

$$(p^* - a_i) \cdot q = q_i.m.$$

which determines p^*.

If marginal costs are negatively proportional to market shares (something that is related to economies of scale in production), then the national champion, with a larger market share, will earn "super-profits," or rents, beyond the mere payment of a fair share of R&D

Table 3.   Manuafacturers market shares in Europe

	Siem.	Eric.	ITT	Alca.	Ital.	Ples/ GEC	ATT/ Phil.
Germany	.70	0	.30	0	0	0	0
France	0	.15	0	.85	0	0	0
UK	0	.20	0	0	0	.80	0
Italy	.2	.2	.2	0	.6	0	0
Spain	0	.3	.7	0	0	0	0
Belgium	.2	0	.8	0	0	0	0
Netherlands	0	.25	0	0	0	0	.75
Denmark	0	.80	.20	0	0	0	0
Portugal	.5	0	.5	0	0	0	0
Greece	.4	0	.4	0	0	0	.2
Ireland	0	.4	.2	.4	0	0	0

Source: Quatrepoint (1984), with later estimations

costs. Also, the more equally the market is divided between the two sources, the lesser are these rents. With fair division (50/50) the rents are nil (see Appendix 2 for computation).

In order to compute the "rents," we need some information about markets and market shares. Table 3 shows the current market shares in most European countries.

Finally, Table 4 is an estimation of market sizes of the European countries for the period 1985–1994.

It is possible, then to compute the margins given by the carriers to the European manufacturers, in Europe, to recoup their R&D costs. Table 5 summarizes the computations.

Table 4.   Size of European markets (1985–1994) for digital exchanges (% of World market)

Germany	5.85
France	6.67
UK	6.84
Italy	5.34
Spain	2.78
Belgium	.77
Netherlands	1.62
Denmark	.86
Ireland	.43
Portugal	.43
Greece	.21

Source: Northern Business Information (1985)

Table 5.   R & D financed on European market by European firms ($ milions)

ALCATEL	$649
PLESSEY/GEC	565
ITT	488
ERICSSON	408
SIEMENS	388
ITALTEL	192
ATT/PHILIPS	120

Noticeably, Alcatel has, after its merger with Thomson but before merger with ITT, the higher European financing, because of the size of its market (France) and its dominant position in this market. Siemens, on the other hand, is handicapped by a delayed digitization of the German network and a lower market share (70%, against 85% for Alcatel in France). However, Alcatel has to maintain two digital systems—E 10 of Alcatel and MT 20 of Thomson—and this costs probably around 1.5 times the price of a single system. Therefore, the financing of R&D by system in Europe can be calculated and is shown in Table 6.

European markets alone are not sufficient for European firms to recoup their R&D costs, if the latter are as high as $1 billion. Also, Ericsson and ITT, although installed in most European countries, do not benefit fully from this situation, compared to national champions, because they cannot earn extra margins from dominant positions. After the ITT/Alcatel merger, the new Alcatel NV entity has an R&D financing of $1,143 million, for approximately 2.5 systems; that is, $457 million per system. This does not give a leading position to this firm, unless it can streamline its product image.

Table 6.   R & D financed by digital system ($ million)

PLESSEY/GEC	$565
ITT	488
ALCATEL NV	457
ALCATEL	432
ERICSSON	408
SIEMENS	388
ITALTEL	192

Conclusion

We have tried to evaluate the position of the European industry in public switching. We have shown that deregulation and opening markets to second sourcing does not prevent the survival of "rents" to national champions. The often publicized statement of the European Commission that national markets are insufficient to finance R&D is correct but useless: Even if entry were free, most PTTs would limit their purchase to two sellers, and continue to pay extra profits to incumbent firms. The major impact of second sourcing is to reduce the market size of the national champion, and to force it to get exports to maintain its production. Also, concentration has nothing to do with market openings, as the ITT/CGE, ATT/Italtel mergers have shown. But are some mergers more efficient than others?

POTENTIAL ALLIANCES BETWEEN EUROPEAN FIRMS

The Situation in the Late 1970s

Digital switching has not emerged in a single stroke. Some firms have been innovators, some followers, but it is recognized that there are too many products in the market. By 1983, 13 digital switches had been announced by as many companies, and, by 1986, all but 3 were in production.

The innovators in the digital market were Alcatel, Northern Telecom, and Ericsson, which had collectively captured 72% of the digital lines installed by 1985 (Chavelet, 1986).

With two European innovators (Ericsson and Alcatel), the question may be raised whether some followers had an interest to merge with one of the two, to avoid R&D expenditure. Since the British firms, although not innovators, had long been involved in digital switching, they were unlikely to abandon a project where their main customer, the Post Office, was involved.[2] Other European firms, Siemens, Italtel, Philips, ITT, and Thomson could have formed alliances with innovators. The results in terms of R&D financing are summarized in Table 7:

ITT was an ideal partner for both innovators, because it offered wide European market coverage. Also, Ericsson would have been a better partner to ITT than Alcatel. So the best alliance, in the late 1970s, was between ITT and Ericsson. A second best would have been a partnership or merger between ITT and Alcatel-Thomson, which happened in 1986. One can say that the merger would have been much more effective in the late 1970s.

Table 7.   Gains from alliances in the '70s in Europe ($ millions)

ERICSSON WITH:	PHILIPS	SIEMENS	ITT	ITALTEL
R & D financed	$404	490	978	445
ALCATEL WITH:	PHILIPS	SIEMENS	ITT	ITALTEL
R & D financed	239	356	827	247

Finally, were alliances or mergers made in 1978 instead of 1984 or 1985, higher margins would have been generated and competitiveness would have increased. In a sense, the Commission's statement that market fragmentation has prevented an adaptation of the European industry to new market conditions is correct. There was, at the end of the 1970s, a real potential for improving the competitiveness of the European industry through a series of real concentration and mergers between innovators and followers. The latter, instead, have developed their own system and joined the international competition. But if the followers, Philips, ITT, Italtel, Siemens, and Thomson, could have improved their position through a merger, no innovator/follower team would have been sufficient to reach the $1 billion barrier. Even at the end of the 1970s, exports were necessary to recoup costs.

Possible Configurations in the Mid-1980s

It might be interesting to look at the potential alliances between the remaining firms, once a first series of concentration movements occurred at the beginning of the 1980s: Thomson and Philips dropped out of the public exchange market, ITT has merged with CGE.

However, the situation is now very different from the former one. Previously, some firms offered a digital exchange while others did not. Now, all have a digital exchange. Any merger will permit economization of some costs at the margin, but the gains will be limited and the adaptation costs in social terms will be higher: layoffs and plant closings will be the consequence of streamlining the product range after mergers.

We have tested two configurations of coalitions.

The first one includes Alcatel and Italtel on the one hand, and Siemens and Ericsson the other. The second hypothesis is a coalition of Alcatel and Siemens on the one hand, with a second coalition grouping Ericsson, Italtel, and the British firms on the other. In the latter hypothesis, the German Bundespost would seek a second source, AT&T or Northern Telecom. We suppose that APT (ATT/Philips joint venture) would get the market. Table 8 summarizes the results of our simulation.

Table 8.   Gains from alliances in the 1980s ($ millions)

First configuration:	ALCATEL + ITALTEL	SIEMENS + ERICSSON
R & D financed by systems	$413	394
Second configuration:	ALCATEL + SIEMENS	ERICSSON + ITALTEL + GEC/PLESSEY
R & D Financed by system *	480	423

*It is assumed that ATT or Northern takes 15% in the German and British markets (second source after mergers).

Although it would be more interesting for Alcatel to team with Siemens rather than Italtel, this coalition is unlikely, given the cultural differences between ITT's subsidiaries and Siemens. Noticeably the "big coalition" Ericsson/Italtel/British companies would have a comparable market share to Alcatel NV. But here again, transaction costs of running this coalition make it unlikely. Hence, the second configuration: Alcatel/Siemens on one side, the other European on the other, is less likely than the Siemens/Ericsson and Alcatel/Italtel configuration.

Generally speaking, our computations suggest that Alcatel NV is the pivotal element of coalitions. Ericsson also has an equivalent role, but the potential benefits are lower.

CONCLUSIONS

In this chapter we have tried to simulate the functioning of public switching markets in Europe. We have shown that deregulation and market opening have had a minor impact on the industry behavior. More important has been the impact of technology evolution (digitization, soaring R & D costs) on the market structure. We have shown that, at the end of the 1970s, concentration offered great possibility for the improvement of market structures and firms competitiveness in Europe. This opportunity, however, has been missed, probably because of market fragmentation and the defense of national champions.

Some concentration efforts were made at the beginning of the 1980s, but the coalitions were not optimal from our point of view. In the mid-1980s, the markets that remained were as fragmented as in the 1970s, and the second sourcing could not generate overwhelming benefits for the industry as a whole.

In the late 1980s, the concentration game can still be played, but our optimal configuration (a duopoly of Alcatel with Siemens on the one hand, and Ericsson and British firms and Italtel on the other) is impossible to set up. Instead, Italtel has teamed with ATT, and GEC and Siemens are bidding for Plessey. Four major groups will thus emerge in the 1990s in Europe: Alcatel, Siemens/British Firms, Ericsson, Italtel/Philips/ATT. The reason why our model could not predict the eventual configuration are numerous:

1. The entry of the U.S. firms has been neglected, since we were interested in the improvement of the European industry only.
2. Ericsson and Siemens are competing against one another to penetrate the U.S. market. This makes a coalition between them very unlikely.
3. Our model does not claim to encompass the diversity of production situations, the diversity of the products, or the impact of political factors: In France for example, the choice of a second source, Ericsson, has been mainly a political decision.
4. Innovations are still underway in the public switching business. Broadband switching is investigated at the firm level as well as the cooperative level (the European research program RACE). It may impinge on the firms strategies.
5. We have not investigated the position of the firms outside Europe. There are also protected markets (e.g., ex-colonies, or countries where a firm has long been present) that enable firms to generate extra margins for paying their costs.

The aim of this chapter was to link market structure, market behavior and technological evolution in a market where the hypothesis of perfect competition, or even Cournot or Bertrand oligopoly, do not apply. The rather theoretical exercise undertaken here may help to understand firms' decisions, and to show the boundaries in which these decisions are made. We could easily generalize our method to the world market, in order to answer the question: what is the optimal number of digital exchange systems in the world market?

APPENDIX 1:
SOLUTION OF THE REPEATED
PUBLIC TENDER GAME

The carrier, each year, raises an amount, q, of orders from its two suppliers. It pays the price of the lowest bidder and has an incentive scheme, where the market shares are function of the bids. Hence, the profits can be written:

$$Max \ (Inf \ (p_1,p_2) \cdot f \ (p_1,p_2) - c_1 \ (f \ (p_1,p_2))$$

$$p_1$$

$$Max \ (Inf \ (p_1,p_2) \cdot (q - f \ (p_1,p_2)) - c_2 \ (q - f \ (p_1,p_2))$$

$$p_2$$

with linear functions

$$f \ (p_1,p_2) = \overline{q}_1 + a \ (p_2 - p_1)$$

$$c_1 \ (f \ (p_1,p_2)) = k_1 + c_1 \cdot (\overline{q}_1 + a \ (p_2 - p_1))$$

$$c_2 \ (\overline{q} - f \ (p_1,p_2)) = k_2 + c_2 \cdot (\overline{q}_2 - a \ (p_2 - p_1))$$

It is obvious that the strategies (p_{t^*}, p_{t^*}) at every time, where p* is the maximum acceptable price by the carrier, are Pareto optimal. We will show that they are Nash solutions for some values of the parameters.

Suppose that a supplier (say number one) begins a price war at $t = 0$. Then, its maximum profits will be:

$$Max \ \pi \ (p_1,p^*) = p_1 \ (\overline{q}_1 + a \ (p^* - p_1)) - k_1 - c_1 \ (\overline{q}_1 + a(p^* - p_1))$$

It can be computed that $\overline{p}_1$ which achieves the maximum profit is:

$$\overline{p}_1 = \frac{1}{2} \ (\overline{q}_1/a + c_1 + p^*)$$

And the potential gain, during period 0, of this price war, is:

$$G = \pi_1 \ (\overline{p}_1,p^*) - \pi_1 \ (p^*,p^*)$$

$$= (p^* - \overline{p}_1) \ (a(\overline{p}_1 - c_1) - \overline{q}_1)$$

Once the price war is unleashed, the second supplier will have an interest to price also $\overline{p}_1$, since its profits will increase: the new equilibrium will be $(\overline{p}_1, \overline{p}_1)$. The potential loss from period 1 onwards for the first supplier is thus (discounted at $t = 0$)

$$L = \sum_{t = 1}^{\infty} \alpha^t \ (\pi_1 \ (\overline{p}_1, \overline{p}_1) - \pi_{1^*})$$

by substitution we find that

$$L = \frac{\alpha}{(1 - \alpha)} (\bar{p}_1 - p^{\cdot}) \bar{q}_1$$

Hence, the price war is not profitable and $(\bar{p}^{\cdot}, \bar{p}^{\cdot})$ is a Nash equilibrium from one's point of view, if:

$G < L$, that is (after computations)

$$p^{\cdot} < \frac{\bar{q}_1}{a} (1 + \frac{2\,\alpha}{1 - \alpha}) + c_1$$

By permutation of one and two, we see that an equivalent relation holds for two. Hence

$$p^{\cdot} = Min\,(\frac{\bar{q}_1}{a} (1 + \frac{2\,\alpha}{1 - \alpha}) + c_1, \quad \frac{\bar{q}_2}{a}(1 + \frac{2\,\alpha}{1 - \alpha}) + c_2))$$

which can be computed by the carrier, gives a Nash equilibrium Pareto optimal.

APPENDIX 2
COMPUTATION OF THE PRICE
ACCEPTABLE BY THE CARRIER

As seen in the text, a reasonable assumption is that the network operator will be prepared to contribute to R&D expenditures in the proportion of its size compared to the world market:

Let α be this proportion. Then, for a supplier i

$$(p^{\cdot} - a_i) \cdot q_i = K_j = (\alpha \cdot K)\, q_i/q$$

where K is the cost of R&D, a_i the marginal (variable) cost of production, and K_j the amount its R&D paid in the market j.

Then $p^{\cdot} - a_i = \alpha K/q_j$ since $q_j - \alpha Q$, where Q is the world market size

$$p^{\cdot} - a_i + \frac{K}{Q}$$

Suppose now that the marginal cost a_i varies with the market share (economies of scale). More precisely let

$$a_i = (n + 1) a_{min} / (1 + n.B_i)$$

Where B_i is the market share, a_{min} the "competitive" price, that manufacturers will get in the world market, n the number of "optimal" suppliers in the world market:

when $B_i \to 0$, $a_i \to (1 + n) a_{min}$
$B_i \to 1$, $a_i \to a_{min}$

If a national champion is alone in the market ($m_i = 1$), it will be able to have a cost comparable to international standards. If a second source is introduced, the carrier has to guarantee to this second source that the margin obtained from this national market will be comparable to "international standards" therefore

$$(p - a_i)/p = (p^* - a_{min})/p^* = m^*$$

Where m is the "standard" margin. This determines the maximal acceptable price p by the carrier. From this we can deduct the margin of the national champion. It can be shown that this margin m is given by the following relation

$$m = m^* + \frac{a_{min} (1 - (n + 1) B_i)}{p^* (1 - n B_i)}$$

Where B_i is the market share of the second source. Clearly $m > m^*$, and national champions get "superprofits." In the numerical application, we have supposed that $n = 10$, that is there are optimally 10 manufacturers in the world market, which is consistent with the assumption that a 10% market share is necessary to recoup costs.

REFERENCES

Aurelle, B. (1966). *Les telecommunications*. Paris: Editions La Decouverte.
Brezzi, P. (1981). *La politica dell'elettronica*. Roma: Editori Riuniti.
Caty, G.F., & Ungerer, H. (1984, December). Les telecommunications: nouvelle frontiere de l'europe *Futuribles*.
Chavelet, E. (1986, December 30). CGE-ITT sur une meme ligne. *Le Figaro*.
Dasgupta, P., & Stiglitz, J. (1980). Industrial structure and the nature of innovative activity *Economic Journal*, pp. 1–28.

Dataquest/Nielsen. (1985, November). The European Telecommunications Industry.

Gilholy, D. (1987, January). The politics of switching. *Telecommunications.*

Golschmann, M. (1986). *L'industrie mondiale des telecommunications.* Publications CESTA, Paris.

Information Dynamics Ltd. (1986). *The European market for public digital telecommunications switching.* Rickmansworth.

Lorenzi, J.H., & Le Boucher, E. (1979). *Memoires volees.* Paris: Ramsay.

Il Mondo Economico. (1982). *Rapporto Mese: Telecommunicazioni.*

Moulin, H. (1981). *Theorie des Jeux pour l'economie et la politique.* Paris: Hermann.

Newstead, T. (1986, March). ISDN: A solution in search of a problem? *Telecommunications Policy.*

Northern Business Information. (1985). *The world public switching market: 1985 edition.* New York: Author.

Quatrepoint, J.M. (1984, May 15). CIT-Alcatel n'a fait qu'une percee limitee. *Le Monde.*

Salaun, J.M., & Sutter, H. (1974, July). L'industrie Quest europeene des telecommunications. *Revue Francaise des Telecommunications.*

Sarrati, L. (1984, February). Lo sviluppo delle reti di telecommunicazioni nel mondo. *Sistemi di Telecommunicazioni,* pp. 18–28.

ENDNOTES

[1] Other innovators in public switching (Ericsson and Cit Alcatel) penetrated the US market in 1982–83 only, when divestiture was announced. There is still skepticism about the variability of a third source to the new regional holding companies (Gilhooly, 1987).

[2] There have been tables, however, between Alcatel and Plessey in 1974 to import, to the UK, Alcatel's E 10, the only digital exchange in the world at that time.

Chapter 8
Asymmetric Deregulation and the Transformation of the International Telecommunications Regime*

William J. Drake

For 120 years, governments cooperated in the International Telecommunication Union (ITU) to maintain an international telecommunications regime which, compared to other international institutions, was remarkably stable. The framework established in the Austro-German telegraph treaty of 1850 was transferred to a multilateral regime with the birth of the International Telegraph Union in 1865, reaffirmed with the transition to the telecommunication union in 1934, and retained virtually unaltered until its transformation during the past three years. Scholars and industry observers have often interpreted this stability as a triumph of functionalist rationality, a view that was encouraged by ITU policy makers (Jacobson, 1973; Renaud, 1986, 1990; Wallenstein, 1976). But while the issues addressed in the ITU lent themselves to a technocratic style of problem solving, functionalism is weak as a causal explanation of regime cooperation in general and ITU cooperation in particular. Among other deficiencies, it overlooks the power and interests of the players involved, as well as the ways in which different collective action problems generate incentive struc-

---

* For their helpful comments on an earlier version of this paper, the author would like to thank George Codding Jr., Douglas Conn, Peter Cowhey, Lisa Martin, Eli Noam, and Anthony Rutkowski.

tures that help define the possibilities for a given style of problem solving in the first place.

The fundamental purpose of the *ancien* regime that has recently been replaced was to balance the demand for national sovereignty over domestic telecommunications with the requirements of international correspondence by standardizing internetwork connections and regulating cross-border service provision. In contrast to other collective action problems such as prisoner's dilemma, this was a coordination game with comparatively few incentives to defect from cooperation. True, network standardization sometimes involved distributional struggles over whose equipment would be chosen as the global model, but once a standard was agreed, nonconformance entailed increased transaction costs from the additional procedures and equipment needed to maintain interconnection which governments generally did not want to pay. Service regulation and provision was made even easier by convergent interests: None of the ITU's member governments wanted foreign competitors to sell international services to their domestic customers on an end-to-end basis, so they created a regime under which these were jointly provided by national carriers with the revenues split on a 50/50 basis. Many additional regulatory rules were developed to buttress the carriers' positions by precluding private sector competition in international services from home or abroad. In short, the regime sanctified an international system comprising mutually exclusive and noncompetitive national segments, precluded the sort of distributional conflicts associated with open markets and trade, and became the world economy's oldest and most stable multilateral institution.

An essential feature of the *ancien* regime was that its jurisdiction was strictly delimited to international correspondence. Members could organize their domestic telecommunications industries (and socioeconomic systems) however they pleased, and while almost all chose a public monopoly, a few opted for private monopolies or varying degrees of regulated competition. All that mattered was that they played by the same rules in organizing cross-border traffic. Thus the regime accommodated asymmetric regulation at the national level, but required symmetric regulation at the international level. In principle then, the asymmetric deregulation of domestic markets in the 1980s that is explored elsewhere in this volume might have been compatible in purely functional terms with retention of the *ancien* regime. In practice, the political and economic forces that catalyzed domestic change did not stop at the border, but pushed on into the international sphere and undermined the symmetry of national preferences and practices therein, upon which the regime rested. The result has been a deep transformation in the overarching principles and norms of the regime, from the age-old assumption that international interconnection and transmission were best organized by national monopolies providing joint services, and to the assumption that these objectives should be realized through a more market-based system which favors the interests of competitive corporate suppliers and users.

This chapter explores the evolution and transformation of the international telecommunications regime, and the role of policy (a) symmetries in that process. I argue that for 120 years, the administrations of the major capitalist countries had a shared interest in maintaining absolute control over their national telecommunications systems, and succeeded in devising regime procedures and policies that reflected and reinforced that control. To be sure, the communist and less developed countries (LDCs) were not happy with northern domination of the equipment industry and accompanying standards process, or with the relative conditions of their own networks and services. But to the extent that they were or became sovereign, their administrations also benefited from a regime that blessed national monopolies and joint service provisioning. The main losers in this arrangement were corporations that might have preferred a more liberal system, although the historical record is unclear about just how strong that preference really was in an age of comparatively limited technical conditions and market opportunities.

However, the information revolution provided the private sector with strong incentives to push for competitive supply and flexible use of networks, equipment, and services. Beginning in the United States, a coalition of influential transnational corporations (TNCs) mobilized to pressure governments for change, first in domestic policy arrangements, and later in the international regime. Their campaign was aided immensely by a deep shift in the intellectual environment, as industry analysts from around the world became convinced that the conditions which had justified monopoly control in the past no longer applied in an increasingly dynamic information economy. The globalization of the new corporate interest configuration and intellectual outlook in the 1980s led governments to redefine their interests and embrace varying degrees of liberalization in accordance with their specific domestic institutions and market conditions. Hence, policies of international liberalization, and the fact of their asymmetric character, have undermined the pillars of a uniform and restrictive regime framework and resulted in its transformation in the past three years (1988-90).

To access a transformation process, we need a baseline of prior conditions against which to measure change. However, there have been precious few theoretically informed studies of cooperation in the ITU to provide a clear picture of the *ancien* regime (Cowhey, 1990). Accordingly, the first part of the chapter attempts to fill this void. The first section examines the role of symmetric preferences regarding international regulations in ensuring regime stability. The next section assesses the organization of power relations within the ITU, and the third section shows how this impacted the policy process. The section following that then lays out the key regime principles, norms, and rules which resulted. The second part of the chapter turns to the contemporary process of regime change. The first section assessed briefly the driving forces behind global liberalization, while the final section details the impact on regime procedures and policies.

SYMMETRIC REGULATION AND THE ANCIEN REGIME

Convergent Interest and International Stability

Historically, governments cooperated in the ITU to maintain two interrelated arrangements: the telecommunications regime for network standardization and service regulation and provision; and the radio regime for the division among nations and services of frequency spectrum and geostationary satellite orbital slots. The ITU is a complex organization comprising numerous specialized bodies and functions; here we are concerned solely with three bodies and corresponding instruments that defined the *ancien* telecommunications regime. The Plenipotentiary Conference was the ITU's supreme body, and convened roughly every 7 to 10 years to renegotiate the treaty-level International Telecommunication Convention. The Convention was the governing document for the organization and its regimes, and comprised broad principles and norms specifying the overarching purposes and procedures of cooperation. The World Administrative Telegraph and Telephone Conference (WATTC) convened roughly every 10 to 15 years to renegotiate the treaty-level International Telegraph and Telephone Regulations. The Regulations comprised a mix of norms and rules clarifying how states should act in the regulatory sphere to implement the Convention's intent. The International Telegraph and Telephone Consultative Committee (CCITT) was a permanent organ that met continuously in 4-year study periods demarcated by quadrennial meetings of its governing body, the Plenary Assembly. The CCITT developed detailed Recommendations, or voluntary standards and regulatory rules for network and services.*

The ITU and its regimes were designed by and for the European countries' Ministries of Posts, Telegraph and Telephone (PTTs). Nothing in the Convention explicitly precluded membership for counties where private firms were dominant, as long as these abided by the rules of international correspondence. However, a straightforward reading of formal instruments does not reveal the intersubjective meanings and politics behind them, as "Nationalization or complete control over telegraph was always an unwritten prerequisite for membership" (Codding, 1952, p. 42). Indeed, the United Kingdom was not admitted until it nationalized telegraphy in 1868, as continental administrations felt it would be easier to coordinate with a like-minded public agency. In this context, the United States was the odd man out. With its comparatively liberal domestic institutions and greater private control, the United States did not fit the domestic model elsewhere, and regarded the ITU's international arrangements with hesitation and even hostility. The first meeting attended by an American was in 1871, and he was a businessman operating in a personal capacity with no brief from the State Department. The American ambassador to Russia attended the 1875 meeting in St. Petersburg, but only as an observer. The Europeans were torn by the fact that while the United States had failed to nationalize its systems, its participation was nonetheless functionally necessary for international communications. For example:

> Secretary of State Hamilton Fish originally asked the presidents of two private companies to attend the conference but both declined, so then Fish asked [the ambassador to Russia]. Sec. Fish said the Russian *charge d'affaires* in Washington "has been very urgent for us to be represented at the proposed telegraph congress in St. Petersburg."

---

* Two comments are necessary here. First, it is important to distinguish between the telecommunications and radio regimes. While both are negotiated in the ITU and are closely interrelated, they are based on separate legal instruments devised in different ITU bodies, and involve distinct functional problems and national interests. And while the International Consultative Committee on Radio (CCIR) does produce technical standards for wireless communications, this function accounts for only about 15% of its activities, and can be treated as ancillary to those of the much more prominent CCITT. Second, as is discussed in the chapter's final section, the three bodies and corresponding regime instruments mentioned above were changed in the late 1980s. The narrative in the first four sections is concerned with the period prior.

When it was explained to the Russian that a person sent by the United States could not speak for the private companies, the Russian "then intimated a disposition to receive delegates from private companies." (Feldman, 1976, p. 18)

Dealing with the new world upstart was not easy. The American ambassador made no effort to conceal his distrust of the Europeans at St. Petersburg, and argued in his post-conference report to the State Department that

The interests of the public who use the telegraph seemed to be entirely subordinated to the interests of the state and to the administrations; that is, to a fear lest any improvement might produce less revenue that is got at present, and lest it might throw more work on the telegraph bureau. (Codding, 1952, p. 65)

In successive meetings, American delegates consistently challenged PTT proposals, and "participated to the extent of practically nullifying whatever the conferences hoped to accomplish" (Feldman, 1976, p. 7). But by the turn of the century, hostility began to give way to pragmatism. The government sent more people to ITU meetings and took an interest in policy developments. After World War I, Woodrow Wilson's administration even attempted to play a leadership role *vis.* the telegraph and radio arrangements by proposing a consolidated Universal Electrical Communications Union. When the telecommunication union was born in 1934, the United States finally agreed to join subject to three conditions. First, it demanded that the Convention by changed to enhance private sector input. Second, it signed the Convention to attain membership, but issued numerous reservations to those articles it deemed objectionable. Third, it refused to sign the Regulations, claiming it could not legally bind American firms to some of the rules therein.

Passage of the 1934 Communications Act of America relaxed these constraints on participation. Further, the creation of the Federal Communications Commission (FCC) had an important effect on the composition and outlook of American delegations to the ITU. The State Department officials leading prior delegations lacked the technical training, institutional support, and stability of postings necessary to attain sufficient competence. The policy process was controlled by private companies involved in international correspondence, and they often advanced positions at the ITU that were wildly at odds with those of foreign PTTs. With the launching of the FCC, the latter felt they finally had an official counterpart who spoke the same language and had similar objectives. The Act also gave the American Telegraph and Telephone Co. (AT&T) and a few international record carriers

(IRCs) officially sanctioned dominant positions in the markets, and their preferences regarding international regulation, service provisioning, and network interconnection generally fit with those of the PTTs. In short, the United States moved into rough conformity with the PTT model and the regime's major purposes. This constituted a relative shift in the balance of state-society relations, as the private sector now operated within a framework of federal and international rules. Of course, the FCC was heavily dependent on AT&T and the IRCs, and many observers believe this constituted regulatory capture. But in the ITU, the differences between the United States and other countries were now primarily on the means, rather than the ends of international policy. For the next 45 years, the United States endorsed the regime's broad outlines, if not all its particulars.

While the errant lamb had joined the flock, its refusal to sign the Regulations remained a problem. The Regulations contained some detailed rules on charging and accounting that were distasteful to AT&T and the IRCs, whose tariff structures and procedures differed somewhat from those of the PTTs. Other provisions were thought to stifle technomarket development even within the accepted monopoly framework. True, the United States was participating in ITU fora, and its carriers complied with enough of its norms and rules to facilitate interconnection and avoid undermining the regime, but the American approach also made the joint planning of facilities and services a cumbersome affair. It was difficult to undertake new multilateral actions if AT&T, the world's biggest carrier from the world's biggest market, was not in step. ITU members concluded that if the United States refused to play by the rules, it would be necessary to modify them.

Deformalization of the Regulations was the solution. The 1949 WATTC recommended that the Regulations be amended so as to negate American legal concerns about the treaty being too restrictive. Following changes in the details of accounting, transmission prioritization and so forth, the United States signed the Telegraph Regulations for the first time, albeit with some important reservations. But it still did not sign the Telephone Regulations, which it viewed as constraining the rapidly expanding service. At the 1958 WATTC, several delegations suggested transferring most of the Regulation's elaborate provisions to the Recommendations. This would appease the Americans, and facilitate the continuous amendment of detailed rules and standards as new technologies required. Nevertheless, some members remained unconvinced that they should bend so far for the United States, and the idea was referred to the CCITT for further study. Finally, after 15 years of consideration, deformalization was enacted at the 1973 WATTC. The impact was substantial: The Telegraph Regulations were reduced from 151 to 13 pages, and the Telephone Regulations from 35 to 8 (Rutkowski, 1983). What remained were mostly norms general enough for all governments to comply with. Detailed rules on each category of service were relegated to the Recommendations, which provided states with leeway in national application. The United States for the first time signed both sets of Regulations, with only one reservation.

The above leads to four conclusions. First, given vested interests, issue complexity, and a tradition of consensual decision making, it took a long time to achieve a new multilateral policy equilibrium in the ITU. "This kind of slow evolutionary change over many years has been fairly characteristic of the ITU and the associated domestic regulatory bureaucracies which coalesce under its roof" (Codding & Rutkowski, 1982, p. 37). When change did occur, it was *within* rather that *of* the regime's overarching purpose: The key principles and norms were unaltered, while the rules and decision-making procedures to operationalize them were adapted to new circumstances. Second, the deformalization underscores the sources and limitations of national power. The size and centrality of its market provided the United States with the means to induce change, but it took 40 years to win a partial accommodation of its position. Deformalization did not alter the regime's impact on the global market; it only changed the legal status of certain injunctions to increase flexibility and win American adherence. The PTTs' symmetric commitment to the regime made it impossible for any one government, no matter how powerful, to force its counterparts to alter their basic objectives.

Third, the United States government's impact on cooperation was uneven. From 1865 to 1934, its policy toward the International Telegraph Union was one of benign neglect, and its role was marginal at best, obstructive at worst. In many meetings, American delegates did little more than alienate the majority. Nevertheless, the United States conformed with the regime's main injunctions when this was necessary to achieve interconnection, and AT&T played a progressively greater role in decision making. With its accession to the modern ITU, the government became more involved and jettisoned much of the rhetoric and positions that had marred the telegraph meetings. Regime adherence became more consistent because the American institutions and international objectives now roughly approximated the global model. However, the United States still pressed the PTT majority for more general and flexible policies so as to make that adherence politically sustainable at home. Where the multilateral framework was deemed too restrictive, it established bilateral correspondent relations which deviated somewhat from the norm.

These kinds of involvement appear to characterize what might be called the general, long-term approach of the US toward international telecommunication arrangements. It is a policy of minimizing the specificity of arrangements, diminishing the role of international organization, and effecting bilateral alternatives. (Rutkowski, 1982, p. 34)

But the asymmetry of domestic regulations between the United States and other countries was attenuated substantially at the international level, and did not disrupt the cooperative framework.

Fourth, the reverse impact of the regime on the United States was arguably stronger. While the regime preserved the right of sovereign states to govern their domestic systems as they wished, it constrained sharply the participation of American firms in the international market. If AT&T or an IRC wanted operating agreements for "landing rights" on foreign soil, they had to negotiate with PTTs committed to applying the rules strictly. And as these required that rates between two countries be the same regardless of the route taken, it was impossible to compete by offering a more efficient pathway between two counties. This cartel-like coherence precluded arbitrage, and all American firms could attain was a joint provision arrangement that divided the attendant revenues evenly between corresponding carriers. Further, the regime implicitly legitimated and reinforced monopoly control, so they could not sell services directly within a foreign market. The national and international realms were clearly delineated, and the comparatively competitive dynamics of the United States market were kept at bay by the dual force of PTT policies and the international regime.

The last observation leads to another key point. In a sense, the regime endogenized its "exogenous" operational environment by constraining and directing the technical and market changes it was to manage. The regime-sanctioned monopsonistic organization of demand was of special importance due to the high costs and time requirements of producing equipment and establishing networks. Moreover, terminals, switches, and transmission lines had to be compatible both in design and over time. Administrations' prior decisions therefore constrained what it was rational to invest in subsequently, since they needed to amortize investments before stepping up to a new generation of equipment. For example, while the telephone was adopted in some countries in the 1880s, many PTTs were slow to follow because of their sunk investments in telegraphy, and this regulatory "stickiness" was reinforced in the international aggregate. The development of multilateral standards and operating agreements for telephone in the International *Telegraph* Union did not begin until the 20th century, which in turn limited the new technology's diffusion. When there was potential competition between old and new media, the entrenched interests of monopsonists in and out of the ITU tended to favor the former. Technical change and network interconnection were driven by the demand patterns of political institutions rather than by a competitive supply pattern in the market. The rate of change was paced by capital constraints, so the gap between invention and innovation was often wide. The substantive direction of change was skewed toward those products demanded by PTTs, such as large network switches and uniform telephone handsets, and away from potential diversity. The diffusion of change was constrained by nationalistic procurement policies and regime-sanctioned protectionism; since the major industrialized countries' markets were essentially closed, there was no dynamic global market upon which to base manufacturing plans. These equipment trends also constrained service availability. The incremental development of technology yielded only telegraph, telex, and voice transmissions that were broadly homogeneous across countries, and the pace of international diffusion was limited by the slow-moving process of multilateral coordination. In sum, the international regime shaped its own operational environment, and hence the conditions of its own reproduction. Functionalist accounts which view technomarket change as an exogenous force which determines cooperative outcomes are therefore inadequate. The century of stability was due a international interest configuration that marginalized technological, economic, and political forces which might have upset the status quo.

The Players and the Playing Field

From this background flow three observations about the organizational dynamics that shaped the *ancien* regime. First, the ITU's structure and procedures reflected and buttressed states' dominance in the policy process. ITU instruments did not endow the permanent organs, such as the General Secretariat, with powers to compel governments to behave in any particular way. Like its predecessors, the 1982 Convention began by "recognizing the sovereign right of each country to regulate its telecommunication," and subsequent provisions simply bade them to cooperate in providing interconnection and services (ITU, 1982, p. 1). Only national administrations could vote in ITU bodies. "One nation, one vote" was the rule, and while a simple majority was required for an initiative to carry, many decisions (especially in the CCITT) were taken on the basis of unanimity due to the lack of fundamental disagreement associated with the national monopoly/joint services system. Moreover, states could issue reservations to objectionable provisions of the Convention and Regulations; and the Recommendations, while generally followed, were not legally binding. These rules preserved state interests and facilitated cooperation.

The Convention specified decision-making procedures that were exclusive as well as inclusive. Corporations and other interested entities could not exercise formal authority in the process of regime development. An active role in deliberations was accorded to recognized private operating agencies (RPOAs), which were private common carriers from the relatively small group of countries that did not have government monopolies. RPOAs were bound by ITU instruments when their respective home governments acceded to them, but did not have an independent vote. However, they could in some cases represent their recognizing governments. A few RPOAs had a decisive impact on policy, as the practical significance of their formal procedural limitations was mitigated by market conditions. AT&T was a major player in the CCITT because it developed many of the key technologies, was the largest participant in correspondent relations, and dominated American delegations. Finally, since the CCITT strived to reach consensus during the study periods, RPOA positions were accommodated before recommendations were approved at the plenaries.

The decision-making process was more exclusive with regard to other parties. In the Convention, advisory participation in the CCITT was allowed for "international organizations and regional telecommunication organizations which coordinate their work with the International Telecommunication Union and which have related activities" (ITU, 1982, p. 58). These included the specialized agencies of the United Nations, regional carrier groups, nongovernmental standards bodies such as the International Organization for Standardization (ISO), and corporate user lobbies like the International Telecommunications User Group (INTUG). An advisory role was also allowed for scientific or industrial organizations (SIOs) "engaged in the study of telecommunication problems or in the design or manufacture of equipment for telecommunication services" (ITU, 1982, p. 59). Interestingly, neither corporate users nor SIOs appear from the available historical record to have challenged with much vigor the procedures or policies of the ITU. Certainly both would have preferred enhanced roles in ITU deliberations, and presumably users would have liked lower tariffs and better operating conditions, while manufacturers would have liked greater access to foreign markets. However, monopoly control was the known universe, and technical and market conditions did not provide strong incentives to push for a more competitive system. That would change with the information revolution, as these same players came to challenge vocally the legitimacy of the ITU arrangements with which they had lived in the past. But until that time, "while the logic of including manufacturers and private users...[was] strong, government entities are rarely willing to share international decision-making responsibilities so openly" (Codding & Rutkowski, 1982, pp. 99–100).

Second, while the ITU's formal structure provided every nation with an equal vote, actual control over regime design was a heavily weighted affair. Advanced capitalist countries held almost all of the cards: They were the main sources of the technologies requiring technical and operational standardization; of the new market dynamics and entities which occasioned regulatory deliberations; of the bulk of the ITU's budget; and of the information, resources, and expertise required for effective participation. And because of the mixed nature of their economies and the role of private firms, they had the largest stakes in the particulars of standardization and regulations. These countries could set the technical, operational, and regulatory agendas, effect policies which promoted their objectives, and prevent the adoption of objectionable initiatives. Correspondingly, governments from other regions were less central to regime development. Communist states were very active and distinctly consequential in purely distributional bargaining over the radio regime's divisions of spectrum and satellite slots, but they were less independently important in designing the telecommunications regime's provisions on network and services. On the broad parameters of international standardization, regulation, and joint service provisioning, their interests largely paralleled those of the advanced capitalist countries which took the lead. As the information revolution widened the gap between East and West and raised to the forefront issues of public-private competition in advanced systems and services, their significance in such discussions would attenuate further.

That the Third World was also of marginal significance might seem surprising. In other economic issue areas such as trade, investment, monetary, and natural resource policy, LDCs formed a fairly coherent bloc in the post-colonial era to press for international regime rules that would redistribute wealth and power. However, in the ITU, North-South distributional bargaining was confined to two areas distinct from the telecommunications regime. One was the radio regime, wherein the LDCs demanded a shift from the "first come, first served" system of allocations and assignments favored by the North to a planned system guaranteeing their access to spectrum and satellite orbital slots. The powerful North refused to accept a fundamental transformation of this overarching principle, although it did accept some changes within the regime involving the planning of certain frequencies where its key interests were not threatened. The other was technical assistance. Beginning in the 1950s, the LDC coalition sought in the Plenipotentiaries to make development promotion a recognized and well-supported ITU function. It succeeded in the former objective, but not in the latter. Primarily under the aegis of the General Secretariat, the ITU created a number of new organs concerned with development and initiated technical training and resource transfer programs.* However, the actual levels of financial assistance were generally paltry in relation to the need, as the industrialized countries refused repeatedly to volunteer significant contributions or to accept mandatory transfers through the regular ITU budget. Moreover, there is a difference between an international organization and a regime negotiated therein, just as there is between a national parliament and its laws. Technical assistance became a new programmatic area of the ITU as a corporate actor and forum, but it did not become part of the regulatory-standardization regime through which governments coordinate their daily telecommunications relationships. To the contrary, the regime was shielded from North-South redistributional bargaining and principles. There were a number of reasons for this, but two are of particular importance here.

One reason was the nature of the functional problem and cooperative solution. International regimes for trade and money could promote redistribution by providing LDCs with preferential access to Northern markets or exemptions from otherwise binding obligations. International regimes for natural resources could promote redistribution by providing LDCs with preferential allocations of spectrum, satellite slots, ocean waterways, mineral deposits, and so on. But the telecommunications regime was designed to standardize systems and regulate services between administrations on a nonmarket basis. Neither of these problems lent themselves to redistribution, as there were no rules of competition to be skewed preferentially or common resources to be reallocated. Insofar as the regime legitimated national

---

* Among the initiatives approved by the Plenipotentiaries during the ancien regime were: the addition of the phrase, "foster the creation, development, and improvement of telecommunication equipment and networks in new or developing countries by every means at its disposal" to Article 4 of the Convention, "Purposes of the Union"; the expansion of the Administrative Council to include more southern delegations in organizational management; the establishment of the World Plan and regional plans for networks; the addition of development-oriented Special Autonomous Working Parties in the CCITT; and the creation of the Special Fund, the Special Voluntary Program for Technical Cooperation, the Center for Telecommunications Development, and ITU regional offices in the South.

monopolies and barred threatening international competition, the LDCs also had a stake in preserving the basic framework. The only way to incorporate concessionary transfers into the regime rules would have been to alter the accounting and settlements procedures through which administrations divided evenly the costs and revenues from jointly provided services. For example, the settlements formula could have been changed from a 50/50 to a 51/49 revenue split, with the LDCs reaping the larger share. Recommendation D.150 allowed for asymmetric settlements on a voluntary basis, and some European administrations offered such concessions to their former colonies. What is interesting is that the LDCs did not demand in a collective and consistent manner that this be the standard practice in all relations until the 1982 Plenipotentiary. There they succeeded in adding to the Convention Opinion 2, which suggested "that developed countries should take into account the requests for favorable treatment made by developing countries in service, commercial or other relations in telecommunications" (ITU, 1982, p. 344). However, opinions are not binding upon the membership, and the industrialized countries were unwilling to contemplate a firmer commitment. As we shall see, this issue has been raised anew with greater force in recent years.

The lack of action on accounting and settlements points to the other factor insulating the regime from North-South bargaining: power. As noted, the advanced capitalist countries controlled both the industry and the ITU budget, and could not be forced against their will to accept redistribution. Moreover, Northern power rested not only on these material capabilities, but also on immaterial capabilities such as the control of knowledge, information, and the policy discourse in which problems were defined and tackled. The North maintained that there was no empirical economic evidence that would justify asymmetric payments; and that in any event, the ITU was a purely "technical" body in which "policy" considerations like redistribution were inappropriate and disruptive of its mission. Indeed, development aid was referred to in ITU instruments as "technical assistance," a term preferencing training and information dissemination as opposed to resource transfers. In this context, it was difficult for the LDCs to legitimate and press a welfare-oriented agenda.

In parallel, the Third World lacked the capabilities necessary to participate effectively in the technical fora such as the WATTCs and CCITT wherein regime rules were devised. To some extent, they also lacked interest: For most, problems like the standardization and regulation of increasingly advanced systems and services appeared irrelevant to their immediate problems (Renaud, 1987). If, as of 1984, two-thirds of the world's population had no local access to basic telephony, why devote scarce money and trained personnel to discussions about the latest technological advances in the North (ITU, 1984, p. 13). Hence, for example, in 1979, "44 countries took part in the 17 regular CCITT study groups; of these, only 15 could be classified as Third World, and only one had attended a majority of the study groups" (Codding & Rutkowski, 1982, p. 104). The rise of the newly industrialized countries in the 1980s has changed this situation somewhat, but the CCITT remains the almost private preserve of the rich countries, and most LDC attention is focused on the Plenipotentiaries where budgetary issues are addressed. Thus the sort of debates and bargaining dynamics associated with the New International Economic Order and New World Information Order campaigns of the 1970s did not impact the telecommunications regime. The South pursued the expansion of technical assistance programs and access rights in the radio regime, but left largely unchallenged the arrangements for international networks and services. This constituted a sort of "hegemonic compromise," in which the North offered various side payments to keep the South in the fold, deflect potential disruptions to its core agenda, and ensure the stability and universality of both the regime and the global network of national networks.

The third key point concerns the precise identities and interests of the players. Due to the technical nature of the issues, the lack of "high politics" competition, and the notion that telecommunications was a mere utility, high-level political elites showed little sustained interest in ITU activities. Most governments, as *principals*, selected PTTs as the *agents* to represent their national interests (Pratt & Zeckhauser, 1985). Most of the PTT representatives were engineers whose professional ethos and training led them to view systems planning in a technocratic perspective that took policy objectives and institutions as given. Allowing them to contemplate technological problems in a routinized and orderly setting, monopoly control comported with their shared world view and work habits. They saw themselves as specialists in a purely "technical" organization, as if state control was not "political." The result was an expert community ill-disposed to entertain subsequent corporate criticisms of the economic implications of their standards and regulations. Its exclusivity was an important source of power and stability, and was reinforced by procedures which barred the press and other outsiders from attending meetings or accessing internal documents. The rationales were sometimes bizarre; for example, the General Secretariat reportedly argued that, "the more people one admits to meetings, the greater the chance there is that an individual who might wish to harm one or more of the delegates could be in attendance" (Codding, 1984, p. 10). It strains the imagination to believe that anyone was really concerned about terrorists masquerading as researchers in order to harm engineers on the premises. It should be noted that the ITU has become much more open and accommodative in recent years, although outsiders are still barred from decision-making fora. In sum, during the ITU's first 120 years, administrations from the advanced capitalist countries carved out a policy space in which they could shape the regime free of supranational pressures from above, intragovernmental pressures from the side, and corporate pressures from below. They organized international interdependence as an extension of the domestic sphere: on a semicorporatist basis, with themselves at the apex of an institutionalized alliance. This arrangement had the support of central governments, national manufacturers, political parties, trade unions, regulatory economists, and other groups, all of whom believed these arrangements to be appropriate at the time.

The Policy Process

These organizational attributes shaped the way ITU participants responded to the post-war information revolution. Administrations were slow to appreciate the implications of the merging of telecommunications and computers for the balance of public and private power. Up to the 1980s, ITU policies remained uncontested, and new techniques were understood as opportunities to be managed within the institutional status quo. Administrations expected exclusive control of the new markets: Advanced telecommunications and information services were slow to emerge outside of the United States, and were not anticipated to be provided independently of or in competition with themselves. Natural monopoly conditions may no longer have existed in a purely economic sense, but monopoly still seemed natural politically.

International data transmission was considered at the first CCITT plenary in 1956, and a working party was set up to devise the necessary standards. At the third plenary in 1964, the CCITT began discussing recommendations on modem standards, signalling between computer terminals, network interfaces, transmission qualities, service characteristics, operating agreements, and related aspects which would allow administrations to integrate digital components into their networks. Because the expensive construction of separate systems optimized for "value-added" services was still in the future, the initial focus was on upgrading telegraphy and telephony. Progress was slow; nobody knew where the technology would lead, so it was difficult to make long-term plans. The V Series Recommendations were not formally approved until the Sixth Plenary Assembly in 1976, by which time some administrations were already building switched data networks. These allowed PTTs to develop new services, expand their operations, and play leading industrial policy roles in the telecommunications and computer industries. As early as 1965, the CCITT estimated that the demand for data transmission might put strains on extant telegraph and telephone circuits. Special study groups and questions were established at the 1968 and 1972 plenaries to consider the issues, and work on system design and interworking continued into the 1980s. The initial result was a plethora of detailed rules contained in the X Series Recommendations approved in 1976.

Data networks took on additional importance with the growing power of TNCs in the information revolution. During the 1960s, large users attained leased lines to develop private networks for telephone and telex between their branches and with fixed suppliers and customers, as they had done in the United States. Dedicated circuits provided alternatives to the overloaded and error-prone switched networks, and the PTTs were willing to comply so long as the flat rate charges could be set high enough to maintain revenues. Accordingly, the CCITT set rules for their allocation, denial, or rescindment. But as the merging of computers and telecommunications progressed, the significance of leased lines increased. American-based TNCs now wanted to send data and other new services across borders to increase their global efficiency and control. They could already do this within the United States, where the FCC had loosened conditions for the attachment of customer premise equipment (CPE) and service use. For a TNC user with substantial investments in Europe or elsewhere, the optimality of its network would be constrained if it lacked these possibilities between its various markets. A learning process and demonstration effect were underway. Competitors abroad began to see that the creative use of networks and information systems would enhance their own strategic positions. Soon, PTTs were confronted with a growing number of requests for flexible arrangements under which TNCs could upgrade their internal networks. Since the public networks could not yet satisfy users' demands, they found themselves making concessions which reduced their total control over the telecommunications environment. These pressures had not cohered into a broad political challenge, but were a harbinger of things to come.

Hence, the push to construct public data networks was in part an effort to preemptively capture new markets. Better to have large users employing public systems at standard rates than private circuits at flat rates. To strengthen their grip, CCITT members approved a variety of preemptive regulatory recommendations at the plenaries. Conditions were set on the use of leased lines; resale was proscribed, and sharing circumscribed; information service firms were barred from engaging in transmission functions; and on and on. Most governments applied these rules vigorously at both the national and international levels, although the United States and later other industrialized countries began to selectively liberalize certain domestic applications in the 1970s. But the regime rules barred similar actions in the international segments, and liberalizers could not unilaterally open markets without the consent of corresponding administrations abroad. The CCITT also devised standards for the burgeoning variety of private attachments, a task that required increasingly close contact with the ISO and related private standards organizations in computers and electronics. Past jurisdictional boundaries were eroding, and the ITU found itself sharing turf with other multilateral agencies with different social constituencies and agendas.

Growing technomarket diversification raised new problems for administrations. Technically, launching new services often required separate, dedicated networks. End users had to buy equipment and secure connections for each specialized offering, while carriers had to standardize an expanding range of systems and devise elaborate interfaces. As technological progress continued, administrations could look forward to a continuous and cumbersome process of replanning to accommodate change and maintain interconnectivity. Economically, establishing service-specific networks involved massive R&D and expenses. Proliferation generated the kind of redundant facilities that monopoly provision was supposed to avoid. Further, it was not always clear that there would be sufficient demand to make a given service profitable and help recover previous investments. PTTs aspiring to offer the full range of technically feasible services were faced with difficult choices. Politically, pressures for liberalization seemed poised to grow, especially when users could argue that switched networks were insufficient for their increasingly advanced, specialized needs. Public data networks were a viable response in some cases, but not others. To retain control, PTTs had to adopt restrictive policies which could not be justified on purely technical grounds. Clearly based on self-interest, such policies seemed likely to become more controversial and difficult to defend. The capacity and flexibility of national systems needed to be enhanced significantly to stem growing corporate pressures.

The key PTTs and their national manufacturers devised an answer: the integrated services digital network (ISDN). The ISDN was conceived as a unified, end-to-end "digital pipe" that could carry all traffic regardless of its technical requirements. When the concept was introduced in the 1973–76 study period, CCITT planners had only a vague vision and little sense of how it could be implemented. Indeed, "when the international systems designers first began to meet and discuss ISDN, they frequently represented it with nothing more than a simple cloud-like diagram" (Rutkowski, 1985, pp. 40–41). Following the standardization of public data networks, the 1976 plenary proposed that the CCITT undertake formal studies of the ISDN. As the discussions proceeded, participants came down from the cloud and began to develop the details of the network's components. At the 1980 plenary, the CCITT adopted Recommendation G.705, which set the guidelines for future study and development. Among these were that the ISDN would: evolve from digital switched networks, comprise services compatible with 64-kbit connections, incorporate computer intelligence for key functions, be accessible via a layered set of protocols that might vary from case to case, take several decades to construct, and be interworked with existing networks in the transition period (Rutkowski, 1985, pp. 40–41). These principles charted the course for the 1981–84 study period, and formed the basis of what became the I Series Recommendations. It is beyond the scope of this chapter to discuss the ISDN's technical attributes, but a few comments on its political-economic implications for the regime are relevant here.

From a technical viewpoint, integrated digital networks made sense. However, the connotation that "integration" meant not only interoperability and interconnection, but also PTT provision of all future services, was obviously controversial. By the early 1980s, monopolies were under growing attack and liberalization partisans were quick to see the ISDN as a PTT effort to preclude competition. The very term "ISDN" had a monolithic ring which suggested that each country would have one comprehensive network, so these players dubbed it, "Innovations Subscribers Don't Need." One critic even argued that the ISDN was designed with a "hegemonial" purpose by PTTs given to "benevolent authoritarianism" in the name of redistributive social policy (Noam, 1986b, pp. 45–46). And indeed, a unified system could benefit small business and residential users, who were unlikely to invest in advanced private systems. The ISDN would also be good for trade unionists working for national carriers, and for protected manufacturers seeking exclusive, long-term contracts for a new generation of systems. Above all, it was desirable for the carriers, who could defend their extant monopolies while expanding their roles in both new communication and information markets, and in industrial policies for "high-tech" goods. But was it in the interest of the large corporate users and new suppliers seeking competitive entry and control? The PTTs did not address this question publicly. In the CCITT, new design possibilities were a sufficient rationale for a sweeping upgrade of switched networks. When pressed, the PTTs asserted that telecommunications remained a natural monopoly, and that ISDN provided the economies of scale and scope needed to make new services viable. The ISDN allowed PTTs to at least claim competence in fulfilling all new service requirements, and to challenge the technical rationales for separate private systems. It was a potentially centralized solution to the growing challenge of TNC power. Of course, the ISDN did not have to be implemented in this manner; it could instead have served as a flexible infrastructure within which PTTs allowed varying degrees of private competition and control. However, some proclaimed their intention to retract leased circuits and use the ISDN to push corporate users back onto public networks, and the suspicion was widespread among corporate managers that this would happen elsewhere as well.

In the early 1980s, the most controversial issue was where the computerized intelligence would be located. If it was in a customer's CPE, then the network would simply serve as a medium for user-defined applications. If instead the network switch could perform all the intelligence functions, private CPE would play a lesser role. Attention therefore focused on the boundary line between the network and the customer's premises. The United States wanted standardization only at interface point U, at the external boundary of the user's connection to the network. The PTT majority wanted standardization to extend all the way to the S/T interface, or farther out into the network. While U interface standardization would allow CPE to control intelligence functions, the S/T option would favor the network. The CCITT proceeded with a standard at S/T, thereby eliciting widespread corporate concerns that customers would be forced to rely on the PTTs for all their needs, and that the potential market for specialized attachments and services would be stunted.

In addition to the determinacy of state interests, three other observations flow from the above. First, the CCITT process was technically effective yet slow. Information-age issues were more complicated than those of the past, and the regime-making states wanted to promote the standards and approaches of their national administrations and manufacturers. This yielded substantial coordination problems, and some study questions raised as early as 1958 were not answered with recommendations until 1976. But the dynamism of the computer and microelectronics industries was subsuming the once sleepy world of telecommunications, as new systems emerged rapidly and competitive pressures spilled across sectoral boundaries. Administrations and manufacturers were increasingly loath to forestall network development until multilateral agreement could be reached at the quadrennial plenaries. Hence, from 1968 recommendations with only *provisional* approval of the study groups were sometimes used to guide national construction programs. This provided greater flexibility, but the incremental codification of rules favoring public procurement and control still constrained R&D. We cannot test the counterfactual thesis that innovation would have been faster in a market-driven environment, but close observers on both sides of the regulatory debate concede the point.

Second, a shift occurred between the digitalization of telegraphy and telephony and the development of public data networks. Historically, PTTs and RPOAs had proceeded from the "bottom up" with national R&D and only afterwards worried about international standardization; this was true of data transmission over extant networks. As one CCITT participant has noted, "If the problem of international interconnection had been considered earlier in the national development of such networks the tasks of the CCITT in the past would have been very much easier" (Okabe, 1978, p. 233). In contrast, ISDN planning proceeded from the "top down," as the CCITT devised standards in parallel with and even prior to national programs. The top-down approach underscored administrations' growing desire to collectively shape the rate, direction, and diffusion of technomarket change through anticipatory planning. By developing recommendations before the fact, they hoped to avoid the arduous task of interconnecting incompatible systems, and to ensure that construction programs would yield guaranteed returns on investment. Third, the growing stakes in a rapidly expanding marketplace were beginning to render the standardization process more conflictual than in the past. At times the CCITT had to resort to issuing dual or multiple standards because national preferences could not be coordinated. This was the case with videotex, and American insistence on the U interface for ISDN may effectively constitute the same outcome (Savage, 1989, pp. 201–210). At the same time that easy end-to-end interconnectivity was increasingly being demanded by corporate users, PTT and manufacturer efforts to control new markets were at times pushing in the opposite direction.

The Product

The *ancien* regime's overarching social purpose was to balance sovereignty with international interconnectivity and joint service provisioning. These objectives were almost universally interpreted as requiring monopoly control at the national level—nowhere did ITU instruments mention competition as a means for their achievement. To understand how national interests were reflected in the regime, we next present a snapshot of its major regulatory injunctions as codified in its three key instruments circa the mid-1980s. The definitive principles and norms below have, in one formulation or another, been contained in the various Conventions and Regulations negotiated since its inception, and the detailed rules for new networks and services contained in recent Recommendations derive logically from them. As such, the following serves as a roughly accurate depiction of the regime in place from 1865 to the late 1980s.

Article 4 of the 1982 Convention included three general principles derived from the ultimate purposes of sovereignty and interconnection. These were the need for progressive and coordinated technical improvement of facilities to expand network capacity; efficient systems operation to keep user rates as low as possible, while "taking into account the necessity for maintaining independent financial administration; " and services to be made generally available to the public as far as possible (ITU, 1982, pp. 3–4). The Convention also contained other principles of state control over national extensions in its General Provisions Relating to Telecommunications. Among these were that ITU member governments should ensure the right of the public to communicate via public correspondence on a nondiscriminatory basis; could stop any transmission which appeared contrary to their laws, national security, and public order; could suspend transmissions indefinitely subject to notification of other members; accepted no responsibility toward users, particularly as regards claims for damages; should ensure the secrecy of private transmissions, save where violations of national laws and international treaties were involved; should provide the best technical means of public correspondence at their disposal, in accordance with the procedures experience had shown to be best; could allow the use of secret language in private telegrams, and should ensure the right of governments to use secret languages (ITU, 1982, pp. 17–22). Clearly, the law codified here was primarily international, not transnational; its subjects were nation-states, not the global public. While users had a general right to correspond, this guarantee pertained solely to public networks, and administrations could determine the conditions thereof. TNCs or other entities had no right to provide or utilize alternative facilities and services. Similarly, the provisions on the stoppage, suspension, and secrecy of transmissions provided administrations with broad leeway and control. All these principles were established when telecommunications meant telegraph, telex, and telephone services under monopoly control, but remained in place even as competition in advanced communication and information services, equipment, and private networks began to spread. The regime's operational environment was changing while its overarching purposes and provisions were not, a fact that would later generate challenges from the partisans of global liberalization (Naslund, 1983).

The 1973 Telegraph and Telephone Regulations, which remained in force until 1989, included provisions which exhorted members to comply with the Recommendations in implementing them; required that certain classes of intergovernmental transmissions be carried;

allowed administrations and RPOAs to place international circuits at the exclusive disposal of users in those relations where circuits remain available after the needs of the public services had been met; allowed members to enter into bilateral and regional agreements; required that the accounting rates for financial settlements between countries be the same regardless of routing; and encouraged members to make efforts to avoid too great a dissymetry between the charges applicable in each direction of the same connection (ITU, 1973, pp. 6, 11). The Telegraph Regulations included the additional provisions that administrations and RPOAs could refuse private transmissions in secret languages, but must allow these telegrams to pass in transit to another country; could require users to provide their secret codes; should stop transmissions to reforwarding agencies serving third parties in attempts to avoid full payments to administrations for routing; and must prohibit any rebates on the officially agreed rates (ITU, 1973, pp. 7, 9, 12). These clauses restricted competition, but were more permissive than those before deformalization.

It is difficult to provide a representative overview of the Recommendations' key rules. The principles and norms of the Convention and Regulations were general enough to remain in place after infrequent meetings, but the Recommendations evolved continuously with technomarket change. They were complex, numbered in the thousands of pages, and covered in minute detail a vast array of technical, operational, and regulatory issues. Nevertheless, the major nontechnical provisions relevant to regulation, competition, and control are found primarily in the D Series, the 1984 Red Book version of which is examined here.

The rules of facilities were the most restrictive, as the underlying network was both the main source of PTT/RPOA power and regarded as fundamental to national sovereignty. But the steady expansion of user demands for leased lines in the 1960s and for specialized networks, services, attachments, and interconnection rights thereafter compelled the CCITT to spell out conditions buttressing the primacy of public networks. For example, Recommendation D.1, Section 1 included provisions to the effect that leased circuits were generally to be made available only after the needs of public services were met; administrations could withdraw such circuits when they deemed it to be in the public interest; leased circuits were generally to be made available only after the needs of public services were met; administrations could withdraw such circuits when they deemed it to be in the public interest; leased circuits could be used only between fixed points for a designated purpose relating to the customer's nontelecommunications business; customers could not resell excess capacity; equipment connected to private circuits had to meet conditions specified by the administration; and administrations should refuse to provide leased circuits where the customer's usage would infringe on the provision of public services to others (ITU, 1985, p. 6). Recommendation D.1., Section 5 on private networks constructed by linking leased circuits contained similar provisions. For example, switching and transmission were to be the exclusive functions of administrations, and private networks were only to be allowed when they could not meet a customer's specialized requirements; administrations reserved the right to provide such networks, on an exclusive basis if they chose, and accepted no responsibility for the quality of transmissions; users could not make changes to the facilities without the administration's consent; and the interconnection of two or more private networks required the administration's approval (ITU, 1985, pp. 9–10).

The interconnection of private leased circuits to public networks was covered by Recommendation D.1., Section 6. Among its provisions were that administrations could choose whether to authorize such interconnection, subject to the consent of the other relevant administrations; had the right to refuse interconnection on their side of the circuit; should ensure that transmissions pertained solely to the circuit's approved purpose, and was sent only to approved public network subscribers; could levy special charges for public network access; should not consider financial claims resulting from failure in the public networks to which a private circuit is connected; and were not obliged to guarantee the quality of transmission to or from the public network over a leased circuit (ITU, 1985, pp. 10–11). Recommendation D.1., Section 7 covered the use of private circuits in conjunction with CPE or data-processing centers to provide information services to other parties. A key provision here was that private leased circuits terminating at one end in a data-processing center were to be allowed public network access only if the information was not exchanged on a store-and-forward basis; the data-processing center did not switch and transmit messages between users; the list of connected users was provided to the administration on demand; and the participants did not provide a telecommunications service (ITU, 1985, p. 11). Finally, Recommendation D.6 on the shared use of facilities by closed user groups held that administrations could exceptionally provide facilities for uses not authorized under other recommendations which were not met by existing public services until such offerings became available; and the user groups could not be engaged in the telecommunications business (ITU, 1985, pp. 22–23).

These and other provisions of the D Series were intended to preserve the *ancien* regime's traditional objectives in a rapidly emerging global information economy otherwise characterized by increasing corporate control. Large firms were recognizing the competitive benefits of strategically developing and applying new systems and services, and in some countries—especially the United States—were incrementally winning the right to do so at the national level. Things were different at the international level, where the almost all ITU members remained committed to a strict interpretation of the Convention's and Regulations' incontestable mandate of providing the general public with global interconnection and joint services. What was not incontestable from a corporate standpoint were two assumptions behind that interpretation. The first was that international private networking and services were a threat to the technical and economic prerequisites of interconnection. In the 1980s, TNCs would increasingly argue that both private joint and end-to-end services provided on a competitive basis were viable alternative means of achieving the same goals while simultaneously meeting unsatisfied corporate requirements. Private and public systems were complementary, not contradictory as the administrations asserted. Second, while the regime's formal jurisdiction was purely international, the vast majority of PTTs were also vigorously applying the same restrictive rules within their national networks in order to preserve their monopolies. The ITU's instruments did not explicitly require monopoly control, as domestic regulation was a sovereign choice. But this was certainly how most members chose to organize their systems, and CCITT Recommendations were routinely taken as both a guideline and justification of national regulations. As such, overturning these rules would become a primary demand of the new corporate interest configuration in the 1980s.

The role of recommendations on equipment was complex. Again, the regime's stated purpose was solely to promote interconnectivity and joint service provision: How administrations chose to compose their networks and the extent to which they allowed competition in the hardware market was entirely up to them. Since its instruments contained no explicit statements on the issue, one might conclude that the regime did not cover the regulation of equipment markets. But in practice, the regime's standards and other provisions had trade-enhancing or distorting effects that were clearly understood by all the participants and an essential if unacknowledged part of the underlying political bargain among its members (Cowhey, 1990). Advanced countries that could produce equipment were free to protect their markets, while those which could not were free to import; the result was a "global" market open to entry only at the margins.

Two types of recommendations were relevant here. First were those establishing conditions for investment in and control over network components. Because administrations did not want to acknowledge economic issues and interests, they never used terms like "trade" or "competition." But for example, Recommendation 1, Section 5 reserved most switching and all transmission for administrations, meaning only they could own, operate, and hence purchase central office switches and related main network elements. Users could not, so producers could not sell it to them. In contrast, the arrival of CPE required new regulations. In the 1970s, many administrations refused to allow such attachments due to technical and economic concerns, but by the decade's end, public networks were upgraded to lessen the threat of technical harm, and domestic producers in the advanced capitalist countries became more competitive with the American manufacturers which had dominated the market. Hence, regulations on terminals, modems, PBXs, and so on were loosened substantially, making this perhaps the most dynamic and competitive market niche under the *ancien* regime. The many recommendations relating to CPE reflected this trend. In general, they did not say that "users may or may not attach items xyz," but rather left this choice to administrations. But they say that the attachment, upgrading, and maintenance of CPE required authorization, and type of approval and related procedures varied widely. Moreover, Recommendation 1, Section 5.7 stated that administration could require that some of the equipment used be located on their own premises, and/or be provided by them (ITU, 1985, p. 10). In short, the rules allowed PTTs and RPOAs to determine both the extent of foreign producers' market access and the users' latitude in applications.

The second relevant type of rules were technical standards. The Recommendations contained a multitude of standards for equipment design, operation, and interconnection for telephone (i.e., Series E, M, P, and Q), telegraph (Series F, H, R, T, and U), and data (Series I, V, and X) networks. In each case, interfaces, multiplexing, signaling, switching, transmission speeds, communication between diverse terminals, and so on were coordinated to promote compatibility and basic quality levels. While the range of topics covered is too broad to go into here, a key point must be underscored: These standards applied first and foremost to the internetwork gateways of the global system, rather than across the full range of equipment employed in national networks. The recommendations were designed historically to promote both interconnectivity and the protection of national markets, as the standards employed within the latter were often incompatible across countries. However, the ISDN would later draw CCITT standardization deeper into national systems, thereby raising the stakes in the process.

Finally, the Recommendations had a distinct impact on service markets. Who could provide and utilize which services on what basis was determined by the above rules on networks and equipment. In general, basic services were the exclusive domain of administrations, while markets for newer value-added services were shaped by the provisions on leased lines, private/public network interconnection, resale and shared use, and so on. The level of openness for value-added services was much less than for CPE, but the onset of liberalization was roughly similar. Fears of private cream skimming generated opposition to competition when the new services appeared, but in the early 1980s a few PTTs began to open those domestic market segments in which they or other national firms were competitive. Still, they could not allow such services to be provided from their territory to another country without the latter's consent; the regime precluded unilateral liberalization, so advanced private services thrived primarily among a few countries (e.g., the United States, Britain, and Japan) who were willing to jointly authorize them. In contrast, to the extent that a boundary line between information enhancement and transmission was identifiable, data services remained formally unregulated and continued to grow despite telecommunications restrictions, although probably less rapidly than they would have absent regulation.

The Recommendations dealt at length with financial aspects (e.g., the collection charges or tariffs levied on customers) and the accounting and settlements procedures employed between national correspondents. Charges and accounting were so important that some general norms were contained in the treaty-level Regulations, while the detailed rules needed to operationalize them were in the D Series. A key guideline was Recommendation D.5, which held that administrations' income for the totality of services offered should cover all technical and administrative costs; the rates should not foster "harmful" competition between services; for political or social reasons, the rates for certain services could be below the cost of their provision; administrations should protect their overall financial balances by charging above cost for some services so as to cross-subsidize those charged below cost; and the "increase factor" in such cases should depend on the value of a service to a given user as determined by the administration (ITU, 1985, pp. 21–22).

Tariffs comprised two elements: access charges, which included the initial fee for subscriber hook-up and regular rental payments for terminals and/or connection; and utilization charges, which depended on the time, distance, and duration of calls and for some services, additional variables. While the D series established formuli for tariffs, variations in access charges and in the means of calculating utilization charges often resulted in asymmetries such that "charges for a telephone call between two countries may vary by as much as 100% without either of the countries concerned departing from the CCITT

Recommendations" (Neumann, 1987, p. 389). To avoid interservice competition and recover network costs, the methods used in setting rates also varied across services. Recommendation D.1 did not explicitly endorse a set means of tariffication for leased lines, but most administrations provided these to TNCs at flat monthly rates. In contract, Recommendations D.6 on shared use by common purpose groups, D.10 on dedicated public data networks, and D.11 on packet-switched public data networks all provided for tariffs which were volume-sensitive, and hence more costly for large users. The rules also allowed for additional charges based on service and switching class, additional user facilities, transmission routes, bit rate and bandwidth, and so on.

While the rules on charging provided administrations with leeway, those on accounting and settlements were more rigorously harmonizing. It was acceptable for a carrier to impose high charges on its customers, but not for it to profit in relations with another carrier—this was the fundamental bargain of the joint services regime. Accounts were to be settled on a bilateral or regional basis, and in principle, revenues were split 50/50 between sending and receiving administrations. If one transit country was involved, the split was 40/40/20; if two were involved, it was 40/40/10/10, and so on. If the facilities and costs on either side differed substantially, administrations could use a different formula. The key was that traffic units were added up on a monthly basis, and the carrier whose outbound traffic exceeded its inbound traffic reimbursed its counterpart to achieve equity. As we will see, asymmetric deregulation in the 1980s would upset the political bargain underlying the arrangement. Figure 1 summarizes our overview of the *ancien* regime's major regulatory provisions:

Figure 1. Principles, Norms and Rules of the *Ancien* Regime

Overarching Purpose: National Sovereignty balanced with International Interconnection and the Joint, Noncompetitive Provision of Services, Preferably by National Monopolies

Convention
*Modernization of facilities and services
*Efficient operation and maintenance
*Services generally available to the public
*Right of the public to communicate, normally in secrecy
*Stoppage, suspension, monitoring of transmission if national security threat
*Special arrangements allowable if not of general concern

Regulations

*Compliance with Recommendations encouraged
*Priority of transmissions related to government and safety of life
*Leased lines only when public requirements have been met
*Common accounting rates regardless of route, reduce assymetries in charges
*Restrict harmful competition from third-party traffic

Recommendations

*Provision and conditions of leased lines restricted
*Leased lines only for business of the customer, upgrading restricted
*Interconnection of private networks restricted
*No private resale of excess capacity; shared use restricted
*No private infringement on functions of Administrations
*Exclusive control of circuit and message switching, transmission
*No responsibility for transmission quality regarding private circuits
*Interconnection of private and public networks, subscribers restricted
*Data service firms may not perfom telecommunications functions
*Customer premise equipment restricted, acceptable pending type approval, authorization etc.
*Standardization of equipment in international segment
*Value-added networks and services restricted
*Cost or value-based pricing, cross-subsidization acceptable
*Rates unaffected by routing
*Common accounting rates and settlement procedures

ASYMMETRIC DEREGULATION AND REGIME TRANSFORMATION

Divergent Interest and International Instability

Even as delegates to the 1984 Plenary Assembly were approving the above recommendations, the ground was shifting rapidly under their feet. Pressures unleashed earlier in the United States were spilling across national borders, resulting in a growing and unsustainable discrepancy between the international regime and the operational environment it was meant to govern. Those pressures led to change first and most forcefully at the national level, as many governments groped toward new deregulatory mixes of public and private control, but they also began to eat away at the formerly firm and symmetric commitment of ITU members to a uniform and restrictive regime for international correspondence, and by the late 1980s had gathered sufficient force to result in its transformation.

Some analysts see technological change as the driving force of this global liberalization, but as a causal explanation, technological determinism remains suspect for at least four reasons. First, technologies are social constructions generated by specific institutional environments and actors; to anthropomorphise and argue that "the technology requires" liberalization obfuscates the interests involved. New techniques expand the range of feasible actions to choose from, and may even make one option more cost effective than another. But the choosing is still key, and in our case the relevant choices were those of corporate managers seeking to advance specific types of objectives in relation to their competitors and state regulators which determined new telecommunications technologies' local effects. Second and relatedly, technologies are also in a sense social relationships, and TNCs' ability to employ new systems and services was at least in part dependent on the decisions of those regulators. In view of the industry's history, it seems strained to argue that states suddenly became powerless in the 1980s. For example, one observer has asserted that "with the advent of super-microcomputers and fast-packet processors, there is no way governments can maintain control over [network-based] data processing even if they try. They can barely maintain control over telecommunications" (Solomon, 1987, p.3). But this is true only insofar as governments permit the use of such systems in the first place, or are unwilling to pay the political and economic costs of denying such use. Administrations faced few constitutional barriers to prevent them from adopting restrictions; indeed, their authority to do so was enshrined in ITU instruments and reflected in the ISDN concept. The real issue is how governments assess the relative costs and benefits of allowing companies to supply and use new systems and services in particular ways, and that is a political-economic process involving pressure and power. Third, consider the primary source of technology-driven proclamations: The claim that institutional change "must happen" because of new innovations has become a hallmark of corporate speech for a reason. If technology renders regulation "obsolete" and "counterproductive," it is a short jump to the proposition that the only "pragmatic" response is liberalization. Finally, if technology was an adequate independent variable with which to explain deregulation, then the global diffusion of new telecommunications systems and services in the 1980s should have elicited the same responses across countries, rather than the sort of asymmetries studied in this volume.

If strategies and institutions shape technological choices and effects, one might argue that global deregulation is explained by relative state power. By this account, the United States government employed its disproportionate power to force open foreign markets through bargaining, trade threats, preferential arrangements with liberalizing countries, and so on (Krasner, 1991). These instruments of state power were sometimes important, as the government had behind it large firms prominent in the standardization process and a huge market central to correspondent relationships. But as before, it was confronted with an entrenched PTT majority that rejected many of its demands, and with regime rules that limited the scope for unilateral initiatives. Moreover, the Reagan Administration's tone and style did little to convince other states that liberalization was in their interest as well, and its negotiators were at times less than effective. Certainly the government helped to put and keep liberalization on the agenda, but its efforts were not a sufficient condition—perhaps not even a necessary condition—of change, without which nothing would have occurred.

The driving force in the transformation of national and international telecommunications institutions derives from the economic sphere. It has been observed that capitalism "is less notable for how it manages extant institutions than for how it creates and destroys them," and that is true here (Schumpeter, 1942, p. 84). The advanced capitalist state's success in promoting private capital accumulation helped to undermine the legitimating conditions of monopoly regulation. The constraining parameters of the institutions which nurtured telecommunications in an earlier era were bust by subsequent processes, thereby reversing the historical relationship between the political and economic spheres. The evolution of capitalism from one stage to the next gave rise to new technical possibilities, transaction patters, and market structures which altered corporate interests regarding regulation. The post-war expansion of firms in many industries into unfamiliar and often highly competitive markets placed a premium on the comprehensive management of information and services to ensure control and growth. This resulted in a learning process, in which TNC users in particular came to see the traditional regulations as antithetical to their interests (Schiller, 1982). Arrangements which favored the interests of administrations at the expense of such users, who comprised a vastly larger grouping central to macroeconomic development, became unsustainable economically and politically. At the same time, the very success of public network development and service penetration increasingly negated the logic of natural monopoly regulation and made it difficult to defend. "The driving force for the restructuring of telecommunications has been the phenomenal growth of user demand for telecommunications, which in turn derives from the shift toward [an information and] service-based economy" (Noam, 1987, p. 33).

While users' changing interests were critical, it is unclear whether they could have overturned a century-old regulatory tradition on their own. But they did not have to, because technical possibilities provided other firms with similar incentives. In particular, strategic decisions to pursue the development of telematics and the integration of microelectronics generated demands for change from new entrants in systems and services, and even from traditional telecommunications, computer, and electronics manufacturers. Thus was born a new interest configuration of users and suppliers which acted as a sort of "shadow government" that challenged at every turn the corporatist "postal industrial complex" of PTTs, and protected manufacturers and their political supporters (Noam, 1986a). This coalition first emerged in the United States, where decentralized political institutions, a huge and diverse market, and Defense Department support for private innovation combined with other factors to stimulate market forces. It was instrumental in convincing the FCC to begin incremental reform with the 1959 "Above 890" decision, and figured prominently in a series of later decision (Horwitz, 1989; Schiller, 1982). The subsequent transformation of international telecommunications arrangements was most directly a function of the slow but steady globalization of the new interest configuration and its preferred conceptualization of the emerging information economy.

The restructuring process was multidimensional, and consisted of more than pressure group politics. The new coalition's success was based not only on raw market power and political lobbying, but also on seemingly compelling ideas. If its claims had remained fully equated only with the profit motives of particular firms, governments might have remained unwilling to give in to its demands. The linkage had to be broken to provide a receptive conceptual environment for the reevaluation of national interests. It would be a mistake to suppose that the FCC or subsequently liberalizing administrations acted simply as the compliant instruments of big business; policy makers had to be convinced that competition was desirable for their national economies as well. The battle had to be waged at the level of legitimating policy discourses, and victory required a somewhat consensual reconceptualization of the technomarket reality to be governed. The redefinition of telecommunications as an industry characterized by technological abundance and tradelike transactions, central to the dynamism of network-based manufacturing and service sectors, undermined the intellectual foundations of monopoly regulation. The notion of potential economic dynamism stunted by regulation was gradually elaborated by an expanding and diverse expert community of academics, industry insiders, and other observers from around the world, who analyses were taken to be more "objective" and not tainted by direct interests in policy outcomes. In the press, conference circuit, and negotiations, "PTT traditionalists" were depicted as "out-of-touch" neo-Luddite dinosaurs, not simply because big business said so, but also because there were plausible arguments that they stood in the way of new wealth creation. This combination of changing corporate interests and pressures and a new intellectual landscape proved potent.

Up to the 1980s, America's liberalizing deregulation did not have direct and immediate effects on the international sphere, as the new interest configuration focused primarily on opening the domestic market. This localization of priorities was mirrored in the federal government, which had yet to identify global liberalization as a key objective of its foreign economic policy. While administrations abroad regarded the American process with fascination, they deemed it irrelevant to their own circumstances, and the private members of their corporatist postal industrial complexes concurred. Further, the ITU instruments clearly distinguished between national and international jurisdictions, and pertained only to the latter. The Americans could destroy their network if they pleased, but international services remained jointly provided with monopolists abroad. Competition was not only not contagious, it was not yet even an issue.

However, American deregulation had indirect, medium-term effects abroad. The relaxation of political constraints invigorated the American technomarket environment, as the differentiation of supply and demand fed waves of new innovations and applications. In turn, the creation of new techniques provided corporate strategists with incentives to reconsider their international positions. By the late 1970s, American-based TNCs had begun to press foreign PTTs to provide them with at least an approximation of the leeway they were achieving with the FCC. They did so individually and collectively, through such trade associations as INTUG and the International Chamber of Commerce (ICC), and in both bilateral and multilateral fora. They also provided a booming business for American consulting firms, which spewed forth a seemingly endless stream of high-priced reports about how bad things really were out there. That the sky was falling was further evidenced by the concurrent preemptive debate over transborder data flow (TDF) restrictions (Drake, 1993). They were trying to establish a normative presumption that competition was equivalent with western values of freedom and the natural state of affairs, whereas regulation was an unnatural contrivance contrary to those values which could be justified only exceptionally. Getting the world to accept this presumption would broaden and change the criteria by which any given policy was evaluated, thereby placing administrations in a politically untenable bargaining position.

Against this backdrop of TNC activity, the American government launched a multipronged diplomatic offensive seemingly designed with maximum friction in mind. Reagan Administration officials marched into numerous multilateral negotiations and conferences to give the sort of "magic of the marketplace" speeches once reserved for Lion's Club conventions. The U.S. Trade Representative (USTR) joined forces with an emerging community of service industry specialists to argue that jointly provided services in fact constituted trade, and as such should be covered by the General Agreement on Tariffs and Trade (GATT) (Aronson & Cowhey, 1988). The Commerce Department released an inflammatory report blasting foreign practices and questioning whether the United States should leave the ITU (NTIA, 1983). Even the FCC entered the fray. It had previously issued a number of decisions—eliminating for IRCs the voice/record and domestic/international dichotomies, extending Computer II's provisions on VANs to international service, and so on—which partially opened up the American side of the half circuit (Frieden, 1983). In doing so, the commission was mindful that its jurisdiction was purely domestic, and that the assent of foreign administrations was necessary for new joint services. But in 1980, it announced unilaterally its intention to extend resale and sharing to international circuits, despite the fact that almost every administration restricted these functions in accordance with the Recommendations. CCITT Director Leon Burtz promptly sent a strongly worded letter noting the "surprise" and "deep disappointment" within the ITU, stating further:

> It seems to me an extremely dangerous situation when one country, and what is more, the leading country with regard to the number of subscribers, the extent of its services and its telecommunications technology, can help to undermine the work of the CCITT. (Schiller, 1982, p. 185)

Many PTTs sent similar messages, some of them declaring that if the FCC proceeded, they would in turn revoke TNCs' access to leased lines. Frantic, American businesses bombarded the commission with calls to reconsider, and it retreated with egg on its newly extended profile.

This episode underscores some of the factors which hindered the globalization of new interests and ideas at the decade's outset. Grudging adherence to the theory of natural monopoly remained strong, no coherent conceptual alternative had yet emerged, and the postal industrial complex was embedded in the fabric of domestic polities abroad. Further, that it was primarily Americans rather than indigenous firms leading the charge deprived claims about the necessity of change of any generalizable legitimacy as an accurate and unbiased depiction of a new reality. This made it easy for PTTs to conclude that the emerging discourse about "restrictive trade barriers," "abuse of dominant position," and "excessive regulation" reflected the interests of large American firms poised to swoop down on their presumably vulnerable markets.

The presumption of vulnerability derived from many sources. For example, while Europe had a number of prominent telecommunications equipment manufacturers, years of reliance on nationalistic procurement and trade policies deprived them of the experience and commercial orientation needed for open global competition. In the computer and microelectronics industries, efforts to foster competitive "national champions" had generally failed. In advanced services, monopoly practices slowed the creation of private firms capable of taking on American entrants. Similar problems existed in varying degrees in other countries, North and South. Moreover, the prevailing intellectual winds in Europe and the Third World were blowing in the opposite direction. In the early 1980s context of stagflation and growing surplus capacity in traditional industries and the lack of competitiveness in the "industries of the future" generated *info-angst* about the broad structural changes underway. This was heightened by a recognition that telecommunications, as a key infrastructure, and information, as a key factor of production, were becoming ever more central to competitiveness throughout the manufacturing and services sectors. A prominent report to the French president adopted a wholistic approach to the emerging complexity of the information economy, and argued that failure in the "telematics sector" would have profound implications across many user industries (Nora & Minc, 1980). The Commission of the European Community (EC) agreed in its 1979 "Dublin Report:"

> Control over the "telematics system" as a whole is slipping away from Europe to an ever-increasing extent...domination of the telematics industry by the United States and Japan would, in the more or less short run, result in:
> —the final loss of European control over an essential field;
> —damage to the competitive position of the Community, both in Europe and in the rest of the world;
> —the loss of the potential for new jobs, which should compensate for loss of jobs caused by the new technologies;
> —a reduction in our independence in decision-making in all walks of public and private life. (EC, 1979, p. 12)

Many governments began to consider and sometimes enact regulatory, trade, and industrial policies for telecommunications and information that the new interest configuration damned as protectionist. Hence, the early 1980s were marked by growing discord and drift in bilateral and multilateral policy discussions. Within and without the ITU, PTT engineers were aghast at being described as undemocratic cartel managers conspiring against the free market, since commercial considerations had never been an acknowledged criteria for evaluating standards and regulations. They were doing as they had always done, but were suddenly being castigated for it.

The emerging gap between the United States and the rest of the world rendered problematic for the first time the principles and efficacy of the international regime. If it widened into a gulf, the United States might have reduces its involvement in and compliance with those ITU processes and rules deemed contrary to its new objectives. Technically, this would make if difficult to devise international standards for new systems and services. Economically, it would increase the costs of achieving interconnection, as special operational arrangements would need be devised on an ad hoc bilateral basis; and provide American-based TNCs with incentives to attempt to bypass regulations in search of "gray markets." Politically, the disagreement was beginning to undermine the universal legitimacy of the assumption that national monopolies were a necessary or desirable basis for building international interconnection. Further, the cracks in the dike could turn into a flood. Finding themselves competing with invigorated American counterparts, other states might be tempted to follow suit and defect from the historical consensus in order to attract TNCs to their turf. If they were pushed into a liberalization sweepstakes, regulatory arbitrage could spread and the symmetry of national regime objectives would decay. In this light, the United Kingdom's early decision to bilaterally open certain international market segments with the United States was viewed almost as an act of betrayal by some European administrations. Britain wanted to promote domestic competition, attract network-based service industries, and deepen its role as a hub for transatlantic traffic, and the conditions it offered businesses were both more permissive than those on the continent and contrary to the spirit if not the letter of some CCITT rules. Some European PTTs sought to keep her in the fold, lest their own policies appeared overly restrictive in comparison. Japan also began a somewhat similar path to bilaterally negotiated change in certain relations.

If national asymmetric deregulation had continued to spread to international correspondence in this matter, the result might have been regime decay, rather than transformation. Retention of the general principles and social purpose which defined the *ancien* regime in the face of consequential defections from the United States, Britain, Japan, and others would signify a disjuncture between collective commitments and actual practice. Effective regimes require coherent compliance lest a minority cause problems for the majority, and the ITU had no means to compel conformity. The incipient spread of asymmetric deregulation to international connections implied that a new agreement would be necessary, as the regime was decreasingly "neutral" regarding national choices.

> As long as competition among service providers had been generally excluded, the recommendations restraining competition served as a means to protect mutually the spheres of influence of national monopolies. But in an increasingly competitive environment, the recommendations create market distortions to the benefit of incumbent service providers and to the detriment of potential entrants. It is this change in the function of the ITU recommendations that represents probably the most important impact of national liberalization on the regulatory activities of the ITU. (Witt, 1987, p. 362)

The growing challenge to these rules needed to be accommodated if the system was not to fragment into a patchwork of uncoordinated specialized arrangements, yet sovereign states do not readily give in to foreign demands when this implies jettisoning long-held objectives. However, by mid-decade, changes in the political equations at home and the spread of new thinking about the information economy were leading many of the key regime-making states to reevaluate their positions regarding both national and international institutions. Frustration with weak macroeconomic performance and a conservative political wind set a larger context in which these pressures became doubly compelling. Two in particular merit brief mention here.

First, corporate demands for deregulation were taking on a truly international profile. Firms abroad which had initially been either lukewarm or hostile to the American agenda, especially large users, were reconsidering their positions. TNCs, especially those in financial and other services, found themselves competing with American-based counterparts which were benefiting from the efficiencies and enhanced range of choice in systems and applications associated with liberalization. Market incentives therefore pointed to the desirability of achieving similar gains with their home PTTs, and of extending these gains to cross-border services. Further, a conceptual realignment accompanied these users' shift to more globally oriented profiles. They now saw themselves to have similar interests as American users in relation to states, insofar as they were more concerned with accessing the best resources than with buying nationally. If foreign-based services were more appropriate than those of local suppliers, they wanted lower tariffs and easier interconnection. If foreign CPE was better for their customized needs, they wanted open standards and liberalized attachments. Hence, the regulatory preferences, negotiating agendas, and intellectual orientations of large users across the industrialized world began to converge around imported focal points, which substantially broadened the support for and impact of the efforts of INTUG, ICC, and similar industry alliances.

A parallel shift was occurring on the market's supply side. The rapid globalization and differentiation of demand generated new opportunities which could be realized best in a liberalized international market. Traditional telecommunications manufacturers and new entrants, whether medium-sized startups or large computer and electronics firms crossing market niches, could not recover the rising R&D costs of advanced CPE and network equipment without foreign sales. Potential private service suppliers could not lure customers to their new offerings unless they could ensure end-to-end connectivity. As locally based users began to procure more widely, success at home necessitated resources and expertise not attainable solely through monopsony purchases. National competitiveness therefore required international competitiveness. Where states were slow to change, TNCs devised novel solutions to access barriers, such as joint ventures and other resource-sharing arrangements. These were piecemeal responses to an uneven transition in which some suppliers still clung to their PTT patrons. But those companies seeking international profiles wanted the predictability of a "flexible" and liberalized multilateral framework.

Second, the emerging reconceptualization of telecommunications' role in economic activity raised the question of whether PTTs should retain their exclusive jurisdictions. If indeed it was not merely a public utility, but was now the nervous system and catalyst for the full range of user industries, other state agencies whose turf was affected by telecommunications wanted a say in national policy. By virtue of their professional training and organizational objectives, the personnel of such agencies were more receptive to liberalization than those of the PTTs. Key trade ministries thought that many cross-border transactions constituted trade and were under their jurisdiction; industry ministries wanted to support national firms, but that held for users as well as producers; competition ministries saw the possibility to extend their antitrust policies; finance ministries wanted to cut expenditures through privatization; and so on. Moreover, such ministries had ties to different social constituencies that the PTTs, and were the targets of effective lobbying by the new interest configuration.

While the resulting interagency divisions over regulation paled in comparison to tradition of turf wars in the United States, they did render telecommunications policy a contested intellectual and bureaucratic terrain, which in turn added to the reform pressure. PTTs no longer had an automatic claim to exclusive and unquestioned jurisdiction over the field. Hence a changing configuration of corporate and intrastate interests and ideas was taking root. These pressures were forcing administrations to reexamine the efficacy of the regime, and would probably have been sufficient to catalyze change in the ITU. However, two further initiatives added supporting external pressures to the mix.

One was the GATT's launching of the Uruguay Round in 1986. The notion that international services exchange had tradelike properties first emerged in the early 1970s, and by the early 1980s the United States was pressing other governments to negotiate services rules as part of a larger trade package. This decision reflected both new corporate interests and ideas about the global economy and national welfare (Drake & Nicolaïdis, 1992). The new interest configuration in the United States supported strongly the government's position, and indeed played an important role in its formulation. After all, the principals and agents involved in GATT negotiations were more procompetitive than those in the ITU. Trade policy tended to receive greater attention from central governments and mobilize broader corporate constituencies which lacked stakes in the postal industrial complex. Moreover, the concepts and terms of reference employed in GATT discussions were more congenially loaded. Trade policy was about establishing rules of fair competition, opening up market access to a multitude of players, and circumscribing narrowly the conditions under which access may legitimately be constrained. The very act of viewing telecommunications as part of a larger category of services transactions to be "traded" according to common rules created a strong conceptual bias toward openness, and set a new yardstick for evaluating telecommunications regulations as simple nontariff barriers to be removed. Hence the GATT was an attractive venue in which to push for a new multilateral framework that would deal with the economic dimensions of international correspondence, as well as a means of pressuring administrations in the ITU to reform the extant regime.

When the United States first raised the issue in 1982, most GATT members were reluctant or hostile. At this point, suspicion was widespread that the Americans wanted negotiations for their own particularistic ends, but over the next four years, an interesting process took place. After undertaking studies of their national capabilities in services, the EC and many key countries learned that they were not helpless before the American threat, and could in fact fare well in freer competition (Drake & Nicholaïdis, 1992). In the years since the round's launching, opposition in principle to some type of telecommunications trade deal has virtually evaporated, although governments continue to fight over precisely how open the market should be in accordance with which rules and commitments. At the time of writing, negotiations on a General Agreement on Trade in Services (GATS) and its Telecommunications Annex are stalled along with the rest of the round. While the particulars of the Annex are discussed below, a key point is relevant here: Its impact is not entirely dependent on its final form. A treaty would be important in codifying and reinforcing change, but the negotiation process itself had already altered the world of telecommunications policy by the mid-1980s. It was becoming clear that telecommunications would increasingly be thought of and bargained over in trade terms, and that corporate demands for market access would become politically difficult to ignore. As with contested markets among firms, a contested market among policy makers helped lead to anticipatory action. To avoid being swamped with criticism and legal challenges, PTTs needed to get out in front of the wave and prepare for the eventuality of trade by injecting some competitive advantage into their operations; deregulation was in part a response to that need. Simply by taking up services, the GATT had already played a supporting role in laying the seeds of change in the ITU.

The other contributing factor was the launching, also in 1986, of the EC's 1992 program of internal market unification. For over a century, it had been European PTTs which provided the dominant orientation of ITU instruments regarding regulation and standardization, but with the commission's conversion to the cause of a single market in telecommunications and information, those PTTs now found themselves confronted with a higher proliberalization force backed by substantial legal and political authority. In the past five years, the commission has undertaken a wide range of initiatives to push institutional and policy change which have impacted heavily the major national markets and ITU's internal politics.

As a result of these factors, deregulation and liberalization have become a global movement since the middecade. It took root first and most deeply in the domestic systems of the advanced capitalist world, where the pressures and capacities for change were strongest, but it has recently begun to spread rapidly to LDCs and formerly communist countries, as well as to international connections. The characteristics of national deregulation are discussed in the other contributions to this volume, and need not be recited here. What is important to this chapter is the impact on regime cooperation in the ITU.

Institutional Adaptation: Organizational Procedures and Regime Policies

The American move toward domestic deregulation in the 1960s and 1970s did not have a substantial impact in the ITU. But as the government and its corporate constituents turned their attention to international liberalization in the early 1980s, the issue slowly began to creep into the ITU. The first major venue at which it could have been addressed was the 1982 Plenipotentiary in Nairobi. However, plenipotentiary conferences generally concentrate on questions of organizational management and leave detailed standardization and regulatory issues to the administrative conferences and consultative committees. Moreover, after Third World decolonization, they had generally been dominated by North-South conflicts over development assistance (or the lack thereof), the budget, the regional allocation of elected positions in the permanent organs, and so on. At Nairobi, these divisions were deepened by the LDCs' dissatisfaction with the results of the 1979 World Administrative Radio Conference (WARC) and by their high-intensity effort to expel Israel from the meeting, which was narrowly defeated after the Americans threatened to leave (Codding, 1983; Segal 1982). In a sense, the Plenipotentiary had more in common with the United Nations General Assembly than with the CCITT, and liberalization issues received little or no sustained attention from the majority of members. However, the conference did take two steps—one innocuous, the other controversial—that would have important consequences for market liberalization and regime change in the years to come.

First, it retained in the Conventional a provision allowing members to formulate "Special Arrangements." Article 31 held that "Members reserve for themselves, for the private operating agencies recognized by them and for other agencies duly authorized to do so, the right to make special arrangements on telecommunications matters which do not concern Members in general." (ITU, 1982 p. 22) With mild variations in language, this provision dates all the way back to the first ITU treaty in 1865, and has remained in every convention since (ITU, 1866 p. 33). Its retention in 1982 was not expected to cause problems for members, and hence was not a subject of debate. How then could it figure in regime change?

The answer highlights how the actual intersubjective meaning and policy impact of formal institutional rules depends on the context in which they are interpreted and implemented. During the long century of national monopoly control, the special arrangements provision was seen as a mechanism by which administrations and RPOAs could exceptionally cut deals that deviated somewhat from the otherwise uniform rules of the game. At the outset, this appears to have been intended to allow pairs of continental European countries like Prussia and Bavaria to set tariffs, standards, and operational procedures that catered to their special network and traffic conditions if—and this was crucial—their doing so did not negatively impact the revenues and other interest of third parties. Insofar as monopoly control and joint service provisioning still prevailed, such deals did not undermine the regime's overarching political bargain. In subsequent years, the special arrangemnets provision also appears to have been important in experimentally developing some new services, including those governed by the radio regime, as well as in facilitating the progressive incorporation of American private carriers with unique network characteristics and operating procedures into the regime.

In contrast, the provision would begin to take a new meaning and significance amidst the assymmetric deregulation of the 1980s. As the United States and Britain jumped out ahead of the wave and began to extend liberalization their bilateral relations, Article 31 would provide their TNCs with a legitimating legal basis for launching international VANs, relaxing D Series restrictions on intracorporate leased circuits and so on. Although these were still bilateral deals, the rapid growth of basic and enhanced traffic from the liberalized British hub to the continent now put pressure on continental PTTs to follow suit. Moreover, as TNCs began to increase pressure for liberalization of international relations across the industrialized word in subsequent years, special arrangements provided rationale for an increasingly varied set of agreements that did not comport with the historic regime objective of uniform and restrictive rules. In this sense, Article 31 would play a role in evolving actual market practice away from what the regime rules looked like on paper. Finally, as we will see below, the notion of special arrangements would, by the end of the decade, be reformulated and invoked in an ITU treaty in such a manner as to actively promote the shift toward a multivendor, user-oriented market.

The second step was the decision to convene a WATTC in 1988. The plenipotentiary could not address the new regulatory issues on the horizon, but an expert meeting six years hence with sufficient preparatory committee work could. In separate proposals, the Nordic countries and Japan argued that the rapid growth and differentiation of computer-enhanced, nonvoice services was occurring in a policy void. As the primary treaty instrument for record transmissions, the International Telegraph Regulations on 1973 provided less and less guidance in a value-added world. Proliferation without clear rules for each class of new offerings could, from a PTT standpoint, encourage destructive competition between services and even administrations; the benefits of a uniform regime and symmetric regulation would be lost. This was a proposition with obvious appeal to the majority of members, and so Resolution No. 10 stated "that it is advisable to establish, to the extent necessary, a broad international regulatory framework for all existing and foreseen new telecommunications services" (ITU, 1982, P. 239). Fearing new restrictions, the United States unsuccessfully opposed the Resolution.

Beyond these two rather different initiatives, the plenipotentiary left the emerging liberalization issues to the CCITT. By slowly unleashing market forces, national deregulation was altering the regime's operational environment and the process of standardization. Growing user demand for flexible systems and customized applications invited a widening array of manufacturers to develop CPE and network equipment for integration into an increasingly complex infrastructure. The number of firms with stakes in the standards game was multiplying rapidly, and they were attaining RPOA or SIO status in the CCITT. By the early 1980s, the private sector was "beginning to play a preponderant role" in the committee, and its representatives outnumbered those of the PTTs in many key study groups (Cerni, 1982, p. 25). This did not mean that administrations were suddenly powerless, but rather that the style and objectives of the discussions became different from in the past. PTTs and RPOAs were forced to accept that they could not formulate effective recommendations without input and consent from major producers, users, and other standards bodies. Just as the equipment market was shifting from monopsony to differentiated supply and demand, key aspects of regime design were being partially privatized, and influence derived increasingly from market shares rather than age-old political alliances. Moreover, there was a growing tendency, especially in the United States, for TNCs frustrated with CCITT's pace and carrier bias to focus their efforts regarding some standards in alternative private bodies. The model of the *ancien* regime—uniform, global, de jure standards developed slowly by a handful of administrations and their chosen suppliers—was giving way to a varied, application-oriented world of rapidly generated private standards, some of which were established de facto by large firms such as International Business Machines (IBM). These dual processes of internal change in the balance of influence and external challenges to the CCITT's exclusive position would continue to accelerate throughout the decade.

Change in the process meant change in the product. The diversification of interests, markets, and regulations applied pressure on the committee to devise standards that allowed TNCs greater flexibility and control. One major casualty was the original ISDN vision. Given the nature of the technology, truly global ISDN standardization would have to extend more deeply into national networks than was generally the case prior. It was also necessary to provide new service suppliers and users with end-to-end connectivity. But early in the 1981-1984 study period, the United States and its corporate supporters began to lobby heavily against the centralized model favored by European PTTs (Schiller, 1985). At American insistence, the 1980 definition was altered substantially by 1984. No longer was ISDN to be defined as a "public" network. Rather than a single standard user/network interface, there would be a "limited set of connection types" (Rutkowski, 1985). These changes meant that ISDN could be implemented through a number of reference point configurations in accordance with varying national preferences, but at the cost of reduced or more expensive and cumbersome global interconnection. The FCC endorsed the U interface as devised in the private T1 standards committee, and ruled that Network Channel Termination Equipment was CPE rather than network equipment. The United States had opted for multiple private ISDNs rather than "the ISDN." This met the demands of specialized service suppliers, computer manufacturers, and users, all of whom have been very active in American standards fora, but meant that the United States would not support the S/T interface developed in the CCITT. The other rapid liberalizers, the United Kingdom and Japan, also adopted ISDN configurations that were not fully incompatible with the CCITT standard.

In contrast, the European PTTs proceeded with S/T and the original "one nation, one network" vision (Noam, 1986b). Even so, their specific designs sometimes varied, and the shifting political-economic context preclude adopting the sort of measures that had been anticipated and vigorously attacked by the new interest configuration. Forcibly withdrawing leased lines and pushing customers back onto the public network was no longer possible; the PTTs now had to make ISDN more attractive than private alternatives. Some attempted to upgrade their switched networks, offer enhanced Centrex in competition with CPE-defined services, and provide virtual private networks that approximated the same levels of control associated with leased circuits. The EC commission entered the game with money and directives in 1987, announcing that coordinated ISDN development would be central to its 1992 plan. Nevertheless, corporate pressures had resulted in ISDN being absorbed into a more market-oriented supply and demand structure, and customers were increasingly free to choose whether to support it. Thus far, most have not. Capital constraints and soft demand have resulted in repeated delays in implementation, and the EC's hopes of a 5% penetration rate in the community by 1992 are unlikely to be fulfilled. In short, the grand plans for uniform and centralized networks, a logical extension of the *ancien* regime, have been superseded by asymmetric deregulation and the social forces behind it. The CCITT's ISDN standards are incomplete and unstable, and actual implementation varies widely across the industrialized countries (Wigand, 1988).

Many other trends in network technology and the political-economic context affected CCITT standardization in the 1980s, two of which merit brief mention. The limitations of narrowband ISDN became even more apparent with the shift to Integrated Broadband Network development (IBN). With their megabit capacities, IBNs could carry virtually all forms of information, including full-motion video and high definition television signals (HDTV), but uncertainties remain about its technical design and eventual political control. A major breakthrough came in 1988, when the CCITT adopted a network node interface standard based on the Synchronous Optical Network design (SONET). SONET was generated in the American T1 committee and opposed by the Japanese and Europeans, some of whom favored a rival technology. A compromise approach was taken that may again result in varying national interfaces for some signals. As with ISDN, the user/network interface proved controversial, and a decision was delayed to the 1989-92 study period, in which IBNs have received extensive attention. Hence while there could be substantial capacity improvements over the narrowband ISDN conceived in the 1970s, the fundamental questions of competition, control, and the prospects for truly global standardization were unresolved in the early 1990s.

Whether broadband is defined and implemented in a carrier or customer-oriented fashion will depend in part on another trend: the rise of open network regulatory concepts. In its 1986 Computer III decision, the FCC embraced an Open Network Architecture (ONA) design that would give VAN operators equal access to common carriers' network resources in exchange for allowing the latter to compete in enhanced services without having to form separate subsidiaries. Building on AT&T's Intelligent Network/2 technology, ONA essentially treats networks as aggregations of advanced capabilities that can be drawn on, optimized, and combined by customers to fit their specialized needs on a case-by-case basis. The underlying infrastructure becomes a pool of intelligent, software-based resources for shared interfirm processes, wherein value can be added and new wealth generated. While ONA is difficult to police and recently suffered a setback in the courts, the basic concept spread rapidly. The EC Commission adopted a series of broadly similar Open Network Provisioning (ONP) measures, and the Japanese have their own version (Rutkowski, 1987). To date, the extent of this unpacking and dispersal of functions from the center has varied across counties, as PTTs are uncertain of the financial implications. But some seem ready to gamble that what they lose in terms of control over certain functions, they can make up for by expanding the level of switched traffic in a competitive environment. In short, the emerging trend since the late 1980s seems to be toward a configuration in which national administrations retain control over the underlying facilities but allow a widening array of independent suppliers and users greater market access and applications control in services. This is likely to affect many ITU activities in the future.

While CCITT standardization was rapidly impacted by the emerging order, movement was slower on its regulation of international services. In the first half of the 1980s, a growing number of northern PTTs began to experiment with selective liberalization of specific domestic market niches in the hope of satisfying their awakening corporate constituencies. The result was a complex mosaic of increasingly asymmetric regulatory and market structures that aggravated globally oriented corporate managers, who wanted clear, consistent, and permissive rules wherever they operated (Bruce, Cunard, & Director, 1988; Eward, 1984). Indeed, rather than satisfying corporate appetites and achieving a new and marginally more open equilibrium, such experiments provided influential TNCs with additional incentives to press onward with further demands across unstable regulatory boundary lines. But in the CCITT, there was no consensus for accommodating these pressures in the international order. To the contrary, the 1984 Plenary Assembly adopted the D Series, cited above, over adamant objections to its restrictive provisions from INTUG and other business lobbies. More surprisingly perhaps, virtually the same D Series provisions were retained in the Blue Book approved at the 1988 plenary at Melbourne, by which time the consensus for change was otherwise stronger (ITU, 1989b).

Many administrations were still loath to rescind rules that protected their monopolies over lucrative international traffic that was a major source of revenue with which to cross-subsidize domestic programs. Especially with value-based tariffs for corporate customers, these services remained an important cash cow and source of authority in an era when such resources were eroding at the national level. Even by 1988, fundamentally altering a collective arrangement devised to fit the least-common-denominator interests of all members would have been difficult because they varied widely in the speed and depth of reform. Increasingly asymmetric regime preferences presented two distinct options. The CCITT could undertake the conflictual task of trying to jettison, in an organization that takes decisions by consensus, rules which some members continued to favor. That would reduce their room to maneuver, as it would be politically easier to legitimate selectively liberalizing departures from the existing restrictive baseline than to legitimate restrictive departures from a new liberal baseline. And insofar as many PTTs used the recommendations as guidelines for domestic policy, changing the D Series would make it difficult to resist similar changes at home. Alternatively, the CCITT could retain the common framework but allow those administrations who wished to grant firms new rights to negotiate bilateral special arrangements with like-minded counterparts. The latter course would not disrupt the affairs of third parties or remove the safety net of collective legitimation upon which some PTTs depended in their dealings with TNCs. However, it did mean that insofar as administrations agreed to selectively depart from them, the recommendations were truly becoming recommendations, rather than rules that were automatically and uniformly applied as in the past.

That the 1988 plenary kept the old D Series language intact despite substantial pressures for change was also due to the committee's preoccupation with two other issues. One, the restructuring of the standards process, is discussed below. The other was the WATTC conference to be held just afterwards, also in Melbourne. The regime's three instruments—the Convention, Regulations, and Recommendations—are structured in a logical and legal hierarchy. Accordingly, the Recommendations are interpreted in light of the Regulations, the status of which was unclear because of sharp divisions over what type of new treaty rules would be applied to "all existing and foreseeable services." The Preparatory Committee established to draft the new agreement was deeply and bitterly divided between the partisans of sweeping liberalization and a majority favoring more incremental and limited reforms. Pending the outcome of WATTC-88, reconsideration of the D Series was effectively on hold.

The PrepComm comprised about 35 of the ITU's then 165 members, and was dominated by a coalition of PTTs. In four meetings during 1985-1987, they inserted provisions into the draft which hard-line liberalizers found extremely objectionable. At the May 1987 meeting, the PrepComm text was adopted over objections from the United States, Britain, and Kuwait. There were many contentious issues, but the key ones concerned the scope of services (and by extension, networks) and domain of entities to be covered in the new regime treaty (Drake, 1988). The Regulations would apply to the provision of services to the public, and Article 1.2 defined this public as meaning the population, including "governmental and legal bodies within the territory in whole or part of a Member." Similarly, Article 1.7 provided that

> Members shall endeavor to ensure that any entity, established in their territory, using the international telecommunication network to provide an international telecommunication service: a) is so authorized by the

Member, b) complies with these Regulations, and c) to the extent considered appropriate by the Member, complies with the relevant Recommendations. (ITU, 1987, p. 53)

The PrepComm minority asserted that latent in this jargon was a grand plan by the PTTs to not only preserve their existing market positions and regulatory authority, but actually expand them into new domains of the information economy. They argued that it could be taken as codifying new rights for administrations to apply restrictive conditions to any type of service provided by any company to anyone else. Specialized suppliers such as private VANS, and perhaps even large users who employed internal capabilities to service their geographically dispersed operations, could be forced to attain official approval for any operation. This was not the case with the 1973 Regulations. Written in the precompetitive era, their scope encompassed clearly only telegraph and telephone services, their domain only PTTs and RPOAs. New services and suppliers had arisen subsequently, and were covered primarily by the recommendations. The minority saw bad news here, too, as the language seemed to require full compliance by everybody with the recommendations, implicitly elevating their status from voluntary to mandatory rules. Finally, they maintained that the draft expanded the regime's scope beyond telecommunications transmission to information services. Article 4.2 stated in part that, "Types of international telecommunication services are defined in the relevant CCITT Recommendations" (ITU, 1987, p. 56). This was in deference to administrations that had unsuccessfully sought to include a detailed list of all services to be regulated, which was impractical amidst rapid innovation. But some services discussed in the recommendations were not unambiguously "telecommunications," as they were concerned more with information's enhancement than its transport. Indeed, a highly-publicized report by prominent American consultants blasted the ITU for allegedly seeking to attain regulatory control over all network-dependent services firms, from banks and consultancies to data processors and beyond; and implied that the Secretary General, Richard Butler, was engaged in a personal power grab (Bruce, Cunard, & Director, 1987).

In truth, such charges were probably a bit exaggerated, and several factors make it unclear just how restrictive the PrepComm text would have been in implementation. First, the policy environment had changed rapidly since it was first drafted in 1985. While the Americans alleged that the PrepComm was seeking mandatory conformity with a uniform and onerous global framework, the PTTs were already engaging in asymmetric deregulatory programs that would make such an interpretation difficult, and many of their own domestic constituents and governments would have opposed this. Moreover, while a few PTTs such as the French and their African clients argued strongly for the language, support from others was wavering or soft; the document did not necessarily reflect the coherent and committed determination of all PrepComm members. Second, it is debatable whether the authorization of entities would be required and conform to some single, rigid procedure; PTTs might choose the degree of flexibility which matched their increasingly diverse policies. Third, Article 1.2 said the Regulations included "underlying telecommunication transport," and while "include" could be read to mean "but are not limited to," it would be extraordinarily difficult for PTTs to extend their reach to financial and all other network-based services as the Americans feared. In short, the draft's open-ended wording provided support to those PTTs wishing to adopt telecommunications restrictions, but it did not consistently require them to do so. It was again a least-common-denominator instrument designed for members' baseline interest in preserving national sovereignty as fit their needs.

Nevertheless, the impending WATTC became a major controversy that brought the ITU to the front page of newspaper business sections. The organization that had always been cited as the paragon of smooth apolitical international cooperation was now the locus of a major struggle over the rules of the game in the global information economy. From mid-1987 to mid-1988, a worldwide pressure campaign was launched against the PrepComm text. The American and British governments denounced it, the former intimating that it would return to its old status of nonsignatory to the Regulations. In the business press and conference circuit, analysts depicted the WATTC process as an almost cosmic struggle between free market good and PTT evil. Most importantly, the fight focused the minds of corporate managers around the world on their common political interests, and helped solidify the transnational front to an unprecedented degree. Multinational lobbies and their domestic counterparts voiced strong opposition. Powerful firms in the United States filed submissions with the FCC saying the United States should not sign the accord, and foreign companies whose home PTTs had supported the draft applied similar pressures on their governments. Some TNCs intimated publicly that they would attempt to customize their CPE and leased circuits so as to bypass any new restrictions. The PrepComm majority was clearly going to have to back off, but needed a way to do so without losing all face.

A few months before the conference, Secretary General Richard Butler proposed an alternative draft which made the inevitable concessions to the PrepComm minority. The "Butler Draft" underscored that sovereign choice rather than a mandatory and uniform global framework was the basis of national policies; deleted the controversial definition of the public in draft 1.2 and the "any entity" provision of 1.7; explicitly restricted the Regulations' domain to PTTs and RPOAs; reaffirmed that compliance with the recommendations was not mandatory; and added a new Article 9 based on Article 31 of the 1982 Convention. It held that members could authorize their administrations, RPOAs, and "any other organization or person" to enter into special arrangements with counterparts abroad, subject to national laws, "for establishment of special networks, systems, or applications, including the underlying means of telecommunications transport, to meet their own international communication needs or those of others" (ITU, 1988a, p. 10). This positioned the ability of new suppliers and users to conclude special arrangements for any type of facilities and services as an overarching regime principle in light of which the other provisions should be considered. Of course, government approval was still needed, but refusal to provide it would now be more difficult if PTTs could not hide behind treaty commitments. Not surprisingly, some ITU members reacted cautiously to the Secretary General's suggestions. The United States stridently demanded firmer commitments to competition, while some in the majority grumbled that the changes were a "giveaway" to the Americans. But adherence to some variant of his language was the only path to a successful negotiation: Too much pressure had been mobilized to allow a return to the PrepComm draft, and many key administrations had concluded that change was unavoidable.

While 112 members were represented at Melbourne, most of the important decisions were taken by a small, ad hoc group of mostly advanced capitalist countries working long into the night behind closed doors. Many LDCs balked at the exclusion of their concerns about officially blessing private interconnection and service provisioning, but these were pushed aside into a series of nonbinding resolutions and opinions. Like all the regime negotiations before it, this was a game between the rich and powerful. After much heated debate, the meeting concluded a new treaty by majority vote, rather than by consensus. "Fittingly, the Town Hall where WATTC took place was cleared immediately afterwards for a performance of Handel's Messiah" (Williamson, 1989, p. 18). The final text drew heavily on the Butler draft, with a few compromises for the PTTs. It was "neutral" insofar as it required neither open markets nor strict regulation; that choice was left to individual states. But in the current policy context, this makes it a de facto liberalizing agreement. Now a single treaty—The International Telecommunication Regulations—applying general principles beyond the realm of telegraph and telephone, it establishes a normative presumption that PTTs will accommodate a multivendor, user-oriented environment, and deprives them of any collective rationale for imposing new restrictions. Left to fend for themselves, many PTTs would find corporate demands difficult to ignore.

Article 1 on "Purpose and Scope of the Regulations" says the Regulations cover services offered to the public, the underlying international telecommunication transport, and administrations and RPOAs. It invokes at the treaty's beginning the right of members to allow special arrangement, which is elaborated by Article 9 in keeping with the Butler formulation. Article 1 goes on to say that the Regulations are to facilitate global interconnection and interoperability, and the efficiency, usefulness, and availability of services, which is understood to involve a complex mix of public and private entities; that references to the Recommendations do not give them the same legal status as the Regulations, and (only) administrations and RPOAs must comply with them "when possible;" and that members may require that administrations and POAs serving the public be authorized and, where appropriate, will encourage compliance with the Recommendations by such suppliers. Other notable provisions were contained in Article 3, "International Network," which holds that any user has the right to send traffic; Article 4, "International Telecommunication Services," which says that administrations and RPOAs should provide a minimum quality of service for access to the international network, private leased facilities and services, and interworking between services; Article 7, "Suspension of Services," which implies that any suspension shall be temporary; and Appendix 1-1, "Accounting Rates," which calls for the revision of rates taking into account cost trends for each specific service (ITU, 1988b, pp. 3–4, 7–8, 11, 13)

These and other provisions largely met the demands of TNCs and government favoring sweeping liberalization. Only the retention of authorization language could be viewed as a small setback. However, it does not obligate authorization, but simply recognizes a member's right to require it should it decide to do so; is clearly limited to firms supplying underlying transport services to third parties; and does not apply to the internal operations of users. "In practice, the new language merely recognizes what has already been a part of the sovereign rights of Members," and there is no evidence that Article 1.7 has constituted a new impediment to TNCs since the Regulations were adopted (U.S. Department of State, 1988, p. 8). Underscoring its position on the regime's scope, domain, and jurisdiction, the United States declared in the Final Protocol that it did not

Accept any obligation to enforce any provision of the domestic law or regulations of any other Member; endorse, in any way, domestic procedures of other Members which would require approval for providers of telecommunications services and services dependent on telecommunication transport seeking to do business outside of the United States of America; [or] accept any obligation in respect of the application of any provision of these Regulations to services other than public correspondence services. (ITU, 1988c, p. 16)

For their part, EC members arrived at Melbourne deeply divided along North-South lines, with the former group having moved away from the PrepComm language. France and its African clients were the only remaining strong advocates of expanded regulatory powers, and their major initiatives—mandatory access charges for private network interconnection and international cooperation in implementing namely national policies. TNCs—failed to pass. Moreover, they wanted to proscribe economic harm to third parties from special arrangements, but:

Several developed countries argued that this addition was beyond the scope of the ITU since the ITU, they said, was a purely technical institution that should not be involved in economic matters. Obviously, a much controversial argument since, throughout WATTC-88, economic issues were discussed extensively. (Raveendran, 1989, p. 37)

Power prevailed, and this concern was relegated to a nonbinding opinion.

The international business community and press were pleased with the results. One corporate spokesperson noted that "we can be sure that the needs of users will dictate the ultimate effects of WATTC" (MCI's Lawrence Codacovi, quoted in Williamson, 1989, p. 19). Another prominent observer noted:

WATTC 88 represents a victory for operators and users of private networks, and for the ITU...the regulations recognize that there are special networks, systems and applications which do not conform to conventional telecommunications networks.... These are "permissive" arrangements between participating parties according to national laws. WATTC represents a transition into a multiprovider world....It also lends legitimacy to claims by trade experts that telecommunications services are indeed traded, and should be governed by a trade regime. (Pipe, 1989, p. 21)

By adopting a formally neutral agreement, the conference did open a space for the GATS negotiators, thus side-stepping the widely anticipated problems of contradictory treaty instruments. It also set an entirely new tone for the ITU's internal workings. The bruising fight over the PrepComm text demonstrated the breadth and intensity of corporate demands for continuing liberalization and a greater voice in ITU affairs. Administrations could no longer expect to retain their exclusive control over the policy process, or to devise instruments that were sharply out of synch with an increasingly privatized marketplace. The treaty signalled the transition to a new international regime under which global interconnection and service provisioning would involve a complex competitive mixture of public and private entities. That transition gathered momentum with five subsequent events: the restructuring of the standards process, changes approved by the 1989 Plenipotentiary, liberalization of the D Series, current pressures to reform the accounting and settlements procedures, and progress in the Uruguay Round on the GATS Telecommunications Annex.

Throughout the 1980s, the CCITT's historical dominance of international standardization had been progressively slipping away. Liberalization and the technical convergence of telecommunications and information systems radically increased the number of diversity of players in standardization. Frustrated with the slow pace and PTT control in the CCITT, these firms were often looking to national standards bodies such as the American National Standards Institute (ANSI), T1 committee of the National Exchange Carriers Association (NECA), and Corporation for Open Systems (COS) in North America, and the Technical Telecommunications Committee (TTC) in Japan; and to regional standards bodies like the EC's new European Telecommunications Standards Institute (ETSI) and the European Standards Commission (CEN). Dozens of other industry-oriented groups entered the game, resulting in the CCITT's position suffering centrifugal devolution, and end-to-end global interoperability became more difficult to achieve (Drake & McKnight, 1988). To address these problems, CCITT Director Theodor Irmer spearheaded a two-pronged program designed to make the committee more responsive to the demands of a privatized marketplace.

The first prong consisted of internal reforms of the CCITT's working methods. Manufacturers, service suppliers, and users all complained that the industry could not wait for the finalization of standards at the quadrennial plenaries. At the 1988 assembly, Irmer argued that some recommendations should be adopted quickly via balloting, as was the practice in many private bodies. The Soviet Union and some LDCs expressed strong concerns that while this would suit the industry in the advanced capitalist countries, it could reduce even further their ability to have a say in the process. Some procedural compromises were offered to partially allay these fears, and the plenary adopted by consensus a "Spirit of Melbourne" Resolution on "Approval of new and revised Recommendations between Plenary Assemblies." Essentially, the new "accelerated procedures" allow that when needed, standards can be adopted if seventy percent of CCITT members responding approve them within three months of the Director's circulation of a proposal. This is an important shift from the slow consensus building process of the past. The 1988 plenary also approved a number of other changes to CCITT working methods designed to improve coordination among study groups, drop obsolete questions and recommendations, streamline documentation, and increase the use of electronic networks in the standards process (Drake, 1989). More are possible at the 1992 plenary, including a formal move to flexible project teams and even the abolition of the quadrennial study-period cycle and associated multivolume books of recommendations, many of which are out of date by the time of publications.

The second prong involved improved coordination between the CCITT and external standards bodies. Despite hopeful resolutions at the 1988 Plenary Assembly and WATTC endorsing its "pre-eminence" in global standardization, the CCITT was recognized to have a different and somewhat diminished role in the future. Rather than being the a priori locus of most activity, the committee will serve as a sort of clearinghouse or central switch for a global network of organizations devising standards in accordance with varying market conditions. Important steps toward this policy architecture were taken at the first Interregional Telecommunications Standards Conference (ITSC), held a Fredericksburg in February 1990. There Director Irmer laid out a three-step plan in which other standards bodies will consult with the CCITT (and where relevant, CCIR) to set plans and priorities, engage in networked problem solving, and submit consolidated proposals to it for possible multilateral adoption. This "upstream" flow will generate global standards for national implementation in the "downstream" stage. Although official delegates to the ITSC were from the CCITT, CCIR, T1, ETSI, and TTC, other industry-oriented organizations will also feed into the process. A framework of periodic meetings and continuous, electronically mediated consultations was established to implement the plan.

Some policy makers felt these reforms were not enough. In the months prior to the May-June 1989 Plenipotentiary at Nice, a debate raged in the ITU about whether to merge the standards functions of the CCITT and CCIR. Proponents included the Secretary General and other key ITU officials, some advanced capitalist countries, and many LDCs. In essence they argued that wired and radio technologies were increasingly integrated and require coordinated planning; many

CCIR activities were redundant, and could be rationalized in a manner that freed up tight funds for other activities such as technical assistance; and the CCIR was both generationally and intellectually slow-moving and out of touch with the world of advanced systems and service, and falling further and further behind the CCITT in terms of productivity. Opponents included the United States and other Northern governments and influential TNCs, especially American broadcasters and service providers. They maintained that: even with growing integration, wired and wireless issues remained functionally different and involved specialized expertise; there were few real cost savings to be realized through a merger; and that the (off-the-record) attacks on the CCIR really concealed a desire by the Secretary General to somehow centralize his control over standardization. Besides, the Director of the CCIR, Richard Kirby, was an American; the United States did not want to lose a top ITU official in a merger (Drake, 1989).

Accordingly, opponents blocked any movement on the issue at Nice, and in compromise the Administrative Council (AC) was asked to appoint a High-Level Committee (HLC) including representatives of 21 countries to examine in detail the merits of organizational reform. Among the many recommendations in its April 1991 report, the HLC suggested a new tripartite policy structure: a Standardization Sector to comprise the CCITT and the standards functions of the CCIR; a Radiocommunication Sector to include the CCIR's spectrum functions and the International Frequency Registration Board; and a Development Sector consolidating all technical assistance programs. Each sector would have as its supreme body a regularly convened World Conference and be supported by Study Groups (ITU, 1991). These recommendations enjoyed broad support in a subsequent AC meeting. The United States and its corporate constituents remained hostile to consolidating the CCIR's standards functions. Either way, the net effect of all these activities has been to bring intergovernmental standardization more fully in line with a new and more market-oriented international regime.

The 1989 Plenipotentiary took another step in that direction by enhancing the role of TNCs in the CCITT decision-making process. Under the new treaty, SIOs attained membership rights in the committee, subject only to approval by their respective home governments (ITU, 1990a, p. 16). Their official status is still somewhat less than that of RPOAs, who may at times represent their governments and even vote in the plenary assemblies. However, this difference on paper is not too significant in practice, because the vast majority of decision on standards, regulatory, and tariff issues are reached by consensus in the committee prior to the plenaries, which rubber stamp them. As such, future CCITT plans will reflect a broader range of industry interests than in the days of PTT dominance, and could actually accelerate rather than slow the evolution toward a multivendor environment. In a sign of the times, this American-sponsored initiative, which would have controversial at the 1982 Plenipotentiary, encountered little real opposition. If implemented as expected, the HLC's recommendations would deepen this trend by also establishing a Business Advisory Forum "composed of chief executive officers or comparable top management representatives to give [the Secretary General] the views of the private sector on the telecommunications environment and how...the ITU's principal activities can be carried out effectively" (ITU, 1991, p. 19). In addition, the Forum would provide direct input into the work of the three sectors, and of a new Strategic Policy and Planning Unit charged with providing suggestions on overall policy reform to the Secretary General.

Two further events at Nice underscore the shift to a market-oriented ITU. One was the discussion of an influential report by a high-level advisory group on "The Changing Telecommunication Environment." Addressing in particular the LDCs, the report urged ITU members to adjust to the new global marketplace by undertaking such reforms as deregulation and even privatization of their PTTs (ITU, 1989a). Once the bastion of PTT power, the ITU was now presenting its dismemberment as an alternative to be considered seriously. Indeed, a growing number of LDCs have moved quickly in this direction during the past three years, often with the prodding of the World Bank, Northern governments, and TNCs. The other event was the election of Pekka Tarjanne as Secretary General. Strongly supported by the United States and other powerful members, Tarjanne has rapidly set a tone that differs sharply from that of his predecessor. For example, he has spoken widely of the need to move toward open networks and free trade in services, and of "complementarity" between the new ITU and the GATS negotiations. Finally, while less central to the question of regime transformation, the 1989 Plenipotentiary also adopted numerous other changes, two of which merit brief mention. A Bureau for Development of Telecommunications (BDT) was established that is to consolidate existing technical assistance programs, pending approval of the HLC recommendations. The BDT may prove more useful to market-seeking TNCs than previous programs, and they do not need to acquire RPOA/SIO status to participate. Moreover, BDT side payments could help allay some LDCs' fears in the transition to a liberalized environment and prevent disruption of regime activities important to the North. Also, the ITU's basic instruments were divided into a semipermanent Constitution and a more malleable Convention, so that future plenipotentiaries can spend more time on substantive issues and less on rewriting the treaty's organizational rules (Codding, 1990).

With the WATTC and plenipotentiary adapting its two treaty instruments to accommodate corporate demands, pressures mounted for corresponding adjustments to the regime's third regulatory pillar. Participants in CCITT Study Group III finally caved in and agreed to endorse liberalization of the D Series restrictions on leased lines. The move came at a time when the CCITT was taking substantial heat from many sides beyond the usual American and corporate suspects. In early 1990, journalist Hugo Dixon wrote a series of widely noted articles in the *Financial Times* which depicted the committee as a cabal of PTTs who were stifling the market through cartel rules. This unusual and highly critical press attention caught the eye of many governments, which took the matter up with their administrations, and it reverberated throughout the ITU and put people on the defensive. More importantly, the EC Commission's competition direc- torate notified regional PTTs that the D Series appeared to be contrary to the Treaty of Rome and the 1992 program, and that its retention could lead to antitrust litigation. European PTTs were thus forces to abandon the last outpost of the *ancien* regime of which they had been the primary architects. Meetings held in October 1989 and May 1990 examined various proposals, and a draft text was ready by November 1990. After minor alterations to mollify certain PTTs, the March 1991 meeting endorsed the text by consensus and submitted it for full CCITT approval under the new accelerated procedures. These changes will be approved in the summer of 1991.

The agreement essentially derives user-specific rules from the WATTC's general principles. It allows basically unfettered access to and control over internal leased circuits; accepts liberal attachments to and modifications of lines, subject to easier type approval and avoidance of technical harm to facilities; accepts the provision of telecommunications services to third parties; allows the interconnnec- tion of private leased circuits and networks between each other and with public networks; and accepts the resale of excess capacity. On charges, "circuits should be cost oriented and generally established on a flat-rate basis," and any access charges must by "cost-related" and dependent on the administration's own additional expenses from providing the specific mode of interconnection or special routing requested by a customer (ITU, 1990d, p. 6). Changes in conditions such as cancellation or temporary withdrawal of lines are to be done only after substantial consultations. Finally, many of the restrictive sec- tions in the 1988 text were simply dropped from mention, for example, the rules giving administrations exclusive control over switching, limiting communication with data-processing centers, and so on. Administrations may designate certain (public telephony) services as their exclusive domain, and can also choose to retain restrictions under their national laws, but there will no longer be specific prohibitions in the regime to cite as justifying or requiring such actions in either domestic or international planning.

The next domino to fall may be the accounting and settlements procedures at the heart of joint service provisioning. There are many sides to this debate, but for simplicity it can be reduced to two key issues deriving from the gap between asymmetric deregulation at the national level and the uniform international framework. First, it has been the long-standing practice of many administrations to render collection charges for international services that are substantially above cost, so as to facilitate cross-subsidization and so on. It is unclear whether there was actual cartel collusion; many carriers in Europe and elsewhere set their charges at broadly comparable level, but there remained much variation catering to national conditions. Either way, the cost to customers was substantial, and the above-mentioned *Financial Times* series alleged that CCITT administrations collectively overcharge by $10 billion per year. Second, the rates set for balancing of accounts between correspondents were also quite high. This was not a problem in the days of symmetric regulation, but it became one when rapid liberalizers cut their collection charges substantially in the 1980s. Following on earlier studies, the FCC issued a Notice of Proposed Rulemaking in August 1990 stating that the United States had a $2 billion trade deficit from international services in 1988, "with perhaps $1 billion of this deficit being a direct underwriting by U.S. consumers of foreign telecommunications administrations" (FCC, 1990, p. 1). The FCC argued that while American carriers had cut their collection charges close to costs, the PTTs had not. It being much cheaper to call from the United States to abroad than vice versa, American customers were doing so at a level resulting in net outpayments to foreign PTTs under the 50/50 settlement scheme. Moreover, the Commission maintained that by generating such surpluses, artificially high accounting rates reduce PTTs' incentives to lower their collection charges.

Accordingly, the FCC announced its intention to attempt to unilaterally force administrations to reduce their rates, with the possibility of some unspecified retaliation if they did not. The EC Commission's competition directorate opened its own investigation, once again raising the possibility of antitrust proceedings against key CCITT participants. The Organization for Economic Cooperation and Development (OECD) and several governments have also entered the fray on the cost-cutting side. The allegations are being picked up and elaborated in a growing number of reports and conferences, and alternatives to the joint service model of international order—free trade, end-to-end provisioning, and so on—are being widely debated (Ergas & Paterson, 1991). There is evidence that some PTTs are attempting to head off the fight by renegotiating certain accounting rates and cutting their collection charges, especially on leased lines, but despite these pressures and piecemeal reforms, the CCITT has not to date achieved consensus on whether to consider changing the overall framework under the *ancien* regime.

All this came at a bad time for the Third World. The LDCs had asserted periodically that the regime should be changed to formally include a redistributional principle. They argued that due to local conditions, the cost of rendering their halves of joint services were often higher than the costs to correspondents in the North. Hence, they wanted codified in ITU instruments some form of asymmetric settlements system under which, for example, revenues from North-South calls would be divided on a 49/51 basis. This goal was noted in a nonbinding opinion at the 1982 Plenipotentiary, mentioned in the 1984 Maitland Commission report, and reaffirmed in a nonbinding Resolution at WATTC-88. The latter statement called on the Secretary General to undertake a study of the issues to be reported to the 1989 Plenipotentiary. An inhouse, low-resource project, the "cost study" did conclude that there was some evidence that LDCs' costs were higher, but admitted that the methodological problems of comparing costs were so daunting as to qualify substantially the finding (ITU, 1990b). Nevertheless, the South had hoped to press on until the accounting and settlements system came under attack from a very different angle. According to the FCC and similar investigations, the newly industrialized countries and a few other LDCs are in fact major beneficiaries of the payment outflows and trade deficits experienced by the United States and some advanced capitalist countries. Their incoming traffic has risen substantially while their collection charges and accounting rates have not generally shifted downward. This news may have all but killed the Third World's incipient campaign for preferential treatment, and ensured that planned redistribution remains outside the regime's framework. Indeed, a November 1990 telecommunications conference executive committee meeting of the Organization for American States beat a rapid retreat from a proposed denunciation of the FCC's proceedings after American pressure and fears of further public exposure set in.

Finally, the story of regime transformation would be incomplete without returning briefly to the GATS negotiations. They have been an important source of pressure on the ITU; one prominent observer called the campaign for a telecommunications trade agreement "the ultimate bypass" of the ITU (Pipe, 1987). The GATS process impacted the way telecommunications services were thought of and bargained over both nationally and internationally, and provided PTTs with additional incentives to build competitive positions through liberalization. But despite the enthusiasm of free trade advocates, the Uruguay Round launched in 1986 collapsed in December 1990. In the press this is usually attributed to agricultural disputes, but in fact many other issues were far from resolved and the draft texts were still the subject of hot contention. The Telecommunications Annex was one such case. Negotiators had extraordinary difficulty with the complex conceptual task of applying trade principles to networks and services, and they remained divided on how binding these should be at a subsectoral level. The handful of initial market opening commitments offered by about a dozen governments prior to December applied almost exclusively to value-added services, and variations in national definitions of what fit this category made bargaining difficult.

Ironically, the United States helped to slow the process in the summer of 1990 by announcing that, due to asymmetric deregulation, it would not accept the application of the key most-favored-nation (MFN) principle to basic telecommunications. Its concern was that insofar as the draft language did not bar monopolies, it would freeze the regulatory status quo abroad and give foreign entities easy access to the comparatively open American market without requiring reciprocal concessions. The United States therefore insisted on adding a second, separate annex devoted entirely to excluding basic services from MFN coverage. Other negotiators decried the move as blocking progress, although in truth it is not clear how many governments really wanted free trade in basic services. Some of the key liberalizing provisions which might survive in an eventual agreement allow leased line access for TNCs, end-to-end provisioning of value-added services, resale and shared use, cost-based (or less rigorously, "cost-oriented") pricing, and limitations on trade-distorting proprietary interfaces and standards (MTN, 1990). As we have seen, many of these questions have already been addressed in the CCITT, albeit not in a legally binding treaty accompanied by national commitments. If the GATS succeeds, it will add liberalizing bite to the ITU instruments covered above. If it fails, the new Regulations and D.1 Recommendations will stand as primary sources of multilateral order in the global information economy.

CONCLUSION

This chapter has attempted to show that the international regime launched over 120 years ago has undergone fundamental transformation since the late 1980s, and that asymmetric deregulation has figured prominently in the process. This transformation consists of shifts to a new intersubjective understanding and set of formal instruments that allow for and even encourage corporate competition and control in international telecommunications. Gone are the overarching principles that network interconnection and service provisioning are the proprietary domains of national PTTs and RPOAs, and with them many of the detailed norms and rules through which administrations maintained their authority. The extent of the change we have traced can be readily appreciated by looking at Figure 1 and considering how many of these key injunctions from the *ancien* regime are now or are soon to be void. Perhaps another measure is the fact that a prominent ITU official has recently advocated privatizing the organization and issuing shares to governments and TNCs alike; the idea received high-level attention (Rutkowski, 1990).

None of the above means that the international market is suddenly wide open, or that government agencies have disappeared from the scene. Instead, it means that the international regime no longer provides governments with collective legitimation of their regulatory restrictions and market positions; they will have to find for themselves individually against corporate pressures for further liberalization. Public administrations will continue to struggle over market shares, user applications, and màny other issues with the TNCs, and attempt to utilize their control over underlying switched networks to strategic advantage. Perhaps an international version of the FCC's Computer III inquiry on open networks will be the next stage in the evolution toward a privatized order. The issue is not that the precise terms of trade have all been worked out, but rather that they are now the issue. The ideological, economic and political terrain has been recast so as to make state control an exception which must be justified, rather than an unquestioned rule. In this sense, Eli Noam is right to argue:

> The rent-seeking coalition that provided links of shared economic interests across frontiers is steadily breaking down. In this light the turmoil of telecommunications should be understood as nothing more

than a normalization—one of the most tightly controlled sectors is becoming more like the rest of the economy, not necessarily deregulated but more "normal." (Noam, 1989, p. 257)

What I have attempted to show is simply this: International normalization has arrived.

REFERENCES

Aronson, J.D., & Cowhey, P.F., (1988). *When countries talk: International trade in telecommunications services.* Cambridge, MA: Ballinger.

Bruce, R.R., Cunnard, J.P., & Director, M.D., (1987, November). *WATTC–88 and the future of the ITU: Realism about the limits of regulation.* Paper presented at the International Institute of Communications Forum, New York City.

Bruce, R.R., Cunnard, J.P., & Director, M.D., (1988). *The telecomm mosaic: Assembling the new international structure.* London: Butterworths.

Clark, K. (1931). *International communications: The American attitude.* New York: Columbia University Press.

Cerni, D.M. (1982). *The CCITT: Organization, US participation, and studies toward the ISDN.* Washington, DC: National Telecommunications and Information Administration, U.S. Department of Commerce.

Codding, G.A., Jr. (1952). *The international telecommunication union: An experiment in international cooperation.* Leiden: E.J. Brill.

Codding, G.A., Jr. (1983, December). The Changing Nature of the ITU Plenipotentiary. *Telecommunications Policy, 7,* 317–325.

Codding, G.A., Jr. (1984, November). Public Access to International Organizations–The ITU. *Intermedia, 12,* 8–10.

Codding, G.A., Jr. (1990, April). The Nice ITU Plenipotentiary Conference. *Telecommunications Policy, 14,* 139–149.

Codding, G.A., Jr., & Rutkowski, A.M. (1982). *The international telecommunication union in a changing world.* Dedham: Artech.

Commission of the European Communities. (1979, November). *European society faced with the challenge of the new information technologies: A community response* (COM (79) 650 final B.) Brussels, Belgium: Commission of the European Communities.

Cowhey, P.F., (1990, Spring). The international telecommunications regime: The political roots of regimes for high technology. *International Organization, 44,* 169–199.

Drake, W.J. (1988, September). WATTC–88: Restructuring the international telecommunication regulations. *Telecommunications Policy, 12,* 217–233.

Drake, W.J. (1989). The CCITT: Time for Reform? In *Reforming the global network: The 1989 Plenipotentiary Conference of the International Telecommunication Union* (pp. 28–43). London: International Institute of Communications.

Drake, W.J. (1993). Territoriality and intangibility: National sovereignty in the information age. In K. Nordenstreng & H.I. Schiller (Eds.), *Beyond national sovereignty*. Norwood, NJ: Ablex.

Drake, W.J., & McKnight, L. (1988, March). Telecommunications standards in the global information economy: The impact of deregulation and commercialization. *Project Promethee Perspectives, 5*, 14–20.

Drake, W.J., & Nicolaïdis, K. (1992, Winter). Ideas, interests, and institutionalization: Trade in services and the Uruguay Round. In P.M. Haas (Ed.), *Knowledge, power, and international policy coordination* [Special issue of *International Organization*], *45*, 37–100.

Ergas, H., & Paterson, P. (1991, February). International telecommunications settlement arrangements: An unsustainable inheritance? *Telecommunications Policy, 15*, 29–48.

Eward, R.S., (1984). *The competition for markets in international telecommunications*. Dedham: Artech House.

Federal Communications Commission. (1990, August). In the matter of regulation of international accounting rates. *Notice of Proposed Rulemaking, CC Docket No. 90–337, FCC 90–265*. Washington, DC: FCC.

Feldman, M.L.B. (1976). *The United States in the International Telecommunication Union and in pre-ITU conferences*. Doctoral dissertation, Louisiana State University, Baton Rouge.

Frieden, R.M. (1983). International telecommunications and the Federal Communications Commission. *Columbia Journal of Transnational Law, 21*, 421–482.

Global communications in the space age: Toward a new ITU—Report of an international conference sponsored by the John and Mary Markle Foundation and the Twentieth Century Fund. (1972). New York: Twentieth Century Fund.

Gregg, D.C. (1982, Winter). Capitalizing on national self-interest: The management of international telecommunication conflict by the International Telecommunication Union. *Law and Contemporary Problems, 45*, 38–52.

Horwitz, R.B. (1989). *The irony of regulatory reform: The deregulation of American telecommunications*. New York: Oxford University Press.

International Telegraph Union. (1866). *Convention télégraphic internationale de Paris, et Reglements et tarifs et annexes (1965)*. Berne: ITU.

International Telecommunication Union. (1966). *Minutes of the Plenipotentiary Conference of the International Telecommunication Union, Montreux, 1965*. Geneva: ITU.

International Telecommunication Union. (1973). *Final Acts of the World Administrative Telegraph and Telephone Conference (Geneva 1973), Telegraph Regulations, Telephone Regulations: Final Protocol, Resolutions, Recommendations, Opinions*. Geneva: ITU.

International Telecommunication Union. (1982). *International Telecommunication Convention: Final Protocol, Additional Protocols, Optional Additional Protocols, Resolutions, Recommendation and Opinions—Nairobi, 1982*. Geneva: ITU.

International Telecommunication Union. (1984). *The Missing Link: Report of the Independent Commission for World-Wide Telecommunications Development.* Geneva: ITU.

International Telecommunication Union, International Telegraph and Telephone Consultative Committee. (1985). *Red Book, Volume II-Fascicle II.1: General Tariff Principles: Charging and Accounting in International Telecommunications Services, Recommendations of the D Series, VIIIth Plenary Assembly, Malaga-Torremolinos, 8–19 October 1984.* Geneva: ITU.

International Telecommunication Union, Preparatory Committee for WATTC–88. (1987). *Report R 4: Report on the Meeting held in Geneva from 27 April to 1 May 1987.* Geneva: ITU.

International Telecommunication Union. (1988a). The international telecommunication regulations. *Informal Consultations, Information Paper 12.* Geneva: ITU.

International Telecommunication Union. (1988b). *Final Acts of the World Administrative Telegraph and Telephone Conference (WATTC–88)— Melbourne, 1988.* Geneva: ITU.

International Telecommunication Union. (1988c). *Final Protocol of the World Administrative Telegraph and Telephone Conference, Melbourne, November–December 1988.* Geneva: ITU.

International Telecommunication Union. (1989a). *The Changing Telecommunication Environment: Policy Considerations for Members of the ITU—Report of the Advisory Group on Telecommunication Policy.* Geneva: ITU.

International Telecommunication Union, International Telegraph and Telephone Consultative Committee. (1989b). *Blue Book, Volume II–Fascicle II.1: General Tariff Principles: Charging and Accounting in International Telecommunications Services, Series D Recommendations, IXth Plenary Assembly, Melbourne, 14–25 November 1988.* Geneva: ITU.

International Telecommunication Union. (1990a). *Final Act of the Plenipotentiary Conference, Nice, 1989: Constitution and Convention of the International Telecommunication Union, Optional Protocol, Decisions, Resolutions, Recommendations and Opinions.* Geneva: ITU.

International Telecommunication Union. (1990b). *Follow-up Study of the Costs of Providing and Operating International Telephone Service Between Industrialised and Developing Countries.* Geneva: ITU.

International Telecommunication Union, International Telegraph and Telephone Consultative Committee. (1990c). *Report of the Meeting of Working Party III/1, Held in Geneva from 23 to 25 May 1990.* Geneva: ITU.

International Telecommunication Union, International Telegraph and Telephone Consultative Committee. (1990d). *Draft Revision of Recommendation D.1, General Principles for the Lease of International (Continental and Intercontinental) Private Telecommunication Circuits and Networks.* Geneva: ITU.

International Telecommunication Union. (1991). *Tomorrow's ITU: The Challenges of Change—Report of the High Level Committee to review the structure and functioning of the International Telecommunication Union (ITU)*. Geneva: ITU.

Jacobson, H.K. (1973). The ITU: A potpourri of bureaucrats and industrialists. In R.W. Cox Jacobson (Ed.), *The anatomy of influence: Decision-making in international organizations* (pp. 59–101). New Haven, CT: Yale University Press.

Krasner, S.D., (1991, April). Global communications and national power: Life on the pareto frontier. *World Politics, 43*, 336–366.

Kwerel, E. (1984, December). Promoting competition piecemeal in international telecommunications. *OPP Working Paper Series*, 13. Washington, DC: Federal Communications Commission.

Leive, D.M. (1972). *The future of the International Telecommunication Union: A report for the 1973 Plenipotentiary conference.* Washington, DC: American Society of International Law.

Milk, L., & Weinstein, A. (1984). *United States participation in the International Telecommunication Union: A study of policy alternatives.* Washington, DC: Center for Strategic and International Studies.

Multilateral Trade Negotiations, Group of Negotiations on Services, Working Group on Telecommunications Services. (1990). *Possible elements of a sectoral annex on telecommunications* (MTN.TNC/W/35 Rev 1). Geneva: GATT.

Naslund, R. (1983). Some regulatory aspects of matters which will be treated by forthcoming ITU conferences. In *4th World Telecommunication Forum, Part III: Legal Symposium on International Information Networks, Geneva, 28–29 October 1983.* Geneva: ITU.

National Telecommunications and Information Administration. (1983). *Long-range goals in international telecommunications and information: An outline for United States Policy.* Washington, DC: Government Printing Office.

Neumann, K.-H. (1987). The international system of telecommunications tariffs. In E.-J. Mestmacker (Ed.), *The law and economics of transborder telecommunications* (pp. 373–413). Baden-Baden: Nomos Verlagsgesellschaft.

Noam, E.M. (1986a). Telecommunications policy on both sides of the Atlantic: Divergence and outlook. In M.S. Snow (Ed.), *Marketplace for telecommunications: Regulation and deregulation in industrialized democracies* (pp. 255–274). New York: Longman.

Noam, E.M. (1986b, April). *The political economy of ISDN: European network integration vs. American system fragmentation.* Paper presented at the XIV Annual Telecommunications Policy Research Conference, Airlie, VA.

Noam, E.M. (1987, Winter). The public telecommunications network: A concept in transition. *Journal of Communication, 37*, 30–48.

Noam, E.M. (1989). International telecommunications in transition. In R.W. Crandall & K. Flamm (Ed.), *Changing the rules: Technological change, international competition, and regulation in communications* (pp. 257–297). Washington, DC: The Brookings Institution.

Noll, A. (1985). The institutional framework of the ITU and its various approaches with regard to international telecommunication law and treaty conferences. In *The Washington Round: World Telecommunication Forum, Washington, DC, April 18–19, 1985* (pp. 19–53). Geneva: ITU.

Nora S., & Minc, A. (1980). *The computerization of society: A report to the President of France.* Cambridge, MA: MIT Press.

Okabe, T. (1978). Evolution of standards through the ITU (CCITT Recommendations). In H. Inose (Ed.), *Evolutions in computer communications: Proceedings of the Fourth International Conference on Computer Communication, Kyoto, 26–29 September 1978* (pp. 229–235). Amsterdam: North-Holland Publishers.

Organization for Economic Cooperation and Development, Working Party on Telecommunications and Information Policy. (1988). *Trade in telecommunication network-based services* (DSTI/ICCP/TISP/88.2). Paris: OECD.

Pratt, J.W., & Zeckhauser, R.J. (Eds.). (1985). *Principals and agents: The structure of business.* Boston, MA: Harvard Business School Press.

Pipe, G.R. (1987, August). The ultimate bypass. *Datamation*, p. 61.

Pipe, G.R. (1989, January). WATTC agrees on new telecomm rules. *Telecommunications*, p. 21.

Raveendran, L. (1989, June). The politics of international telecommunications: The WATTC momentum. *Project Promethee Perspectives, 10,* 35–40.

Renaud, J.-L. (1986, July). The ITU as agent of compromise. *Intermedia, 4,* 20–25.

Renaud, J.-L. (1987, June). The ITU and development assistance: North, south, and the dynamics of the CCIs. *Telecommunications Policy, 11,* 179–192.

Renaud, J.-L. (1990). The role of the International Telecommunication Union: Conflict, resolution and the industrialized countries. In K. Dyson & P. Humphreys (Eds.), *The political economy of communications: International and European dimensions* (pp. 33–57). London: Routledge.

Rutkowski, A.M. (1982, July). The USA and the ITU: Many attitudes, few policies. *Intermedia, 10,* 33–39.

Rutkowski, A.M. (1983, December). Deformalizing the international radio arrangements. *Telecommunications,* 30–40.

Rutkowski, A.M. (1990). *Privatizing the ITU.* Unpublished manuscript.

Savage, J.G. (1989). *The politics of international telecommunications regulation.* Boulder, CO: Westview Press.

Schiller, D. (1982). *Telematics and government.* Norwood, NJ: Ablex.

Schiller, D. (1985). The emerging global grid: Planning for what? *Media, Culture and Society, 7,* 105–125.

Schumpeter, J. (1942). *Capitalism, socialism and democracy.* New York: Harper and Row.

Segal, B. (1982). *Preparatory study for the 1982 ITU Plenipotentiary Conference.* Ottawa, Canada: Department of Communications, Government of Canada.

Solomon, R.J. (1987, May). WATTC continues never-ending story: Telecom regulation and DP bad mix. *International Networks, 5,* 1–7.

United States Department of State. (1982). *Report of the United States Delegation to the Plenipotentiary Conference of the International Telecommunication Union, Nairobi, Keyna, September 28–November 6, 1982.* Washington, DC: Department of State.

United States Department of State. (1989). *Report of the United States Delegation to the 1988 World Administrative Telegraph and Telephone Conference (WATTC–88), Melbourne, Australia, November 28–December 9, 1988.* Washington, DC: Department of State.

United States Department of State. (1990). *Report of the Delegation of the United States to the Plenipotentiary Conference of the International Telecommunication Union, Nice, France, May 23–June 30, 1990.* Washington, DC: Department of State.

Wallenstein, G.D. (1976). *Collaboration without coercion: The ITU as a model for worldwide agreement-making.* Palo Alto, CA: Program in Information Technology and Telecommunications, Stanford University.

Wallenstein, G.D. (1990). *Setting global telecommunication standards: The stakes, the players, and the process.* Dedham: Artech House.

Wigand, R.T. (1988, Winter). Integrated services digital networks: Concepts, policies and emerging trends. *Journal of Communication, 38,* 29–49.

Williamson, J. (1989, March). International telecom in turmoil: WATTC and beyond. *Telephony,* pp. 17–19.

Witt, D. (1987). The impact of national deregulation policies on the structure and activities of the ITU. In E.-J. Mestmacker (Ed.), *The law and economics of Transborder Telecommunications* (pp. 353–372). Baden-Baden: Nomos Verlagsgesellschaft.

Chapter 9
Asymmetric Re-regulation of Telecommunications Under European Community Law

Joachim Scherer

INTRODUCTION

The regulatory frameworks of the European telecommunications markets are in transition. On the national levels of the member states of the European Community (EC), the traditional regulatory model is organizationally oriented. Telecommunications policy has been, to a large extent, formulated and implemented by dominant public entities (the Telecommunications Administrations), which were regulated by national rather than European Law, and by organizational rather than substantive and procedural rules. In all member states, technological developments and economic pressures have led to considerable re-regulation, or at the very least to discussion about regulatory reforms.[1] The question of *asymmetric regulation* arises from the notion that such reforms are geared toward a more competitive environment for telecommunications.

Asymmetric regulation represents an effort to curtail or control the dominant firm's market power by setting different substantial, procedural, and organizational standards for the dominant firm and its competitors. In general, the dominance of national Telecommunications Administrations in the EC member states is being mitigated by this new regulatory approach.

However, these re-regulatory decisions on the national level require an active Community telecommunications policy if a common telecommunications market is to be established. For this reason, the Commission of the European Communities (the Commission) has launched a supranational telecommunications policy. Concomitantly, and with an eye to developments within the EC, the European Conference of Postal and Telecommunications Administrations (CEPT) is reviewing its organizational structure.

On June 10, 1987, the Commission of the European Communities adopted a Green Paper on the Development of the Common Market for Telecommunications Services and Equipment. This policy paper contains far-reaching proposals for telecommunications policy decisions concerning telecommunications networks and services, terminal equipment, and the regulatory frameworks for telecommunications on both the Community and national levels. The Green Paper contains the following policy proposals[2]:

1. the provision and operation of telecommunications network infrastructures may remain an exclusive right of national telecommunications administrations;
2. the provision of two-way satellite communications systems should be permitted on a case-by-case basis in order to foster the development of transborder telecommunications services, provided that the financial viability of the telecommunications administrations is not substantially affected;
3. the provision and operation of certain telecommunications services considered to be of social relevance may remain an exclusive right of national telecommunications administrations;
4. the provision and operation of telecommunications services not considered to be of social relevance should be opened to competition;
5. standards concerning network provision and definition of network infrastructure will be promulgated by the Commission;
6. network access for providers of competitive services should be governed by a community directive on open network provision containing definitions of network infrastructure provision, interconnect and access obligations for transfrontier service providers, technical standards, frequencies, and tariffing principles;
7. the provision of terminal equipment should be opened to competition;
8. regulatory and operational activities of Telecommunications Administration should be organizationally separated;

9. the operational activities of Telecommunications Administration will be continuously reviewed by the Commission under the antitrust provision (Art. 85, 86, 90) of the EEC Treaty;
10. likewise, the activities of all private providers will be continuously reviewed under Art. 85, 86, in order to avoid abuses of dominant positions.

There appears to be a widespread consensus on the recommendations concerning the provision and operation of network infrastructure and of services of social relevance, as well as the provision of terminal equipment.

Regarding the need for a community directive on open network provision, it was agreed that network access should be governed by European standards based on international standards.

The implementation of these policy goals will have a considerable impact on the respective roles of the national telecommunications administrations and the Commission.

This chapter attempts to give a preliminary answer to the question of whether, and to what extent, re-regulation under European law must and/or should be asymmetric in order to achieve these policy goals.

Part I briefly describes some of the regulatory issues confronting both EC Member states and the Community as a whole, and sketches out some of the emerging regulatory structures.

Parts II and III examine the admissability and scope of the asymmetric re-regulation under European Community law with respect to the provision of networks, services, and terminal equipment. Part IV addresses organizational and procedural aspects of asymmetric re-regulation. Organizationally, the emerging competition between telecommunications administrations and private network and/or service providers seems to require a separation of regulatory and entrepreneurial functions that have traditionally been carried out by the dominant telecommunications administrations. This organizational separation will necessarily lead to procedural consequences. Most importantly, the behavior of network and service providers in the emerging telecommunications marketplace will need to be screened and, if necessary, regulated by administrative bodies on both the national and the European level. This will require new types of administrative proceedings as well as careful consideration of the role of the Commission in the European policy-making process.

THE DOMINANCE OF TELECOMMUNICATIONS ADMINISTRATIONS: REGULATORY ISSUES ON THE NATIONAL AND ON THE EUROPEAN LEVEL

National Regulatory Frameworks in Transition

The traditional regulatory model in the member states of the European Community is organizationally oriented. Telecommunications policy is formulated and implemented by telecommunications administrations, which are characterized by specific organizational structures. In the European tradition, telecommunications administrations are public entities, in that they are characterized by public ownership, but also connected to the government by financial, personnel, organizational, and/or procedural ties. In addition, they are furnished with a double *de jure* monopoly status for provision of networks and of services, and are generally providers of both telecommunications and postal services.[3] According to this model, the European telecommunications administrations provide a public service characterized by the following normative rules:

1. the national telecommunications administration provides both telecommunications networks and services (except broadcasting services) and is obliged to do so at equal conditions (including equal tariffs) nationwide.
2. the telecommunications administration is obliged to guarantee the confidentiality of the information which it transmits.[4]
3. in fulfilling these tasks, the guidelines for decision making are the guarantees of free expression and of access to information.[5]

The traditional European model of telecommunications regulation attempted to achieve these goals predominantly by organizational means, i.e., by formalizing the organizational structure of the telecommunications administrations.

The procedural structures of European telecommunications administrations are clearly underdeveloped in comparison to the high degree of sophistication that characterizes their traditional structures.[6] This becomes evident through comparison with the American regulatory concept (before and after the divestiture of AT&T). The public service concept in the United States model is implemented by means of procedural structures with an independent agency, the Federal Communications Commission. Procedural rules govern the interorganizational relations between this regulatory body and the regulated private telecommunications providers (i.e., network and service).

In contrast, the traditional European regulatory concept is based on organizational structures. The definition of the *public interest*, and its implementation, occur within the organizational structure of the telecommunications administration, and the telecommunications administration itself is considered an instrument of public interest decisions. Consequently, regulatory and entrepreneurial functions are separated within the organizational structure of the telecommunications administration, and not generally entrusted to organizationally separated entities.

The notion of de jure monopolies, with respect to the European telecommunications administrations, is imprecise. These de jure monopolies encompass a multitude of exclusive rights and obligations. Their scope, and consequently the possible targets of deregulation, will become clearer when the monopoly positions are analyzed in terms of decisions and decision-making processes.

The creation of telecommunications networks and services is a highly complex and evolutionary process.[7] As such, it may be divided into several distinguishable procedures that are used to arrive at different decisions.

The traditional de jure monopoly of European telecommunication entities is the sum of these public service-related decisions, or, more precisely, the sum of the exclusive rights to take such decisions. These decisions may be categorized into three groups, including:

1. the planning and standardization of networks and services;
2. the installation of network facilities and telecommunications services; and
3. the provision of facilities and services to potential users.

For the traditional decision-making procedures of the European telecommunications administrations, the distinction between telecommunications facilities and services has traditionally played a minor role. Telecommunications networks were planned, installed, and operated as service-specific networks.

Telecommunications administrations in the EEC member states have been deeply affected by the convergence of telecommunications and data processing into what has become known as telematics (telematique). This convergence has, inter alia, resulted in the erosion of traditional technological boundary lines between telecommunications and computers, networks and terminals, networks and services, and transmission services and processing services. Thus the proliferation of telecommunications services requires changes in network functions, and a higher level of network integration.

The technological option of gradual network integration demands substantive policy decisions on both a national and a European level regarding network standardization and development, competition and access, and network use.[8]

With respect to network integration, the EC member states seem to have reached a consensus on the introduction of integrated services digital network (ISDN).[9] No similar common denominator of national telecommunications policies exists for network competition, standardization, and use.

The proliferation of telecommunications services has led to regulatory problems which may be summed up in the somewhat loaded question: Who should provide what type of telecommunications service, to whom, at what tariffs, and under what competitive conditions? The broad range of options for the location of processing and storage capabilities also necessitates decisions concerning the boundary lines between networks and services, between different categories of services, and between network and service providers. Issues for the near future include the distinction between universal services and non universal services, competition among service providers, and the relations between network and service providers.

As a consequence of telematics, the organizationally oriented model is gradually shifting toward a more procedural model. For this reason, the legal interfaces between the various parts of telecommunications and information systems and their actors will have to be re-defined.

One of the basic policy decisions with respect to the organization of the traditional European Postal and telecommunications administrations—PTTs—is whether or not the organizational and financial ties between postal and telecommunications services should be cut.

The PTTs in many member states provide both postal and telecommunications services and cross-subsidize their postal services with revenues generated from telecommunications services. It may be argued that such cross-subsidization is in the interest of certain user groups of postal services and contributes to the provision of universal postal services at reasonable tariffs. From an economic point of view, it can be argued that the joint provision of postal and telecommunications services does or could create economies of scope. On the other hand, cross-subsidization of postal services may lead to organizational slack. It may prevent cost-oriented pricing of telecommunications services and thus have repercussions on all national telecommunications policies. Moreover, the British experience seems to indicate that a separation of postal and telecommunications services does not necessarily lead to losses due to foregone economies of scope in production and procurement.[10] Those economies of scope may, however, increase with the introduction of new telecommunications services which combine traditional postal and new telecommunications service features.

Also on the organizational level, telematics has led to a considerable pluralization of actors, who now have a stake in the regulatory process. These include new network and service providers; a multitude of administrative agencies, including ministries of economics and industry; data protection agencies; antitrust authorities; standardization organizations; and various organized user groups.

This diversification of industry structures, and therefore interests in the telecommunications sector, can no longer be managed by the traditional organizational structures of the telecommunications administrations. Therefore, new regulatory bodies have been created on the national levels of the member states for the purpose of establishing a formal process for gathering the information necessary for policy decisions. This new procedural approach has been adopted in the United Kingdom with the installation of OFTEL, a regulatory entity operating on the basis of procedural rules. The French Commission Nationale des Communications et Libertes is another example of this approach. Similar regulatory bodies may be established in the Netherlands, in Belgium, and in the Federal Republic of Germany.

The Evolving Community Law Framework

In the law-making process of the European Community, the Council, which consists of representatives of the member states, is the principal legislator of the Community. The general rule of Community lawmaking is that the Commission proposes, the Parliament advises, and the Council adopts. The Commission is essentially the Community's executive. It is involved in the preparation and implementation of legislation and may also exercise law-making powers granted by the Council. In some instances, the Commission also has law-making powers of its own; of particular importance in the telecommunications field is the Commission's power under Art. 90 (3) EEC Treaty, to adopt directives in order to ensure that Treaty rules are applied to public enterprises.

As a prelude to adoption of the Green Paper, the European Commission has initiated five activities related to the main policy objective establishing a common telecommunications market:[11]

- to launch a coordinated plan for the networks and telecommunications services development in the Community and common infrastructure projects,

- to create a Community-wide market for telecommunications equipment and terminals,
- to launch a development program for the long-run technologies required for the establishment of future broadband networks,
- to improve access for the less favored regions of the Community to benefit from the development of advanced services and networks, and
- to coordinate the negotiating positions within international organizations dealing with telecommunications.[12]

With respect to the coordination of telecommunications networks, services, and terminal equipment, the Commission has submitted a proposal for a Council recommendation concerning the coordinated introduction of the *integrated services digital network* (ISDN).[13] The recommendation, adopted by the Council on December 22, 1986[14] proposes: (a) the definition of precise interfaces between public networks and private local networks in order to ensure "total compatibility of terminals at a European level"; (b) that EC members take a "coordinated approach towards the introduction, in particular as regards the timing, of ISDN"; and (c) that a critical mass of subscribers be achieved before embarking on a demand-driven policy by 1988.[15] The Council Recommendation contains detailed guidelines for the introduction of ISDN (subscriber access at 144 Kbits/s and 2 MBit/s); the definition of the interface between public and private networks; and the definition and detailed specification of services to be made available in all member states starting in 1988. The recommendation also outlines general considerations to be addressed for setting tariff levels.

A further effort to coordinate services is represented by the "Council Recommendation concerning the implementation of harmonization in the field of telecommunications," which established a consultative procedure between the governments of the member states before the introduction of any new service "so that the necessary innovation takes place under conditions compatible with harmonization." Furthermore, it was recommended that the member states "ensure that all new services that are introduced from 1985 onwards are introduced on the basis of a common harmonized approach, notably with regard to services between member states, so that compatible services are offered throughout Europe, taking into account the progress of work in CEPT, CEN/Cenelec and ISO."[16]

Building upon this general recommendation, the Commission, in a recent Proposal for a Council Recommendation, has suggested the coordinated introduction of a public pan-European digital mobile communications system.[17] In order to implement this mobile communications system, the Commission has furthermore suggested a Council directive on the required frequency bands.[18] If this directive is approved by the Council, it will be the first binding rule of Community law concerning the introduction of a telecommunications system.

On the organizational level, a new unit—the Directorate General XIII (DG XIII)—has been established within the Commission. The tasks of the Directorate General are loosely described by the terms *telecommunications, information industries,* and *innovation.*

In November 1983, the Council agreed that the Commission would call together a *senior officials group* (SOGT), which has since served as a consultative body in the preparation of the Commission's policy decisions.

The emerging European telecommunications policy is governed by the EEC Treaty and by the fundamental human rights as developed by the European Court of Justice.[19]

The provision of telecommunications networks and services is mainly governed by three sets of treaty provisions: Article 59 et seq. on the freedom to provide services, Article 30 et seq. on the free movements of goods, and Article 85 et seq. on competition. The first set applies mainly to the provision of telecommunications networks and services; the second applies to the production, approval, and sale of telecommunications apparatus, including terminal equipment; and the third applies to both the provision of networks and services and to the provision of telecommunications apparatus.

ASYMMETRIC RE-REGULATION: PROVISION OF NETWORKS AND SERVICES

In the member states of the European Community, the national telecommunications administrations are, in general, the dominant providers of telecommunications networks and services. Consequently, asymmetric re-regulation under Community law would have to focus on the behavior of these administrations. Article 90 (2) of the Treaty of Rome, however, places severe restrictions on asymmetric re-regulation of public undertakings.[20]

This chapter aims to protect enterprises in the public sector in order to resolve conflicts between the member states' interests concerning certain national public interest goals, on one hand, and the Community's interest in creating the Common Market, on the other.[21] Before exploring the scope of the qualified exemption contained in Article 90 (2), this chapter will analyze the general rule concerning the freedom to provide telecommunications networks and services.

The General Rule: Freedom to Provide Telecommunications Networks and Services

Article 59 of the Treaty of Rome guarantees the freedom to provide cross-border services. *Services* are defined, by exclusion, in Article 60 of the Treaty as those which "are normally provided for remuneration in so far as they are not governed by the provisions relating to freedom of movement for goods, capital and persons."

For analytical purposes and with regard to the "cross-border" requirement, it is appropriate to distinguish between two types of services under Article 59:

1. the provision of telecommunications networks, and
2. the provision of telecommunications services.

The provision of telecommunications networks may constitute a service "within the meaning of Articles 59 and 60 EEC Treaty." Whereas the provision of telecommunications networks within a Member state is not subject to Article 59 et seq. of the Treaty, the provision of telecommunications networks which extend beyond the territory of one Member state fulfills all the requirements of a *service* according to Article 59, 60: Establishing and operating the telecommunications facilities—i.e., providing the hardware and the software to fulfill at least certain transmission and switching functions—is neither an activity covered by Article 30 et seq. nor by Article 52 et seq. of the Treaty. Consequently, Article 59 et seq. are applicable.

The establishment of cross-border telecommunications networks as "services" under Article 59 may be particularly important for a satellite carrier that wants to offer cross-border links, as satellite technology is inherently a cross-border technology. Article 59 of the Treaty could be invoked to limit national restrictions on the freedom to provide such a service.[22]

According to an almost circular definition delivered by the CCITT, a *telecommunications service* is "that which is offered by an administration or a Recognized Private Operating Agency to its customers in order to satisfy a specific telecommunication requirement."[23]

This definition, though vague, suffices for purposes of European law. Because telecommunications services, which are offered via telecommunications networks, do not concern the transportation of or exchange of goods, they must be considered as *services* within the meaning of Article 59, 60 of the Treaty.[24]

The Court of Justice, in its Sacchi decision (ECR 1974 p. 409), which concerned the broadcasting monopoly of the Italian broadcasting corporation RAI, has drawn a boundary line between merchandise, under Article 30, and services, under Article 59 of the Treaty, with respect to television broadcasting:

> In the absence of express provision to the contrary in the Treaty, a television signal must, by reason of its nature, be regarded as provision of services."[25]

Television broadcasting being one type of telecommunications service, the Court's decision may be generalized to encompass all types of services which involve the transmission of information by means of telecommunications facilities.

Since Article 59 et seq. are directly applicable, they could arguably be used as legal instruments to create a common market for telecommunications services, forcing member states with a rigid regulatory structure to open their services markets.

The Commission could use the *manquement d'etat* proceedings under Article 169 against any member state that failed to fulfill its obligations under Article 59 of the Treaty.

The Exceptions
Article 90 as a Barrier to Asymmetric Deregulation?

The freedom to provide services, guaranteed in Article 59 of the Treaty, is subject, inter alia, to the following exceptions:

> According to Article 55, the treaty provisions do not apply to activities which are connected with the exercise of official authority in a Member state.

> A further exception is stated in Article 56 for provisions of Member states concerning the special treatment of foreign nationals on grounds of public policy, public security or public health.

> Pursuant to Article 90 (2), the treaty provisions do not apply to undertakings entrusted with the operation of services of general economic interest, in so far as they obstruct the performance, in law or in fact, of the particular tasks assigned to them.

Again, these exceptions may apply to both the provision of telecommunications networks and to the provision of telecommunications services via these networks.

The major obstacle to asymmetric deregulation seems to be Article 90 (2).[26]

In order to examine the scope of this exemption, which according to the European Court of Justice and legal doctrine must be narrowly construed,[27] three questions must be answered:

1. What are the criteria for considering a national telecommunications administration to be an *undertaking*?
2. What are the criteria for considering the provision of telecommunications networks and services to be a *service of general economic interest*?
3. What are the criteria for considering the undertaking to be *entrusted* with the operation of the service?

If and when a national telecommunications administration can be considered to be an undertaking entrusted with the operation of services of general economic interest, the Treaty requires a complex, prognostic assessment of consequences.

The question which must then be answered with some degree of plausibility is: will the application of competition rules or other rules of the Treaty (i.e., the rules of Article 59 et seq.) obstruct, in law or in fact, the particular task assigned to the undertaking?[28] Only when this judicial assessment of consequences leads to the result that the obstruction of the "particular task" is to be expected will the respective rules of the Treaty be held inapplicable.

The primary question is, however, if and to what extent the applicability of Art. 85 seq. of the Treaty is determined by Art. 222.

Art. 222 states that the Treaty is not to "prejudice rules in a member-State governing the system of property ownership". In the British Telecom case, which was decided by the European Court of Justice, Italy had attacked the Commission's decision ordering British Telecom to refrain from applying certain usage conditions concerning telecommunications services on the grounds that the member states were free under Article 222 of the Treaty to determine the extent of the public sector of their economy. The Court held that the purpose of British Telecom's usage conditions, which prevented message-forwarding agencies from providing certain services, was not "to close down private agencies established in contravention of (BT's) monopoly rights, but merely to modify the conditions under which the agencies carry on their activities."

Consequently, Article 222 of the Treaty did not prevent the Commission from assessing the validity of the regulations in question in relation to Article 86,[29] which prohibits abuse of a dominant position within all or most of the Common Market insofar as it may affect trade between Member states. Abusive behavior may, in particular, consist of the following: imposing unfair prices or trading conditions; limiting production to the detriment of consumers; applying dissimilar, discriminatory conditions to equivalent transactions with different trading parties; and making the approval of contracts subject to other parties' acceptance of unrelated supplemental obligations.

This reasoning provides a sound basis for an analysis of the interdependence between Articles 222 and 86/90 of the Treaty and its repercussions for European telecommunications policy: Art. 222 refers to property positions, whereas Articles 86/90 refer to economic behavior. It follows from the former that the member states are free to establish their own systems of property ownership, which, in the field of telecommunications, may consist of rules concerning the property of network facilities. As far as economic activities that exploit facilities are concerned, each member state is subject, inter alia, to the competition rules of the Treaty, including Article 86 and 90. Article 90 allows the member state to grant the exclusive right for the exploitation of a network upon a public undertaking, making it irrelevant whether or not this undertaking actually owns the network.

There are, however, interdependencies between property ownership under Article 85–90 of the Treaty: A member state's "system of property ownership" has repercussions upon the scope of permissible economic activities. As an example, if a member state defines *land property rights* as not including the use of subsoil water, this property ownership rule will restrict the scope of economic activities for all gravel dredging enterprises.[30]

A similar situation may arise in the telecommunications sector: If a member state defines the extent, the elements, and the interfaces of its national telecommunications network, these rules of (public) property ownership may have repercussions upon the scope of permissible economic activities of telecommunications providers.

In sum, Article 222 enables the member states to determine— within the limits of the evolving European fundamental right to property ownership[31]—the scope of permissible economic behavior, and, consequently, the scope of Article 90 of the Treaty.[32]

Since some member states categorically deny that their respective telecommunications administration could be qualified as an *undertaking*, this question will most probably stir some controversy between these member states and the Commission in the years to come.

Two criteria—one structural, the other functional—appear to qualify an entity as an *undertaking* within the meaning of Articles 85–90:

1. Its organization and/or procedures are tied to the member state, and
2. its activities are those that have to be undertaken in the marketplace.

The criterion of organizational and procedural ties between the undertaking and the member state has long been recognized as a basis for distinguishing between private and public undertakings. Article 90 (1) of the Treaty, which concerns the admissibility of measures with respect to public undertakings, presupposes the existence of such ties. The Court has determined their function by stating that the member states' ability to influence the decisions of public undertakings imposes a special responsibility upon the member states.[33]

Governmental influence upon public undertakings may be exercised by a variety of organizational and/or procedural mechanisms, including governmental ownership of some or all of the entity's shares, contractual agreements, or statutory ties.[34] Whether or not the decisions or the undertaking are reached according to public or private law is not a factor in determining status in this case. Entities which are structured by private as well as by public law can be *public undertakings* within the meaning of Article 90 (1).

If an entity has some procedural and/or organizational ties with the member state, a second and more difficult question is whether such an entity may be considered an *undertaking* or part of the *government*. Here, the nature of the entity's activities becomes relevant.

Regulatory activities of an entity are necessary, but not sufficient, criteria to qualify an entity as part of the government. This was confirmed by the Court in the British Telecom case. In its decision, the Court did not explicitly qualify British Telecom as a public undertaking. Rather, the Court applied Article 86 on the grounds that British Telecom's activity was of a business nature, since it consisted of providing telecommunications services to the user for a fee. The fact that BT was empowered to issue regulations (or *schemes*) was deemed irrelevant for the application of Article 86, since the *schemes* did no more than lay down tariffs and conditions for the services offered and were determined by BT itself without any parliamentary interference.[35]

Based upon this reasoning, it could be argued that a telecommunications entity, which is governed by usage regulations subject to parliamentary and/or governmental interference, cannot be qualified as a public undertaking.[36] The Court's judgment in the Radio Luxembourg case, however, seems to indicate that legislative influence on a public undertaking does not necessarily lead to the inapplicability of Art. 86.[37]

This case concerned Radio Luxembourg's attempt to provide exclusive rights to use a specific form of TV advertisement to an affiliated company, thus excluding competitive suppliers. The case focused on telemarketing, in which a viewer is asked to dial a certain phone number at the end of a commercial. According to the judgment, this conduct was in violation of Article 86 EEC Treaty.

What, then, is the boundary line between an activity of a business nature and an activity of a nonbusiness, i.e., governmental, nature?

It appears that no clear boundary line exists. The dichotomy of activities "of a business nature," on one side, and of a governmental nature on the other side, even though very popular in European legal doctrine,[38] is based upon the neoliberal distinction of market and government, which is inadequate to describe, analyze, or regulate the economic behavior in a mixed economy. Drawing a sharp boundary line between traditional governmental activities[39] and business activities would be tantamount to petrifying the existing distribution of tasks between the public and the private sectors.

The dynamics of community law, and those of governmental versus nongovernmental functions in a mixed economy, require a less restrictive, democratic view.[40] The boundary lines between governmental and non-governmental or business activities have to be kept open for substantive, organizational, and procedural changes that will first occur in the regulatory frameworks of the member states, and then within the European law framework.

In other words, entities that fulfill governmental tasks today may have to be qualified as *public undertakings* tomorrow (and vice versa) because of changes in society's perception and, consequently, the regulatory framework of their tasks. For some of the traditional activities of telecommunications administrations, this transition has already begun. If it continues, the legal consequence will be that Article 85 seq. of the Treaty will be applicable to every organizationally and/or procedurally separated telecommunications entity that engages in the activities concerned.

This dynamic conception distinguishing governmental and business tasks is in accordance with the Court's case law concerning the subsequent decision on the boundary line between services of general economic interest and services of private interest. Here, the Court has explicitly deferred the determination of the general economic interest to the discretion of the member states—subject to community law scrutiny of abuses of this discretion.[41]

If a national telecommunications administration can qualify as a public undertaking and enjoy an exclusive right to provide a telecommunications network, is the telecommunications administration an undertaking that is entrusted with the operation of "services of general economic interest" within the meaning of Article 90 (2)? The notion of general economic interest does not refer to the general economic interest of the Community. This follows from the objective of Article 90 (2): Since the general economic interest must be one that justifies an exemption from the application of the Treaty, it cannot be identical with the Treaty's goals. Consequently, the general economic interest must be that of the respective member state. However, the yardstick used to determine the validity of a *general economic interest* is community law.[42]

In its British Telecom decision, the European Court of Justice implicitly confirmed this intricate relationship between national interests and Community law when it rejected the Commission's contention that Article 90 (2) was aimed to preserve only the interests of the Member state directly concerned. The Court rejected that argument, stating that interpretation of Art. 90 (2) was not left to the discretion of the Member state; on the contrary, the Commission, under the Court's supervision, was responsible for application of this article.[43]

The general economic interest under Article 90 (2) is characterized by a substantive and a procedural criterion: The general economic interest is more than the specific economic interest of the undertaking concerned. In other words, the undertaking's interest in profit maximization must be subordinated to the general economic interest.[44] Procedurally, general economic interests are created by or on the basis of legislative decision. It is up to the legislator, or more generally a "measure adopted by the public authorities," to define and delineate the public interest objectives of public undertakings.[45] Consequently, whether or not the provision of telecommunications networks and services is a "service of general economic interest" depends upon regulatory decisions of the member states, subject to community law scrutiny.[46] The member states will have to define and redefine their *general economic interests* with respect to telecommunications networks and services.

Arguably, the provision of a nationwide telecommunications network infrastructure that is linked to international telecommunications facilities is a *service of general economic interest*.[47] Whether or not the same applies to the provision of local networks and to the provision of telecommunications services remains to be discussed.

The Treaty requires that the undertaking must be entrusted with the operation of the service in question. The Court has ruled that entrusting requires a governmental act by the competent authorities;[48] any de jure monopoly of a network provider will therefore ultimately have to be based upon a legislative decision.

Qualification as an undertaking within Article 90 (2) does not, in and of itself, free an entity from the obligations of the Treaty (including Article 59). Its applicability depends further upon the question of whether or not "the performance...of the particular tasks" assigned to a telecommunications administration would be obstructed by application of the rules of the Treaty.

The Court's decision in British Telecom appears to imply that the scope of this exception differs from the scope of the public interest exception developed elsewhere by the Court under Articles 59, 56; whereas the public interest exception applies only to public interest considerations of a noneconomic nature, the "performance...of the particular tasks" assigned to a public undertaking could also be obstructed by economic behavior.[49]

The particular task assigned to a telecommunications administration as telecommunications network provider is the construction and operation of telecommunications networks. The performance of this particular task could, arguably, be obstructed if the telecommunications administrations' exclusive right to provide networks were abolished. This could lead to cream skimming by competing network providers and ultimately obstruct the provision of universal network services by rendering the provision of a nationwide, modern telecommunications network impossible.[50]

The danger that the provision of network services may be obstructed must, however, be clearly demonstrated by the network provider in question.

The task assigned to a telecommunications administration as a telecommunications service provider may consist of the provision of universal services. Again, it is assumed that the performance of this task may be obstructed if competing service providers engage in cream skimming.

The British Telecom decision, as well as previous rulings, shows that the Court will scrutinize assertions of obstruction very carefully.[51] One must keep in mind, however, that the British Telecom case arose in a very unusual procedural setting.[52] The Commission's decision ordering British Telecom to terminate alleged abuse of its dominant position, vis-á-vis the private service provider Telespeed, was appealed, not by British Telecom, but, rather, by the Italian government. Furthermore, the British government intervened on the side of the Commission, thus opposing the Italian government's attempt to fight British Telecom's battle.

Since British Telecom had not availed itself of any legal remedies against the Commission's decision, and since the United Kingdom considered that BT's regulations with respect to forwarding agencies were not necessary in order to fulfill its public service functions, it could hardly be argued that BT's performance of its public service tasks was being obstructed.[53] In other words, the Italian government's argument that Telespeed obstructed the performance of BT's public service tasks lacked plausibility.

The Court could easily dispose of this argument by pointing out that "the Italian Republic has produced no evidence to show that the overall balance of the agencies' activities in the United Kingdom was negative so far as BT was concerned or that the Commission's condemnation would, from an economic viewpoint, prejudice the accomplishment of the tasks assigned to BT."[54] Just how strictly the Court is likely to scrutinize assertions of obstruction in a case where the service provider was in the role of the plaintiff, remains an open question.

Asymmetric Regulation of the Behavior of Dominant Undertakings under Art. 86

The Treaty's main yardstick for asymmetric regulation of the behavior of telecommunications administrations is Article 86, which prohibits "any abuse by one or more undertaking of a dominant position within the common market or in a substantial part of it." Since Article 90 (2) does not summarily exempt the national network and service providers from the provisions of the Treaty, including the provisions on competition, each of their decisions concerning the establishment, extension, and use of their networks has to be considered on its own merits.

The national telecommunications administrations as telecommunications network and service providers are generally in a dominant position that enables them to "impede effective competition" in their respective markets.[55]

According to the Court's case law, the abuse of a dominant position, which is characterized by four types of abusive behavior according to Article 86 (2)(a)(d), is an objective concept relating to the behavior of an undertaking:

> which is such as to influence the structure of a market where, as a result of the very presence of the undertaking in question, the degree of competition is weakened and which, through recourse to methods different from those which condition normal competition in products or services on the basis of the transactions of commercial operators, has the effect of hindering the maintenance of the degree of competition still existing in the market or the growth of that competition.[56]

Such abusive behavior may be directed toward competitors, customers or suppliers, and the public.[57]

The technological developments described above[58] appear to elicit five types of behavior which could be qualified as abusive:

1. extending the network monopoly,
2. extending the service monopoly,
3. regulating network access,
4. tariffing of competing service providers, and,
5. cross-subsidizing

A dominant telecommunications administration may inhibit competitors from entering the market by including certain telecommunications services or terminal equipment, which are not common throughout the network,[59] in its de jure network monopoly, thus excluding competing service providers from the market. Such decisions may, however, be justifiable under Article 90 (2); i.e., it may be considered a matter of "general economic interest" to locate certain protocol conversion services in the network rather than having this service performed by separate service providers in order to achieve a high level of penetration for the respective telecommunications service.

An existing service monopoly may be extended by adding "new" service features to "old" monopoly services (thus adding "value" to that service) or simply by establishing new services and excluding competing enterprises from providing them. Again, such an extension of an existing de jure monopoly may be justifiable under Article 90 (2) if it can be shown that the application of Article 86 would obstruct the performance of the particular task assigned to the telecommunications administration.

Regulations of network access may constitute an abuse of a dominant position with respect to service providers, if the network provider charges unreasonable access fees, or sets unreasonable or discriminatory technical standards for network access. The dominant provider must also refrain from imposing access conditions which constitute unlawful tying practices under Article 86 (d), i.e., by making access to the network conditional on whether terminal equipment or other (network) services are from the network provider as well.[60]

An abuse of a dominant position may also consist in "directly or indirectly imposing unfair purchase...prices" (Article 86 (a)), that is, in setting unfair tariffs for the use of the network providers' facilities by private service providers.[61] A question of particular interest to service providers is whether or not Article 86 of the Treaty prohibits usage-sensitive tariffs on leased (point-to-point) lines. Arguably, the use of volume-sensitive tariffs may be a disincentive for private service providers. On the other hand, flat-rate tariffs on leased lines may (due to the tariff structure of public networks) result in diverting traffic from the public networks, which is considered to be economically inefficient cream skimming.

In its British Telecom decision, the Court did not comment upon the legality of flat-rate or usage-sensitive tariffs under community law, even though the Italian government had raised this issue. Since the Court found no evidence that leased lines had been used, the question of how their use should have been tariffed was moot.[62]

Whether or not dominant network and service providers are also abusing their market position by cross-subsidizing certain competitive telecommunications services with revenues from monopoly services is an open question.[63] Arguably, cross-subsidization per se is not an abuse of a dominant market position and may even be necessary to stimulate demand in order to foster the growth of a telecommunications service and create a market. Additionally, the cross-subsidization of services of general economic interest may be justified under Article 90 (2).[64] Cross-subsidization could, however, could be considered to be abusive if it was used for unfair, "predatory" purposes.[65]

Agreements Among Undertakings: Regulation Under Art. 85

Article 85 prohibits "all agreements between undertakings, decisions by associations of undertakings and concerted practices which may affect trade between member states and which have as their object or effect the prevention, restriction or distortion of competition within the common market." Whereas intergovernmental telecommunications agreements would fall outside the scope of Article 85, it appears that certain types of agreements among telecommunications administrations could warrant the Commission's scrutiny. It has been argued[66] that Article 85 is applicable if and when agreements concluded within the CEPT adversely affect competition in telecommunications services.

Such agreements may concern network structures, the availability and tariffing of leased lines, or interconnection and routing arrangements. Though Article 85 may apply to these agreements, they are not necessarily invalid but could be permitted under an exemption from Article 85 (3). Exemption, however, would allow the Commission to scrutinize and influence, on a case-by-case basis, agreements concerning telecommunications networks and their use.

Regulatory Tools and Sanctions

In a case of anticompetitive behavior of public network and service providers, the Commission has at its disposal two sets of regulatory tools and sanctions. As far as the undertaking is concerned, the regulatory tools and sanctions on the basis of Regulation 17 apply. Regarding the member state, the Commission may use the manquement d'etat proceedings under Article 169 of the Treaty as a regulatory tool.[67] The main tool, however, is supplied by Article 90 (3). On its basis, the Commission is empowered to ensure the application of the Treaty provisions by public undertakings on a case by case basis. Its decisions may order a member state to refrain, in the future, from infractions of the Treaty or to remove measures contrary to the Treaty.

Additionally, the Commission may, within its discretion, take legislative measures on the basis of Article 90 (3). This provision enables the Commission to address "appropriate" directives to member states in order to ensure the application of the provisions of Article 90. A *directive* is a regulatory instrument, which, according to Article 189, "shall be binding, as to the result to be achieved, upon each member state to which it is addressed, but shall leave to the national authorities the choice of form and methods." Just how far a Community law directive—with respect to the provision of telecommunications networks, services, and/or terminal equipment—could re-regulate the national telecommunications administrations is an open question. The case law of the European Court of Justice provides only scant elements for an answer.[68]

ASYMMETRIC RE-REGULATION: PROVISION OF TERMINAL EQUIPMENT

Provision of Terminal Equipment: Art. 37

With respect to the provision of terminal equipment, the Treaty requires asymmetric re-regulation in Article 37:

> member states shall progressively adjust any State monopolies of a commercial character so as to ensure that when the transitional period has ended no discrimination regarding the conditions under which goods are procured and marketed exists between nationals of member states.

According to the case law of the European Court of Justice, a state monopoly of a commercial character is characterized by playing an active role in trading goods.[69] Typically, telecommunications administrations do not trade in goods. Their exclusive right to provide terminal equipment are not tantamount to an exclusive right to sell terminal equipment.

The scope of Article 37, however, is not restricted to trade monopolies:

> The provisions of this Article shall apply to any body through which a member state, in law or in fact, either directly or indirectly supervises, determines or appreciably influences imports or exports between member states. These provisions shall likewise apply to monopolies delegated by the State to others.

The asymmetric regulatory thrust of Article 37 is reinforced by ¶2, which obliges member states to "refrain from introducing any new measure which is contrary to the principles laid down in paragraph 1." Undeniably, telecommunications administrations will "appreciably influence..imports...between Member States" by reserving an exclusive right to provide certain telecommunications terminals.[70] Such exclusive rights will force the producers of terminal equipment to sell all their products or a large part thereof to the telecommunications administration. Likewise, the consumers will be forced to use the equipment provided by the telecommunications administration. Consequently, Article 37 applies to the exclusive provision of terminal equipment.

The Commission has used its powers under Article 37 in the cordless telephones case against the German Federal Post Office (Deutsche Bundespost—DBP).[71] This case concerned an attempt of the DBP to extend its monopoly to the provision of cordless telephones. The Commission did not question the DBP's network monopoly. It did, however, intervene with regard to the extension of this monopoly to a terminal equipment device. The Commission argued that this extension of the existing monopoly constituted a new measure within the meaning of Article 37 PG2, which was directly prohibited by that Article.

The German Federal Post Office accepted the Commission's point of view, notwithstanding its own legal position that the provision of the cordless telephone was a service and not a provision of goods.[72] Consequently, the case was closed without a formal decision, which could have contributed to determine the scope of the exemptions to Article 37.

This provision is subject to Article 36,[73] which provides, inter alia, that import restrictions may be justified on grounds of public policy or public security as long as they do not "constitute a means of arbitrary discrimination or a disguised restriction on trade between Member States." These grounds must be of a noneconomic nature[74] and could arguably encompass valid technological reasons in favor of the exclusive provision of certain terminal equipment devices. The main public policy goal proffered in this context is the protection of the public telecommunications network from harm.

According to the Court's case law, however, exclusive rights to provide terminal equipment would have to be strictly necessary in order to achieve public policy goals.[75] Since the public policy goal to protect the public telecommunications network from harm can be achieved in a less restrictive manner by type approval proceedings, exclusive rights to provide telecommunications equipment are not necessary in order to achieve a public interest goal under Article 36.

Another line of argument attempts to justify the exclusive provision of terminal equipment on the grounds that it serves the goal of consumer protection. The European Court of Justice held, in its Cassis de Dijon line of cases, that consumer protection may justify restrictions upon the free movement of goods.[76] Exclusive provision of terminal equipment is said to facilitate innovation if and when changes in the network infrastructure necessitate changes of terminal equipment.[77]

It is doubtful, however, whether or not exclusive rights to provide telecommunications terminal equipment would pass the Court's rigid "less restrictive alternative" test.[78]

Provision of Terminal Equipment: Art. 86

In the modem case, the Commission challenged the German Federal Post Office's decision to establish an exclusive right for the provision of modems to be connected to the direct call and telephone networks. In this case, the Commission based its proceedings on Articles 37 and 86 in conjunction with Article 90. The Commission argued that the extension of the Bundespost's monopoly fell within Articles 37 ¶2, and that tying the provision of telephone network services to the purchase of modems was an abuse of the Bundespost's dominant position as a network operator under Art. 86 of the Treaty. The case was geared toward addressing a formal decision under Article 90 (3) to the Federal Republic of Germany, thus testing the Commission's regulatory powers under Article 90.

Again, the case was settled without a formal decision. The Bundespost agreed to relinquish its exclusive right and type-approve privately owned modems.[79] When the modem case was settled, the Commission announced that it would consider any exclusive right of a telecommunications administration to provide telecommunications terminal equipment as an infraction of Article 37 ¶2 and as an unlawful tying arrangement under Article 86 of the Treaty.[80]

SEPARATION OF REGULATORY AND ENTREPRENEURIAL FUNCTIONS

On the structural level, the applications of asymmetric regulation to control the behavior of dominant telecommunications administrations may require separation of regulatory and entrepreneurial functions or, at least, procedural and substantive rules governing the Administration's regulatory behavior.

This structural re-regulation, which is deemed necessary in order to abolish existing asymmetries, concerns, in particular, the approval of terminal equipment and the licensing of competing service providers.

Approval of Terminal Equipment

Before being approved for connection to the network, terminal equipment must undergo technical tests in order to establish whether or not certain "essential requirements" are being met. Such approval procedures and standards are governed by the treaty provisions of Article 30 seq. concerning the free movement of goods.[81]

Asymmetric distributions of regulatory and entrepreneurial powers may lead to two different types of infringements upon the principle of Article 30:

1. technical standards may be over-stringent, and not the least restrictive means to achieve public interest goals.
2. the application of technical standards in a particular case may infringe upon Article 30.

The case law of the European Court of Justice as well as Council directives, provide a legal framework for the resolution of these problems.

According to the Court's case law under Article 30 of the Treaty, approval requirements must not be disproportionate in relation to the public interest goal pursued.[82]

With respect to approval procedures, the Court has developed a similar less restrictive alternative test. In the biological products case, concerning the approval of insecticides, the Court held that the importing member states may not require further tests and inspections if the same tests and inspections have already been carried out in another member state and if the results have been made available to the authorities in the importing member state.[83] In the woodworking machines case, concerning the safety standards for woodworking equipment, the Court held that a member state would violate the principle of proportionality if it were to require that imported products satisfy literally and exactly the same technical specifications prescribed for national products.[84]

The administrative due process requirements under European law were further explored in the recent franking machines case; with respect to administrative procrastination in an approval proceeding for foreign franking machines, the Court held that conformity of substantive technical standards with Art. 30 does not suffice. Article 30 is violated when a member state adopts:

> a systematically unfavorable attitude towards imported machines, either by allowing considerable delay in replying to approval applications or in carrying out the examination procedure, or by refusing approval on the grounds of various alleged technical faults for which no detailed explanations are given or which prove to be inaccurate.[85]

The evolving body of secondary European telecommunications law comprises substantive and procedural rules concerning both technical standards for terminal equipment, and the application of these standards, i.e., the type-approval proceedings. The essential requirements which terminal equipment must meet under European law[86] are user safety, safety of employees of public telecommunications network operators, protection of public telecommunications networks from harm, and the interworking of terminal equipment in justified cases. The Council Directive of March 28, 1983,[87] established procedural rules obliging the Member states to inform the Commission of any new approval regulation before it is implemented. This notification procedure enables the Commission and other member states to object to any draft regulations which could be considered incompatible with Article 30 of the Treaty.

The Council Directive of July 24, 1986[88] has introduced the first stage of the mutual recognition of type approval for telecommunications terminal equipment. This first stage consists of the mutual recognition of the results of the conformity test specification.[89] The Directive establishes a procedure for the promulgation of common technical standards ("common conformity technical standards") used in all the Community member states by approval laboratories which must be approved by the restrictive member states. The Directive also contains requirements which the "certificates of conformity" issued by the national approval authorities have to fulfill (Article 7 (3)). If such a certificate of conformity has been issued for a particular type of terminal equipment in one member state, the authorities of another member state must recognize this certificate for the purposes of their own type approval procedures and must not require any further tests (Article 6 (2)).

In sum, the emerging Community telecommunications law with respect to the approval of terminal equipment is characterized by a considerable reliance on substantive (European) technical standards and by procedural rules. The organizational structures of the national approval authorities have not been subjected to (asymmetric) re-regulation.

Network Access

The need for asymmetric re-regulation under European law may also arise with respect to network access and use.

National telecommunications administrations could abuse their dominant positions as network providers by setting discriminatory technical standards for access and use of their networks by competing service providers.

Apart from case by case adjudication of such abuses under Article 86 of the Treaty, the Commission may, within its discretion, take legislative measures on the basis of Article 90 (3).[90] Their legitimate scope, particularly the question as to whether or not Article 90 (3) may become a legal basis for the development of a European open network architecture, similar to the comparable efficient interconnection and open network requirements of the U.S. Federal Communications Commission, will require further legal analysis.

In any event, given the division of regulatory powers between the European Community and its member states, re-regulation of network access will have to be based upon substantive technical standards and procedural rules of secondary Community law rather than on structural separation requirements with respect to the organizational structures of national telecommunications administrations.

CONCLUSION

The question whether or not European Community law requires an asymmetric re-regulation of telecommunications cannot be answered with a simple yes or no.

An analysis of the framework of the Treaty and the evolving European telecommunications law, leads to a set of differentiated answers.

While the American experience is helpful in tracing the problems of asymmetric re-regulation, it does not alleviate the burden of finding European solutions.

ENDNOTES

[1] For analyses of the regulatory developments in Belgium see: B. de Crombugghe/Y. Poullet, La Reglementation des Telecommunications en Belgique, in: Administration Publique, 1986, pp. 187–214; France: Genevieve Bonnetblanc, Les Telecommunications Fracaises: Quel Statut pour Quelle Entreprise ? Paris 1985; Jean Bernard Blaise, Rundfunk-und Fernmeldepolitik in Frankreich. Das neue franzosische Gesetz uber die Telekommunikation, in: Joachim Scherer (ed.), Nationale und europaische Perspektiven der Telekommunikation, Baden-Baden 1987, p. 69 seq.; Federal Republic of Germany: Joachim Scherer, Telekommunikationsrecht und Telekommunikationspolitik, Baden-Baden 1985; the Netherlands: Bernt Hugenholtz/Wouter Hins, The Law and Economics of Transborder Telecommunications: Report on the Netherlands, forthcoming; United Kingdom: Arnulf Heuermann/Karl-Heinz Neumann, Die Liberalisierung des britischen Telekommunikationsmarktes, Berlin 1985. For comparative analyses see: Robert R. Bruce/Jeffrey P. Cunard/Mark D. Director, From Telecommunications to Electronic Services, 2 vol., London 1986 (ed.: International Institute of Communications); Joachim Scherer, Nachrichtenubertragung und Datenverarbeitung im Telekommunikationsrecht, Baden-Baden, 1987.

[2] Cf. Commission of the European Communities, Towards a Dynamic European Economy: Green Paper on the Development of the Common Market for Telecommunications Services and Equipment, COM (87) 290 final, Fig. 3 and pp. 184–192. For a legal analysis of the Green Paper see Joachim Scherer, European Community opens its telecommunications networks: Legal aspects of the Green Paper, in: International Computer Law Adviser, September 1987. For an analysis of the Commission's early "teleinformatics strategy" see Thomas J. Ramsey, Europe responds to the challenge of the new information technologies, in: 14 Cornell International Law Journal (1981), pp. 237 seq.

[3] Postal and telecommunications services were separated in the United Kingdom in 1981. For an in-depth analysis of the economic implications see Arnulf Heuermann/Thomas Schnoring, Die Reorganisation der britischen Pose - Ansatze zu einem Vergleich mit der Deutschen Bundespost, in: Jahrbuch der Deutschen Bundespost 1985, p. 321.

[4] The European Court of Human Rights has decided that telephone conversations are covered by the notion of "private life" and "correspondence" within the meaning of Art.8 of the European Convention on Human Rights and that "powers of secret surveillance of citizens, characterizing as they do the police state, are tolerable under the Convention only in so far as strictly necessary for safeguarding the democratic institutions", Klass case, European Court of Human Rights, Judgement (7 Sept. 1978), Series A no. 28, p. 5, 21. This right of the individual was expanded in the Malone case, Judgement (2 August 1984), Series A no. 4/1983, 60/94, where "reasonable clarity" was required of laws and statutes abridging this right (p. 30) and, in particular, the right of telecommunications was extended to "metering" (i.e., the registration of the numbers dialed on a particular telephone): "The records of metering contain information, in particular the numbers dialed, which is an integral element in the communications made by telephone" (p. 31 seq.).

[5] With the emergence of new telecommunications services and the blurring of traditional boundary lines, the need for regulation in order to protect and enhance these freedoms, has increased.

Cf. Joachim Scherer, Telekommunikationsrecht und Telekommunikationspolitik, Baden-Baden 1985, pp. 681–722 with respect to the regulatory framework in the Federal Republic of Germany. For an evaluation of the implications that freedoms of expression and information under Art. 10 of the European Convention of Human Rights have on technical means of communications see Martin Bullinger, Freedom of expression and information: an essential element of democracy, in: Human Rights Law Journal 6 (1985), p. 338, at 349 seq.

[6] For a comparative analysis of the organizational structures of the European telecommunications administrations see R.R. Bruce/J.P. Cunard/M.D. Director, supra, note 1. For a comprehensive presentation of the organizational structure of the Deutsche Bundespost and its development see Helmut Bielefeld, Organisation, Heidelberg, 1982.

[7] See, for a description of the ISDN evolution from a technical perspective, Anthony M. Rutkowski, Integrated Services Digital Network, Dedham Mass. 1985, pp. 33–175; see also Joachim Scherer, supra. note 5, pp. 368–392, 553–567, describing the evolution of new telecommunications services. A lucid account of the technical evolutions is given by Marvin A. Sirbu, Jr., The Innovation Process in Telecommunications, in Telecommunications and Productivity, ed. Mitchell L. Moss, Reading, Mass: 1981, pp. 184–198.

[8] For an overview see Joachim Scherer, supra, note 1.

[9] For an overview of the ISDN-standardization efforts on the international level see A.M. Rutkowski, supra, note 7, p. 35 seq.

[10] Cf. above, note 3.

[11] Communication from the Commission to the Council on Telecommunications, COM (84) 277 final, p. 14, 20.

[12] For a progress report on these activities see Communication from the Commission to the Council on European Telecommunications Policy, COM (86) 325 final, p. 4–20.

[13] Commission of the European Communities, Proposal for a Council Recommendation on the Coordinated Introduction of the Integrated Services Digital Network (ISDN) in the European Community, COM (86) 205 final.

[14] 86/659/EEC, 31.12. 1986, O.J. L 382/36.

[15] This "critical mass" is proposed to be "about 5% of the 1983 telephone subscriber population in each country". COM 86 (205) final, p. 10.

[16] Council Recommendation 84/549/EEC, November 12, 1984, O.J. No. L 298, 16.11. 1984, p. 49.

[17] COM (87) 35, Feb. 9, 1987.

[18] COM (87) 35, Feb. 9, 1987. Whereas Recommendations do not have "binding force", a Directive "shall be binding, as to the result to be achieved, upon each member state to which the choice of form and methods", Art. 189 (3).

[19] For a thorough analysis of the Court's case-law concerning (tele-) communications and the media see Jurgen Schwarze, in, Jurgen Schwarze (ed.) *Rundfunk und Fernsehen im Licte dre Entwircklung des nationalen und internationalen Rechts*, Baden-Baden 1986, pp. 119–148.

[20] Art. 90 (2) provides: "Undertakings entrusted with the operation of services of general economic interest of having the character of a revenue-producing monopoly shall be subject to the rules contained in this Treaty, in particular to the rules on competition, in so far as the application of such rules does not obstruct the performance, in law or in fact, of the particular tasks assigned to them. The development of trade must not be affected to such an extent as would be contrary to the interest of the Community".

[21] Cf. Ernst-Joachim Mestmacker, Europaisches Wettbewersrecht, Munchen 1974, p. 653.

[22] For the direct applicability of Art. 59 see Case 33/74, van Binsbergen, (1974), ECR 1299; Case 33/74, Walrave, (1974), ECR 1405; Case 39/75, Coenen (1975), ECR 1547.

[23] Recommendation No I.112, ¶201, CCITT Red Book (1985).

[24] See also Bernard E. Amory, Les Monopoles de telecommunications face au droit europeen, in RDAI No. 2 (1986), p. 117, at 129.

[25] Case 155/73, Sacchi (1974), ECR 4C9, Ground 6; see also Commission of the European Communities, Television without Frontiers, Green Paper on the Establishment of the Common Market for Broadcasting, Especially by Satellite and Cable, COM (84) 300 final, pp. 105 seq.

[26] For an analysis of the scope of Art. 55, 56, and the Court's "public interest" exception cf. Joachim Scherer, European Telecommunications Law: The Framework of the Treaty, in European Law Review 1987 (forthcoming).

[27] Case 10/71 Ministere Public of Luxembourg v. Muller (1971) ECR 723, Ground 13/16 (implicitly); Case 127/73—BRT II—(1974) ECR 313, Ground 19 (explicitly).

[28] The non-applicability of Treaty provisions is, in turn, restricted by Art. 90 (2) 2 which requires that the non-application of the Treaty rules must not affect the development of trade to such an extent as would be contrary to the interests of the Community.

[29] Case 41/83 British Telecom (1985), ECR, p. 873, Ground 22.

[30] For a case in point see BVerfGE 58, 300.

[31] Cf. the seminal Hauer Case, 44/79, Hauer v. Rheinland-Pfalz, (1979), ECR 3727, Ground 17–20.

[32] See also Hans Peter Ipsen, Europaisches Gemeinschaftsrecht, Tubinquen 1972, p. 658 (37/8).

[33] Case 190/80 French Republic et al. v. Commission (1982), ECR 2545, Ground 12; for a functional analysis of Art. 90 (1) see also Volker Emmerich, Das Wirtschaftrecht der offentlichen Unternehmen, Bad Homburg 1969, p. 376 seq., 407 seq.; J. Thiesing, in: von der Groeben/Thiesing/Ehlermann (eds.). Handbuch, I A 50, Art. 95, I.4.; Hochbaum, op. cit., n. 21, Art. 90, Note 1, 7.

[34] Cf. Hochbaum, in: von der Groeben/Boeckh/Thiesing/Ehlermann (eds.), Kommentar zum EWG-Vertrag, 3rd ed., Baden-Baden 1983, Art. 90, Note 8; see also J. Megret/J.-V. Louis/D. Vignes/M. Waelbroeck, Le Droit de la Communaute Europeenne, 4., Concurrence, Brussels 1972, p. 84 seq.

[35] Case 41/83, British Telecom (1985), ECR, p. 873, Grounds 17, 19.

[36] Cf. ¶¶14 and 13 of the German Postal Administration Act which provides that tariff and usage regulations are (1) issued by the Ministry of Post and Telecommunications acting in accordance with the Ministry of Economics and (2) subject to the Cabinet's veto.

[37] Case 311/84, Radio Luxembourg-Telemarketing (1985) ECR, p. 3261. Telemarketing.

[38] Cf. Arwed Deringer, Das Wettbewerbsrecht der Europaischen Wirtschaftsgemeinschaft. Kommentar zu den EWG-Wettbewerbsregeln. Dusseldorf 1961, Art. 90, Rz. 26, 27; Hochbaum, supra, note 34, Art. 90, Note 11.

[39] Cf. Hochbaum, supra, note 34, Art. 90, Note 12 with reference to the postal and telecommunications administrations; see also A. Deringer, supra, note 38, Art. 90, Note 27.

[40] Cf. Joachim Scherer, supra, note 7, p. 429–431.

[41] See, in particular, Case 10/71 Ministere Public of Luxembourg v. Muller (1971) ECR 723, Ground 8, 11–15; see also Case 127/73, BRT v. Sabam, (1974), ECR 313, Grounds 20, 23; Case 94/74, IGAV v. ENCC, (1975), ECR 699 Ground 33/35; Case 13/77, INNO/ATAB, (1977), ECR 2115, Ground 34.

[42] 42. Cf. E.-J. Mestmacker, supra, note 21, p. 662 seq.; see also Pernice, in Eberhard Grabitz (ed.), EWG—Vertrag, Munchen 1986, Art. 90, Note 35 with further references.

[43] Case 41/83 British Telecom (1985), ECR, p. 873, Ground 30.

[44] Cf. E.-J. Mestmacker, supra, note 21, p. 662 seq.; Pernice, supra, note 42, Art. 30, Note 36.

[45] Case 172/80, Zuchner v. Bayerische Vereinsbank AG, (1981), ECR 2021, Ground 7; see also case 127/73, BRT v. Sabam, (1974), ECR 313, E.-J. Mestmacker, supra, note 21, p. 662 and Pernice, supra, note 42, Art. 90, Note 33.

[46] See above, n. 40.

[47] Cf.—with reference to infrastructures in general—Pernice, supra, note 42, Art. 90, Note 35. For problems arising in the context of qualifying telecommunications services as services of general economic interest, see below.

[48] Case 127/73 BRT v. Sabam (1974) ECR 312.

[49] Cf. Case 41/83 British Telecom (1985), ECR, p. 873, Ground 33 ("from an economic viewpoint").

[50] For the applicable standard of review cf. Case 10/71 Ministere Public of Luxembourg v. Muller (1971) ECR, 723 Ground 14/15.

[51] Case 41/83 British Telecom (1985), ECR, p. 873, Ground 33.

[52] Cf. Reinhard Schulte Braucks, European Telecommunications Law in the Light of the British Telecom Judgment, in CMLR 23 (1986), p. 39 (47).

[53] Cf. Case 41/83—British Telecom—(1985), ECR, p. 873, Opinion of Advocate-General Darmon.

[54] Case 41/83—British Telecom—(1985) ECR, p. 873, Ground 33.

[55] Cf. Bernard Amory, in RDAI 2 (1986), p. 119. For the Court's definition of a "dominant position" cf. Case 27/76 United Brands v. Commission (1978) ECR 207 Grounds 10–126; Case 85/76 Hoffmann La Roche v. Commission (1979) ECR 461; see also Case 31/80, L'Oreal v. De Nieuwe AMCK (1980) ECR 3793, Ground 26/27; see also Schroter, supra, note 34, Art. 86 Note 9.

[56] Case 85/76 Hoffman La Roche v. Commission (1979), ECR 461 Ground 91; see also Case 31/80 L'Oreal v. De Nieuwe AMCK (1980) ECR 3793, Grounds 26/27; Case 322/81 NBI Michelin v. Commission (1983), 3461, Grounds 29/30;

see also Koch, supra, note 41, Art. 86, Notes 13, 43 and Schroter, supra, note 34, Art. 86, Note 40.

[57] Cf. Koch, supra, note 41, Art. 86, Note 14–16; 42 with references to the Court's decisions.

[58] Part I, 1. d.

[59] Cf. above, II.1.a.

[60] For a case in point see Commission of the European Communities, Information Memo No. IP 86 (379), July 1986, Common Market Rep. (CCH), 1986, 10, 801.

[61] For the Court's standard of review for prices under Art. 86 see Case 27/76—United Brands—(1978), ECR 206, Ground 248/257; see also D. Schwarz, Imposition de prix non equitables par des entreprises en position dominante, in Semaine de Bruges 1977, p. 381.

[62] Case 41/83 Italy v. Commission (1985), ECR Ground 26.

[63] Cf. Volker Emmerich, Anmerkungen zu den Postfinanzen, in Ordo 35 (1984), p.43 (61 seq.); see also E.-J. Mestmacker, supra, note 21, p. 390.

[64] For a more restrictive view see V. Emmerich, Ordo 35 (1984), p. 61.

[65] For a critical assessment of the concept of predatory pricing see Dieter Schwarz, Wettbewerbpolitische Problematik des Predatory Pricing, in Wirtschaft und Wettbewerb 1987, p. 93–99.

[66] by Bernard Amory, RDAI 2 (1986), 122 seq.; see also THomas J. Ramsey, supra, note 2. p. 277.

[67] Cf. Hochbaum, supra. note 34, Art. 90, Note 49; Pernice, supra, note 42, Art. 90, Note 60; Megret, supra 34, p. 91.

[69] Cf. Case 6/64, Costa v. ENEL, ECR X, p. 1254 (1298).

[70] Cf. Aurelio Pappalardo, Die Stellung der Fernmeldemonopole im EWG-Recht, in: Ernst-Joachim Mestmacker (ed.), Kommunikation ohne Monopole, Baden-Baden 1980, p. 201 (210); see also Volker Emmerich, Nationale Postmonopole und Europaisches Gemeinschaftsrecht, in: Europarecht 1983, p. 216 (218).

[71] Bull. EC 3–1985, point 2.1.43; see also 2 C.M.L. Rep. 397 (1985).

[72] Cf. Eckart Wiechert, Das Recht des Fernmeldewesens der Bundesrepublik Deutschland—Staaliche Aufgabe und private Betatilgung im Fernmeldewesen nach dem geltenden Recht, in: Jahrbuch der Deutschen Bundespost 1986, p. 119, 142 seq.

[73] Cf. Manfred Zuleeg, Die Umformung der Handelsmonopole, in: Ernst-Werner FuB (ed.), Der Beitrag des Gerichtshofs de Europaischen Gemeinschaften zur Verwirkluchung des Gemeinsan ? Marketes, Baden-Baden 1981, p. 29 (37 seq.); see also A. Papalardo, supra, note 70, p. 201 (213 seq.); and implicitly Thompson, (1978), ECR 2247 (2275).

[74] Case 7/61, Commission v. Italy, 1961, ECR 695 (720); 95/81, Commission v. Italy, ECR 2187 (2204).

[75] Cf. Case 104/75, de Peijper, 1976, ECR 613 (635); Case 35/76, Simmenthal, 1976, ECR 1871 (1885); Case 13/78, Eggers, 1978, ECR 1935 (1955 seq); Case 153/78, Commission v. Federal Republic of Germany, 1979, ECR 2555 (2564 seq).

[76] Case 120/78, Rewe, 1979, ECR 649 (662); for an analysis see Cassis de

Dijon and its progeny see Alan Dashwood, the Cassis Dijon Line of Authority, in: In Memoriam J.D.B. Mitchell 1983, p. 145 seq.

[77] The German Federal Constitutional Court has acknowledged the validity of this argument in BVerfGE 46, 120 (146, 147 seq.)

[78] Cf. Joachim Scherer, supra, note 7, p. 401 seq.

[79] For a summary of the Bundespost's legal arguments see Eckart Wiechert, supra, note 72, p. 145–150.

[80] EC-Bull. 7/8 1986, 2.1.85.

[81] Art. 30 provides: "Quantitative restrictions on imports and all measures having equivalent effect shall, without prejudice to the following provisions, be prohibited between member states". Art. 36 provides in its pertinent parts: "The provision... of Article 30 ... shall not preclude prohibitions or restrictions on imports, exports or goods in transit justified on grounds of ... public policy or public security; the protection of health and life of humans...Such prohibitions or restrictions shall not, however, constitute a means of arbitrary discrimination or a disguised restriction on trade between member states".

[82] Case 124/81, Commission v. United Kingdom (UHT milk), 1983, ECR 203, ground 16; see also Case 261/81, Rau, 1982, ECR 3961.

[83] Case 272/80, 1981, ECR 3277, Ground 14.

[84] Case 188/84, Commission v. France, ECR 1985, p. 419 Ground 16.

[85] Case 21/84, Commission v. France, ECR 1985, p. 1355 Ground 11.

[86] Council Directive 86/361/EEC, O.J. 1986 L 217/23.

[87] Council Directive 83/189/EEC, O.J. 1983, L 109.

[88] Council Directive 86/361/EEC, O.J. 1986 l. 217/23.

[89] Cf. Commission of the European Communities, Proposal for a Council Directive concerning the first phase of the establishment of the mutual recognition of type approval for telecommunications terminal equipment, COM (85) 230, p. 211.

[90] Cf. Case 190/80, ECR 2545, Grounds 1 seq.

Chapter 10
Departing From Monopoly: Asymmetries, Competition Dynamics, and Regulation Policy

Laurent Benzoni and Raymond Svider

Deregulation modifies old rules of the game in protected industries. One of the most important changes that deregulation brings is the possibility of entry by new players into markets formerly closed. Deregulation usually increases the intensity of competition and subsequently contributes positively to the general welfare. However, theories that argue in favor of deregulation are generally based on the assumptions that a perfect symmetry exists between different actors who operate in the deregulated markets (Baumol, Panzar, & Willig, 1982). There is no doubt that this assumption must be reconsidered, especially in the context of technical change, and capital intensive industries that require delays in installation of capital equipment (Benzoni, 1987; Curien & Gensollen, 1987).

The purpose of this chapter is to investigate the problem of asymmetric deregulation as it applies to the telecommunications industry.

Part I presents a model simulating the entry of a new firm into the previously monopolistic French long distance communication(s) market. Based on this model Part II analyzes the nature of asymmetries and their consequences for competition dynamics. Finally, Part III contains some general conclusions on the conduct of regulation policies in a market environment where asymmetries hardly determine the competitive process.

ENTRY PROCESS IN THE TELECOMMUNICATIONS
INDUSTRY: A SIMULATION

Since 1837, the transmission of any signal in the French public territory has depended on the *Ministry of Posts and Telecommunications* (P&T). Therefore, in France, the telecommunication network and its basic services (telephone, telex, etc.) are managed by a unique public operating company, the *Direction Générale des Télécommunications* (DGT).

General regulatory assumptions need to be made in order to set up the new competitive environment in which the entry would take place. The assumptions are the following:

- The current DGT monopoly on long-distance communications undergoes deregulation by the French government;
- Local and international communications remain the monopoly of DGT; and
- Only one firm has the opportunity to enter the "deregulated" market.

Taking the perspective of the entrant, the following describes the sequence of steps it needs to take to enter the market. To simplify notations, the entrant will be referred to as the *New Operator* (NO) and the formerly monopolistic firm as the *Existing Operator* (EO). Naturally, the sensitivity of NO profitability depends heavily on its competitive advantages compared with EO. So, NO's profitability has to be evaluated by modifying the values of the main exogenous competitive parameters within realistic extreme boundaries. To that extent, we have set up a forecasted 10-year business plan for NO.

Methodology and Presentation of the Model

For NO, the decision of entry requires a market study which must cover both the demand and the supply sides. Let us consider successively these two sides:

Supply: Digital technologies. On the supply side, the first step for NO is to the examine which type of equipment can be used. Obviously, NO must choose the most modern technologies and thus must adopt digital technologies and build a fully digitalized network (transmission and switching). A methodical comparison of the respective advantages between the different digital transmissions means (optical fiber, satellite, and microwave) was undertaken in order to decide which technology will best adapt to the needs of potential consumers. Assuming that NO would not be backward integrated, the same type of analysis was conducted for the different kinds of switching equipment available or to be announced by the world's major manufacturers (AT&T, Northern Telecom, Siemens, Ericsson, Alcatel). This broad review helped envision the technical tradeoffs as well as the design of the fixed cost function for building a nationwide long distance telecommunication network. Table 1 shows a comparison between different means of transmissions.

In order to complete this first approach, we have developed an operating cost function. Finally, in integrating fixed and variable costs we have obtained a global function cost that essentially depends on three parameters: network scope and structure, maximum traffic per trunk, and level of access charges to the network of the EO.

The network scope and structure determines total expenses for the construction and transmission equipment while maximum traffic per trunk indicates variable equipment costs such as multiplexers and personnel costs. Access charges depend on the number of communications and unit level of the charge fixed by EO or regulatory authorities.

Demand: Segmentation and large business users. Two different types of information were analyzed in order to define which market segment(s) are targeted as its primary customer base. We first broke up the data on market sizes and growth by type of product

Table 1. Comparison of different means of transmission

	ADVANTAGES	DISADVANTAGES
SATELLITES	Rapidity of installation Adaptability of capacities Wide territoriality International network Low costs of investments	Poor transmission quality "Double bonds" impossible Uncertainty in the supply of satellite channels High operating costs
OPTICAL FIBER	Good transmission quality Economies of scale Low operating costs	Large investments Difficulties to overhaul the breaks Important landed infrastructure
MICROWAVES SYSTEMS	Rapidity of installation Modulated systems Using of exisiting infrastructure	Difficulties in setting of apparatus Sensitivity to the environment Scarcity of frequencies

(telephone, telex, dedicated lines, data transmission, etc.), type of communication (local, long distance, and international), and type of customers (residential users, small and large business users). This analysis provided important insights that are summarized in Figure 1.

Despite their limited number (approximately 2,000 in France), the large corporate users represent 10% of the total revenues of telecommunications. With a monthly telecommunications bill of $11,800 on average, their consumption per line is by far the highest and is mainly composed on long-distance communications, the market of NO. Moreover, this market segment presents a high growth rate driven by an extensive use of advanced telecommunications services.

On the other hand, the other market segments do not seem as attractive for NO. Much more numerous in terms of total number of customers, and thus more difficult to reach and costly to serve, their consumption per line is lower and concentrated on local communications. The primary service they use—voice—has matured with a growth rate leveling off at around 5%, indicating a saturated market with no significant growth in consumption.

From this first analysis, we conclude that NO would concentrate on the large business users, and more specifically on long-distance communications. Long-distance communications have potentially the

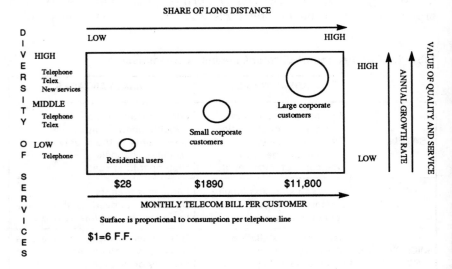

Figure 1.   Telecommunications market segments

highest growth, and also happen to be the most profitable for EO due to cross-subsidies between local and long distance services. Then, in just building a long-distance network, the NO can rapidly offer its services on a nationwide basis, minimize its volume of investment, and thus minimize the financial and economic risks.

To determine how to penetrate the segment of long-distance communications for large business users, we conducted in-depth interviews with a sample of the largest corporate users from various industries, accounting for 30% of the total market for this specific segment. Two major factors were found to concern these customers: quality of service and price. Because they view telecommunications as a critical element in their operations, they refuse to trade off quality for price. Therefore, NO must at least match the recognized quality of the existing operator. However, users need an incentive to switch to NO resulting from the risks involved. Interviews allowed us to measure this risk premium with the following results.

Firms representing 65% of the total communications value of the sample are ready to switch to NO providing a 20% price discount over EO rates that NO would guarantee in the long run (Figure 2). It is important to note that with a 10% to 20% price reduction, NO would not obtain new customers. The importance of fixed costs and investments necessarily implies, for NO, conducting a policy of significant discounts to enter the industry. On the curve represented in Figure 2, the point where 20% price discount meets 65% market shares (in terms of value not in terms of customers) seems a good target for the NO.

Total sample in percentage

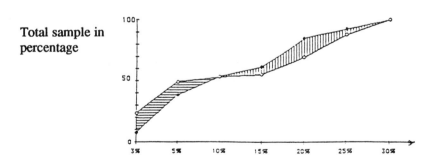

This curve indicates the percentage of firms in the sample which will switch to N.O. if it provides a X% price discount over E.O.

This curve indicates the percentage of telecommunications revenue in the sample which N.O. captures if it provides a X% price discount over E.O.

Figure 2.   Estimation of the N.O.'s demand function

In conclusion, the entry strategy for NO should be to specialize on long-distance telecommunications for large business users and to differentiate its service from those of EO by providing the same quality at a 20% price discount.

At this point, we think that it is important to understand that offering the same quality at a lower price is possible in this case. The reasons for it relate to a general pattern common to many industries. First, due to technological change, NO can utilize more efficient equipment than that generally used by EO. Second, it is not optimal to serve different needs from different customers with the same production and distribution organization. In other words, Rolls Royces and Renault Le Cars cannot be produced cost effectively on the same production line. This applies to the telecommunications industry as well. A strategy of network differentiation is foreseeable (for theoretical principles, e.g., Hotelling, 1929; Thysse & Gabscewicz, 1979). For this reason, despite economies of scale, a more adapted network can offer telecommunication services at lower cost, to a well-defined customer group, provided that the revenue potential is large enough to offset the fixed costs involved in this industry.

Main Results

The network. Figure 3 shows the network of NO, which links 15 major French cities. This network consists of a loop between Paris, Lyon, Marseille, and Bordeaux, with several single "extensions" to cover the northern and eastern industrialized sections. The loop, as well as the Paris-Nancy connection, figures a large capacity 4x140 mbps fiber-optic trunk, while the capacity of the extension is 140 mbps using fiber-optic or microwave technologies. As large corporate users are heavily concentrated in major urban areas, such a network would be able to serve most of their needs. The end-line connection procedure assumed for the purpose of this study is similar to the equal access used in the United States. Moreover, bypass procedures are not allowed, but have been considered to set up an economically justifiable level of access charges.

One central feature of this network is the existence of only four switching stations, which significantly reduces costs. This is made possible by two factors, an excess in transmission capacity and a small number of customers to serve. These stations are located in each of the major cities mentioned above.

The model. An economic model was conceived and implemented to forecast the revenues and profits of NO within the standard 10-year

Physical network   hierarchical structure of the network

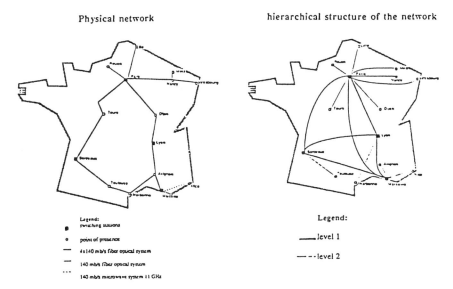

Legend:
● rwitching stauons
○ point of presence
— 4x140 mb/s fiber optical system
— 140 mb/s fiber optical system
··· 140 mb/s microwave system 11 GHz

Legend:
——— level 1
— — · level 2

Figure 3

Physical network   hierarchial structure of the network

period of an investment of this nature. Figure 4 summarizes this model, which can be divided in three parts.

The first two parts result directly from the supply and demand analysis of the new network. The demand function estimates volume of traffic between the cities on NO's network over the time period considered. The fixed-cost function determines the investment expenditure sequence necessary to build up the network. The operating cost function takes into account human, administrative, and technical costs resulting from the demand parameters.

Demand forecasts in volume are compiled by applying the market share evolution forecasted NO to the traffic estimates in the demand block. The market share gained by NO on large corporate users follows a curve in two phases, corresponding to an initial progressive increase (the lead time necessary to convince clients to switch) and a leveling off going to the limit of 65% referred to in the interviews (see Figure 5).

The evolution of tariffs in the marketplace then determines NO's price function and pricing policy, which sets compound to the traffic forecasts to calculate revenues. Access charges go on the expense account of the income statement.

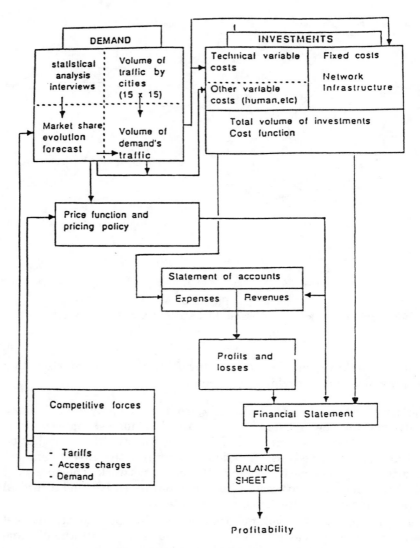

Figure 4.   Structure of the Model

The third block estimates the evolution of the three dynamic factors set by market forces or regulation: *tariffs*, *market share*, and *access charges*. In the model, these variables are parameters for which the values are exogenous. Changes in these values will influence NO's profitability and will be sued in sensitivity analysis scenarios.

Market share
in percentage

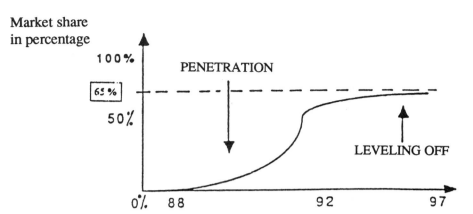

Figure 5.   Market share evolution of the N.O. in the segment of long
distance communications for large corporate users

Scenario hypothesis. In order to run and test the model, a
referential scenario was designed according to values of the exogenous
parameters (demand, tariffs, access charges) that, in our opinion, best
represents the most profitable evolution in case of deregulation. This
scenario brings, for the three parameters, the following values.

1. The evolution of the telecom unit price assumes a sudden rise in
    the EO's local rate accompanied by a decrease in the long-distance
    operations in 1989. This change in prices is simply supposed to
    modify the distribution of EO's revenues without affecting total
    revenues. The continued evolution after 1989 is derived by a two-
    year flat steep curve accounting for a transformation period
    followed by a steady 7% yearly decline due to a productivity gains.
    NO's price has been set up at least 20% below EO's long-distance
    price throughout the period.
2. The level of access charges paid by NO for each communication
    involving EO's connections to the local level is respectively 0.3 of
    the local unit to access for NO's network (threshold above which
    bypass is cheaper for a typical NO's customer) and one local unit to
    end the communication.
3. NO obtains, as it had forecasted, a 65% market share with the
    price reduction of 20% relative to EO's tariffs. To prevent the access
    of its network by small users, NO sets the monthly access charge at
    $300.

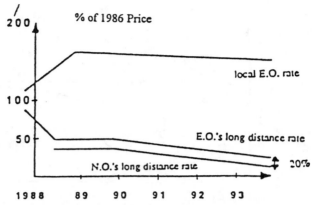

Figure 6. Price evolution of telecom unit in the referential scenario

Even in this referential scenario, we have assumed that EO's reaction is significant in terms of price.

Other scenarios have been studied with more or less hard reactions of EO's in terms of tariff policy, commercial actions (market share), and squeezing behavior (level of access charge paid by EO.). The values of all tested scenarios are related in Table 2.

Table 2 Assumptions on the values parameter in the different scenarios

PARAMETERS		Scenario 1	Scenario 2	Scenario 3
Price	local	1987-88: +70% 1989-97: - 3%	1987-88 + 140% 1989-97: - 3%	1987-88: 0% 1989-97: - 3%
Evolution Scenarios	long distance	1987-88: -40% 1989-90: - 3% 1991-97: - 7%	1987-88:-100% 1989-90: - 3% 1991-97: - 7%	1987-88: 0% 1989-90: - 3% 1991-97: - 7%
MARKET SHARE SCENARIOS		N.O. 65% E.O. 35%	N.O. 55% E.O. 45%	N.O. 45% E.O. 55%
ACCESS CHARGES SCENARIOS		1.3 Unit tariff of local communication	1.43 Unit tariff of local communication	1.17 Unit tariff of local communication

1 Market share: 65% for N.O., 35% for E.O.; level of access charges is 1.3 unit tariff of local communication.
2 For price evolution see Scenario 1 in price scenarios, level of access charges is 1.3 unit tariff of local communication.
3 Market shares: 65% for N.O., 35% for E.O. For price evolution see Scenario 1 in price scenarios.

In the referential scenario, the model indicates that NO's net total cumulative profit on the 1988–1997 period is able to reach $300 million. In this case, the net rate of return of investments is near 14%. We conclude that entry is profitable and thus probably foreseeable.

However, the different scenarios show the critical sensitivity of NO's profitability to its competitive environment. Figure 7 shows the results obtained with the model in reference to the scenarios described above.

First, we can observe that price competition implies an important variation in NO's net profit.

According to diverse price scenarios, it varies from $921 down to $36 million. So, as realistic conclusion is that the entry is certainly not profitable in the case of quasidisparition of cross-subsidies. On the other hand, the potential profitability of entry in the case of low reactions from the EO explains the importance of lobbies in favor of deregulation. On the one hand, firms that want to enter the industry can hope to win a lucrative business. On the other hand, the potential profitability can be used by some categories of users (e.g., large corporate business) or regulatory authorities as an argument to prove the bad resource allocation in the telecommunications industry.

Second, the assumption of entry possibility given to one firm and only one is absolutely necessary to effectively open the telecommunications industry to real competition, i.e., a competition with an effective presence of new competitors in the market. For this purpose, we can observe in Figure 7 that for NO, a 10% market share loss implies a total profit loss of near $160 million! The quasilinearity of that relation (due in part to the underlying model) is fraught with consequences.

Let up suppose that two firms can enter the market, and that the three firms (two NOs and one EO) adopt similar commercial actions that have the same overall efficiency. Each one of them must obtain a 33% market share. For the three firms, their net profit will be null during the period 1988–1997. But one of these firms, the EO, is not specialized in the long distance communication for large businesses. EO operates inside other market segments of the telecommunications industry, as well as local communications, small business, and residential long distance communications. EO can survive the uncomfortable situation in the long distance communications market. However, the two NOs will have a lot of difficulties surviving. Maybe, in anticipating poor gains and failures, they will prefer not to enter. The initial monopolistic structure of the telecommunication industry does not change one way or another because of deregulation process.

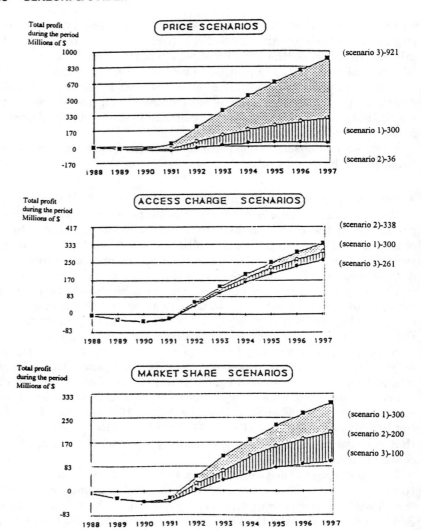

Figure 7.   Scenario Results

In the background, there are asymmetries between actors that induce these paradoxical results. For this reason, we are going to push the analysis in this way.

ASYMMETRIES AND COMPETITION DYNAMICS

The simulation of competition has shown that the profitability of entrants depends heavily on the competitive environment. The model was developed in relation to basic conditions and structures of the French communications market, but similar results would certainly been found in other national telecommunications markets, because in the background, the running of telecommunication industries is quite the same. Cross-subsidies, differences in volume of communications utilized by each category of users, increase of long distance communications consumption, evolution of technologies, and diversification of services are all common factors in the telecommunication industries in developed countries.

The competitive process described in Part I does not differ from the one observed in countries where the telecommunications industry is deregulated. Reactions of dominant firms such as AT&T, NTT, and BT to competition with new firms such as MCI, US-Sprint, DAI-NI-DEN-DEN, and Mercury are the same that DGT will use to compete with NO on its profitable markets. In the new competition, two parameters are particularly important: *price levels* and *market share*. On the other hand, access charge levels do not really influence the results of NO. We can note that, in all cases, *Large users' reactions* to new market conditions will be a determining factor in the competition dynamics. This category of users will play an increasingly important role in the world of telecommunications. This fact is not a minor consequence of deregulation.

In the simulation model, a distinction has to be made between market share and price level scenarios. Market shares depend on EO *and* NO's policies, but also on the possible entry of a second or third new operator. Price levels just depend on EO which, as the dominant firm, is the *price maker*. This evident asymmetry of market power between actors takes root in particular asymmetries that must be studied because they have substantial consequences for the competitive process, and finally, for the regulation of the industry.

Natures of Asymmetries

Table 3 summarizes the diverse nature of market asymmetries that may favor both EO and NO. Lines relate the type of asymmetry, and

Table 3.   The Diverse Types of Asymmetries

Type of asymmetry	Competitive advantage to	
	Entering firm	Existing firm
Technology	X	
Experience		X
Market segmentation/ Structure	X	
Spatial Distribution		X
Public utilities obligations	X	
Image		X
Scale		X

columns relate which firm profits from asymmetry. We can describe more precisely the roots and economic nature of the asymmetries.

The *existing firm* has an advantage in terms of *experience* in the running and organization of complex technologies, and it benefits from a positive effect of "learning by doing" in this field. Also, in terms of *spatial distribution*, a *nationwide* network is owned by the dominant firm. Entering firms must progressively build their network. During a time they can only propose to users some dedicated lines. In terms of *image*, EO enjoys other advantages which include the longevity and intensity of its contract relations with users, the soundness of the firm, the quality products and services of its being well-known, and so on. Obviously, this type of advantage can favor the NO if EO's reputation is not good. But, in the French demand case, we have found, through the interviews, the EO profits from the good reputation of its services and its infrastructures. Finally, EO has an advantage in terms of *scale* and *scope*, due to the number of connected users on the network, the diversity of services, and the large system of commercialization and distribution of services and products.

In contrast, the entering firm profits in a number of way. In terms of *technology*, because of important technological advances, the last firm entering the industry uses up-to-date technologies and can sell a broader variety of services at lower prices than the existing firms. In other words, the telecommunications industry assumes a decreasing cost function in the long run. In term of *segmentation*, insofar as the entering firm can select its customers and its trunk directions and it is not constrained to serve small users and areas with low-density populations. The possibility of differentiation and segmentation is less easy for EO, which continues to support, even after the deregulation, some obligations concerning public utilities.

THE DIVERSE TYPES OF ASYMMETRIES

We are now going to study how those asymmetries can considerably influence the competitive process.

Generic Strategies

Without any asymmetry, that is, with identical of production functions of all firms, with no differentiation of products and services, with no learning by doing, and so on, it is possible to show that, generally, deregulation can bring more social welfare.

But now, using the results of the model, let us consider plausible strategies, in the case of *existence of asymmetries* formerly described and in the case of *pure and perfect* deregulation, that is, a comeback of entirely free competition without any intervention by authorities. We will first consider the EO's strategic approach, and then that of the NO.

Strategies for the existing operator. To deter entry, the existing dominant firm will want to increase barriers to entry into the long distance communications market. The firm will focus on price policies, because they are one of the most determinant parameters in competition in telecommunications. (Figure 7) Now, it is obvious that prices established in a regulated context on the market segment threatened by NO will appear too high following market liberalization. Thus, deregulation is a special instance for which a rising of barriers to entry, generally and paradoxically, requires a *diminishing* of *limit-price*. The dominant firm will continue price cuts until entry becomes unprofitable (example developed as price scenario 2 in the model). This strategy will involve quasidisparition of cross-subsidies between long distance and local communications, supposing that EO balances earning losses in long distance activities by increase of local tariffs. In this way, NO does not enter.

In this scenario, pure and perfect deregulation involves the *stability of a monopoly structure*, but prices for each type of communication (local and long distance) have steadied down at the level of pure and perfect competition equilibrium. Pure and perfect deregulation results in conclusions of a contestable markets theory, where potential competition can be a sufficient threat to enforce monopoly firm to prices as an atomistic and not a dominant supplier.

Unfortunately, business decision makers described in this scenario are guided by short-term concerns. It does not allow for real strategic behavior of a dominant firm making a price policy that maximizes long-term advantages, shaping the structure of the market within which it will operate in future periods. So, in the former strategy, the leading firm erects efficient but very costly entry barriers. In fact, it does not optimize its market power. Other tactics are foreseeable. Therefore, the dominant firm has no incentive to deter immediate entry by cutting out cross-subsidies. After promulgation of deregulation acts, EO can, in a first pass, maintain its price level and structure. Thus, for a potential NO, entry will appear very profitable (price scenario 3). Also, NO will invest in the building of a nationwide network, as referred to in Part I. Then, when the NO network goes into service, the dominant firm announces drastic tariff reductions. Further, it can increase efficiency of strategy in accompanying this price cut with various forms of discrimination.

For example, due to *spatial asymmetries*, it might reduce tariffs only on trunks where the network of NO is going to run; or, due to *asymmetries in scale*, it might raise tariffs for domestic users and reduce tariffs for business users. The dominant firm does not suppress cross-subsidies but changes their nature to compete with NO more heavily. So, cross-subsidies between types of communication become cross-subsidies between principal and secondary trunks, or between domestic and business users, and so forth.

During the phase of cut-throat competition, the dominant firm can adopt a strategy of predatory pricing and provokes its own losses during a significant time. Consequently, NO could rapidly fail. Here, the financial capacity of competitors will be determinant. In this area, the dominant firm is more credible than NO for investors, banks, and so on. In this case, it is obvious that NO will not withstand the competition. The efficiency of the leading firm's strategy is highly related to its competitive advantages due to asymmetries.

For the EO, the strategy using asymmetries is undoubtedly the most efficient to compete with NO. Indeed, on the supply side, the first entrant setback clearly points out market hazards to any potential entrant. On the demand side, users will regard all potential NO's with distrust. Thus, the monopolistic firm prevents entry for a long time. Finally, due to asymmetries, full deregulation implies the possibility for the dominant firm to exert its market power in the long run without a real entry threat. To prevent this undesirable effect of deregulation, the only solution is to introduce control of the competitive process by authorities. This control might relate to tariffs, quality, network structures, access charge, access quality, cross-subsidies, and so on.

Consequently, liberalization results in new regulation to reduce the consequences of asymmetries on the competitive process, especially to protect NO against the market power of the monopolistic firm. But in fact, NO is not without weapons in the competitive process.

Strategies for the new operator. The heterogeneous demand induces a progressive entry. Our demand analysis suggests a specialization of the NO in large corporate long distance traffic. That specificity of the demand allows a strategy of *niche*, which is implemented by the EO. It is based on the high-growth consumption of particular customers and the high sales concentration on a small client base.

Due to the custom characteristics, the market segmentation implies the building of a nationwide network. But the NO's network is not common, but specialized and selective. A lot of services available on the NO's network (e.g., software-defined networks, direct access, centrex, videocommunications) are dedicated especially to NO's customers. The market segmentation is supported by specific technological choices (fully digitalized network, overcapacity of transmission, optical fiber trunks, up-to-date switching stations), and by specific commercial actions (a lot of technology salesmen, price discount, maintenance). In the background, the competition is, in fact, based on differentiation in quality service, discount to attract customers (not to bring prices nearer costs), and technological innovations to create a captive market. For economic theory, that pattern of competition is not pure and perfect competition, but monopolistic competition (Chamberlin, 1933/1956). Nothing proves that, in the long run, this situation will bring more welfare than a situation of regulated monopoly (for an application to the telecommunication industry, see Volle, 1987).

On the contrary, the NO's entry and strategy leads to perverse effects. Cream skimming from the profitable client base is only possible because the regulatory authority, by imposing a public service commitment on the EO without counterparties for the NO promotes unfair competition. The bypass practice appears as an evident case of unfair competition, because it squeezes the EO, which keeps local communications tariffs at a low level ($0.18 in 1987), or else it loses a considerable volume of local traffic as a consequence of the bypass by NO. So, the duplication of a local transmission system certainly does not imply greater economic efficiency.

On the other hand, we have shown that NO cannot support pure and perfect deregulation because of EO's market power. If EO adopts conciliatory behavior in helping NO to penetrate the market, the two firms can implicitly set up a gentlemen's agreement. But if EO adopts aggressive behavior to deter NO's entry, subsequently, regulatory authorities will be likely to protect NO, especially if they are responsible for its creation, implicitly following the rules of the *infant industry theory* (List, 1985). In this case, the authorities are bound by a tacit agreement with NO to prevent the cut-throat competition which would kill NO. It can try to promote rules of competition that favor its particular interest but do not increase efficiency.

When asymmetries represent major data of the market, the consequences of deregulation on social welfare are less clear. The increase of regulation seems necessary to correct distortions in the competition process induces by asymmetries. Finally, we can assume the following paradox: Deregulation movements must always go with an increase of regulatory control—more state control to obtain less state control.

So, to conclude this chapter, we propose some reflections about regulation policies.

CONSIDERATIONS ON ECONOMIC BASES
FOR REGULATION

The problem that derives from the previous analysis is the following: Are there economic bases for "good" regulation in a deregulated market? How can regulatory authorities define rules of fair competition when actors use asymmetries to create mobility barriers, deter entry, and adopt pricing strategies to cut profit outlooks?

In schematizing, a regulatory agency might have a double role. First, it might ensure bases of fair competition in order to select the most efficient firms. Second, it could function to prevent uses and misuses of asymmetries to limit market power effects.

An optimal regulation needs principally to define operational standards in terms of tariffs, access charges, and unfair practices. We know that the protective strategy for the existing firm can take separate forms. The most important consists of using cross-subsidization by product, communication trunk, customer category, and type of communication. To prevent this unfair practice, the nations where telecommunications are liberalized are engaged in different efforts to control the firms.

The theoretical approach to this problem is simple. Regulatory authorities must impose a marginal cost rating for all services provided by telecommunications operators. The marginal cost rating eliminates cross-subsidies in pricing strategies, but we have seen that it reduces the profit so drastically for potential entering firms that, finally, they do not enter. It is difficult to imagine a deregulation without entry of new competitors, because a lot of customers would think that the regulated monopoly became nonregulated. This opinion would be in part justified, because in fact, the marginal cost rating is impossible to control. For this purpose, we must note that it does not seem possible to establish clear rules of accounting to charge fixed costs between different services provided by multiproduct firms such as telecommunication operators. Thus, two approaches can be observed in actual cases.

A pragmatic first approach is to enact a deregulation act where cross-subsidies are impossible because firms provide a single product. The deregulatory process in the United States is a good example of this practice. The Bell system has been broken up into two separate categories of telecommunications operators. Local operators (Regional Holding Bell Operating Companies) preserve the monopoly on the local traffic but they cannot provide long distance and international telecommunications services, or enhanced services, nor can they themselves produce their own telecommunication equipment. On the other hand, long distance operators (AT&T, MCI, and so on) compete in all telecommunication and information markets (services and equipments), but they cannot provide local communication service.

It is obvious that one of the main goals of this regulation is to prevent the use of a monopolistic position by local telecommunication operators to subsidize other telecommunications activities. Thus local operators cannot misuse their monopolistic position, but neither can they use their knowledge and profits to invest in new fields of telecommunications (smart buildings, enhanced services, electronic transfer funds, etc.) Despite technical and commercial advantages, local operators undergo the bypass and are passive bystanders with respect to the development of new services without being able to contribute. There is undoubtedly an anomaly in this situation, because local operators do not enjoy large economies of scope, important in the telecommunications sector. This new type of regulation may not bring the most economic efficiency. For this reason, local operators want the authorization to increase the scope of their activities and bargain continually with regulatory authorities.

However, this type of regulation does not forbid, for long distance operators, the possibility of cross-subsidies between the service provision and other telecommunications activities (equipment manufacturing and so on). AT&T long distance can profit by its dominant position and compete with small firms that meet difficulties in making their investments profitable. AT&T can run economies of scale and scope to investigate other activities such as information and data processing. After an intermediate pass, it is obvious that AT&T will subsidize all types of activity, except local telecommunications, principally by its profits in the long distance telecommunications market. The possible introduction of price cap regulation to substitute the rate of return regulation is a step in this direction.

A second pragmatic approach to deregulation is given by the Japanese and British examples. The former monopolist firm (BT, NTT) continues to provide both local and long distance communications. The new operators choose only to provide long distance communications. The deregulation creates fundamental asymmetry between actors, to favor the entry of NO. To compensate for these asymmetries, the regulatory authorities always give the former monopolies substantial advantages, such as the possibility of entering markets formerly forbidden to them, manufacturing telecommunication equipment, all types of services, and so on. Two major consequences can be observed due to the new market rules.

First, the former monopolies always try to increase the price of local communications to balance price cutting in the long distance market due to competition. Consequently the total profit is not reduced, and now it is used more to rapidly improve many new activities than to increase the telecommunication basis services quality, essentially to the detriment of the small customers.

Second, the regulatory authorities often adopt partial behavior to favor the emergence of one or more NO. Authorities are then implicated in bargaining processes with all the existing and potential competitors. Lobbying, political maneuvering, and international pressure are rapidly becoming a major aspect of the deregulation process.

In conclusion, whatever the type of deregulation, we observe that bargaining power becomes an essential parameter in the deregulation market revolution. It is important to note that the bargaining power of an actor is not proportional to his or her market power. This importance of bargaining power comes directly from the impossibility of economic theory to define clear market rules in a deregulated market when large asymmetries exist between actors. Authorities are obliged to regulate the market but do not know which rules they must invoke. This situation implies a lot of incomplete, contradictory, temporary measures to reduce imperfections of the initial deregulation act.

But finally, will the deregulation give rise to more competition or more regulation? Or both?

REFERENCES

Baumol, W.J., Panzar, J.C., & Willig, R.D. (1982). *Contestable market and the theory of industry structure*. San Diego, CA: Harcourt Brace Jovanovitch.

Benzoni, L. (1988). Industrial organization-industrial economics: Les développements d'une discipline. In E.I. Greco (Ed.), *Traité d'economie industrielle*. Economica.

Chamberlin (1956). *The theory of monopolistic competition* (7th ed.). Cambridge, UK: Oxford University Press. (Original work published 1933).

Curien, N., & Gensollen, M. (1987). De la théorie des structures industrielles à l'économie des réseaux de télécommunications. *Revue Economique, 38* (2).

Gabscewicz, J.-J., & Thisse, J.-F. (1979). Price competition, quality, and income distribution. *Journal of Economic Theory, 20.*

Hotelling, H. (1929). Stability in competition. *The Economic Journal, 34,* (March), 41–57.

List, F. (1985). *The national system of political economy.* London: Longman.

Volle, M. (1987). Qualité des services et équilibre du marché des télécommunications. *Bulletin de l'dDATE, 28* (3).

Author Index

A

Aronson, J.D., 170, *198*
Auerch, H., 85, *103*
Aurelle, B., *134*

B

Baumol, W.J., 47, *55*, 237, *256*
Benzoni, L., 237, *256*
Brennan, T.J., 37, *55*
Brezzi, P., *134*
Brock, G.W., *55*, 57
Bruce, R.R., 182, 184, *198*

C

Carlton, D.W., 38, *55*
Caty, G.F., *134*
Cerni, D.M., 179, *198*
Chamberlin, 253, *256*
Chandler, A.D., Jr., 39, *55*
Chavelet, E., 128, *134*
Clark, K., *198*
Codding, G.A., Jr., 141, 142, 144, 148, 151, 177, 193, *198*
Cornell, N., *103*, 104
Cowhey, P.F., 140, 161, 170, *198*
Cunnard, J.P., 182, 184, *198*
Curien, N., 237, *256*

D

Dansby, R.E., 62, 66, *73*
Dasgupta, P., 124, *134*
d'Aspremont, C., *55*, 58
Director, M.D., 182, 184, *198*
Dixit, A., 84, *103*
Drake, W.J., 169, 175, 176, 183, 189, 190, 191, *198, 199*

E

Ergas, H., 195, *199*
Eward, R.S., 45, *55*, 182, *199*

F

Farrell, J., 38, *56*
Feldman, M.L.B., 142, *199*
Fowler, M.S., 35, *56*
Frieden, R.M., 170, *199*

G

Gabszewicz, J.J., *55*, 58, 242, *257*
Gal-Or, E., *56*, 58
Gensollen, M., 237, *256*
Gilhooly, D., 135, *135*
Golschmann, M., 120, *135*
Granot, D., 40, *56*
Greenbalgh, P., *103*, 104
Gregg, D.C., *199*
Groff, R., 84, *103*

H

Halprin, A., 35, *56*
Haring, J., 98, *103*, 104
Horwitz, R.B., 168, *199*
Hotelling, H., *56*, 58, 242, *257*
Huber, P.W., 35, *56*, 57
Huberman, G., 40, *56*

J

Jacobson, H.K., 137, *201*
Johnson, L., 85, *103*

K

Kelly, D., *103*, 104
Keshane, R.O., 17n, *31*

Klamer, J.M., 38, *55*
Kramer, S.D., 17n, *31*
Krasner, S.D., 167, *201*
Kwerel, E., 75n, 98, *103*, 104, *201*

L
Le Boucher, E., *135*
Leibenstein, H., 85, *103*
Leive, D.M., *201*
List, F., 253, *257*
Lorenzi, J.H., *135*

M
McKnight, L., 189, *199*
Milk, L., *201*
Minc, A., 171, *202*
Moulin, H., *135*

N
Naslund, R., 158, *201*
Neumann, K.-H., 164, *201*
Newstead, T., *135*
Nicolaïdis, K., 175, 176, *199*
Noam, E.M., 155, 168, 180, 198, *201*
Noll, A., *202*
Nora, S., 171, *202*

O
Okabe, T., 157, *202*

P
Panzer, J.C., 47, *55*, 237, *256*
Paterson, P., 195, *199*
Pearce, A., *103*, 106
Perry, M., 84, *103*
Pipe, G.R., 188, 196, *202*
Posner, R., 82, *103*
Povich, L., 93, *103*
Pratt, J.W., 151, *202*

Q
Quatrepoint, J.M., 126, *135*

R
Raveendran, L., 188, *202*
Renaud, J.-L., 137, 150, *202*
Rutkowski, A.M., 144, 145, 148, 151, 154, 155, 180, 181, 197, 198, *202*

S
Salaun, J.M., *135*
Sarrati, L., *135*
Savage, J.G., 157, *202*
Schiller, D., 167, 168, 170, 180, *202*
Schlichting, J.D., 35, *56*
Schmalensee, R., *103*
Schumpeter, J., 167, *202*
Segal, B., 177, *202*
Sharkey, W.W., 40, 46n, *56*
Solaner, G., 38, *56*
Solomon, R.J., 166, *202*
Stiglitz, J., 124, *134*
Sutter, H., *135*

T
Thisse, J.F., *55*, 48, 242, *257*

U
Ungerer, H., *134*

V
Volle, M., 253, *257*

W
Wallenstein, G.D., 137, *203*
Warren-Boulton, F., *104*
Weinstein, A., *201*
Westfield, F., *104*
Wigand, R.T., 181, *203*
Williamson, J., 186, 188, *203*
Williamson, O.E., 113, *118*
Willig, R.D., 47, *55*, 237, *256*
Witt, D., 173, *203*

Z
Zeckhauser, R.J., 151, *202*

Subject Index

A

Alcatel, 120, 122–23, 127–31
Alliances between European firms
  future possibilities, 129–30
  in the 1970s, 128–29
Alternative routing, 38
Ancien Regime, 138–40, 157, 179
Asymmetries, 251–54
AT&T, 33, 35, 142–45, 181
  and the International
      Telecommunications Union
      (ITU), 142–45, 147
  international service, 75, 77–81
  manufacturing, 120–22, 127–31
  PTTs, relations with, 87–90

B

Bertrand pricing game, 44, 46
Boiteux-Steiner prices, 66–68
British Telecom (BT), 77, 122–23
Bundespost, 122–27

C

Collection rate, 60–61, 69–70, 79–81,
    194–95
  matching account rate with, 72–73
  time-of-day, 70, 72
Commission of European Communities
  (CEC), 206
Communications Act of 1934 (United
  States), 25, 142
Competitive markets, 40–41
Competition
  advantages from asymmetry, 249–50
  effect on prices, 83–84
  effect on production costs, 84–85
  effect on product diversity, 84
  in foreign and domestic suppliers,
    52–54
  in international markets, 35–41
  international leases line networks,
    41–44
  international switched service
    markets, 45–46, 54
  model of a firm's behavior under,
    124–25
  strategy under asymmetry, 251–54
  telecommunications, 36
  with fixed costs, 46–52
Contract negotiations, 64–65
Cream skimming, 253
Cross-elasticity, 9–10, 14
Cross-subsidization, 254–55
Customer Premises Equipment (CPE),
  153, 156, 162

D

Directorate General XIII, 213
Dixit, A., 84
Department of Justice (United States),
  33
Deregulation in the United States,
  169–70, 177–78
Digital technologies, 36–37, 39
Direction Generale des
    Telecommunications (DGT), 238

E

Economic Bases for Regulation, 254–56
Economies of Scale, 110
Economies of Scope, 110

Entry in Telecommunication Industry,
model of
digital technologies, 238–39
results, 247–51
scenario hypotheses, 245–47
segmentation, 239–42
Ericsson, 120, 122–23, 127–31
European Conference of Postal and
Telecommunications
Administrations (CEPT), 19, 88
European Community (EC), 205
European Regulatory Structures, 208–11

F
Financing research and development,
124–25
Federal Communications Commission
(FCC), (United States), 142–43,
153, 168–69
and International Record Carriers
(IRCs), 77
Computer III decision, 181
founding, 142
international settlements policy,
90–93, 95–97
uniform settlement rate policy, 60, 69,
90–92
Fiber Optics, 34

G
General Agreement on Trade and Tariffs
(GATT), 175–76
General Agreement on Trade in Services
(GATS), 176, 195–96
GEC, 121–22, 127
General economic interest, 220
Global communications network, 33
in the United States, 33
Global liberalization
and technological change, 166–67
Great Britain, 173
Green Paper, 206
Groff, R., 84
GTE, 121

H
Haring, J., 98
Hierarchies, 113

I
Indefeasible rights of use, 99
Infant industry theory, 253

International accounting rate
efficient, 61–68
matching with collection rate, 72–73
policy implications, 69–73
practices, 60–61, 80–81, 194–95
Integrated Broadband Network (IBN),
181
Integrated Services Digital Network
(ISDN), 155–57, 162, 166, 179–81
development, 154–57, 179–80
introduction, 212
International Business Machines (IBM),
129
International Consultative Committee on
Radio (CCIR), 141n, 191
International deregulation, 172–74, 176
and competition, 175–76
International Frequency Registration
Board, 27, 191
International Organization for
Standardization (ISO), 147, 154
International Record Carriers (IRCs), 53,
142–43, 145
International regimes, 19–22
International stability, 140–46
International Telecommunications Union
(ITU), 17, 19, 25–26, 29, 31,
137–38, 140–44, 146–51, 161, 166,
170, 175, 178
and communist countries, 139, 148
and less developed countries, 139,
148–51, 186, 195
and the United States, 172
Bureau for the Development of
Telecommunications, 192
change of purpose, 144
early history, 142–44
general principles, 158
General Secretariat, 146, 151
International Telecommunications
Convention, 140
Plenipotentiary Conference, 140
Secretary General Richard Butler, 184
structure, 140–141, 190–91
technical transfer, 149–50
United States impact on, 142–45
International Telecommunications User
Group (INTUG), 147, 174, 182
International Telegraph and Telephone
Consultative Committee (CCITT),
39, 140–41, 151, 153–57, 159, 163,
172, 177, 179–81

and Integrated Services Digital
  Network, 154–57
and standardization, 181–82, 189
D series Recommendations, 178,
  182–83, 193
decision-making process, 147, 189–90
interpretation of the Regulations, 31,
  183
leased-line provisions, 159–60, 193–94
Plenary assembly, 140
Recommendations, 141, 143, 161–64
"top-down" versus "bottom-up"
  planning, 157
V series Recommendations, 152
X series Recommendations, 153
International Telegraph and Telephone
  Regulations, 140, 142–44
International Telegraph Union, 137
International Telephone and Telegraph
  (ITT), 127–31
Italtel, 121, 123–24, 127–31

J
Japan, 173, 181

K
Kokusai Denshin Denwa (KDD), 77

L
Land property rights, 217
Local exchange carriers, 77

M
Marginal cost pricing, 62
Ministry of Posts and
  Telecommunications (France), 238
Most-favored nation principle, 196
Multilateral arrangements
  advantages, 20–21, 24
  effect of liberalization on, 28–30
  initiating, 21–22, 25
  stability, 25–27
Multilateral disputes, 31

N
Nash equilibrium, 42–43
Network technology, 181
Northern Telecom, 121–22, 124, 128–29
Nordtel, 88

O
Open Network Architecture (ONA), 181

P
Partitioning added value, 105–18
Peak load prices, 66–68
Perry, M., 84
Philips, 123, 127–31
Plessy, 121–22, 127
Policy cartel, 11
Policy coordination, 11
Public data networks, 153–54
Purchasing policies of European PTTs,
  123–24

R
Recognized private operating agency
  (RPOA), 147
Regulatory colonialism, 13
Regulatory instability, 13–14

S
Siemens, 120, 123–23, 127–31
Spatial competition, 52
Supraregulation, 11–12
Switching technologies, 37
Synchronous optical network (SONET),
  181

T
Tariffs, 163–64
Technical standardization, 29–30
Technical standards, 162
Technological diffusion, 145–46
Telecommunications investments, 24
Telecommunications manufacturing
  in the 1960s, 122
  in 1985, 120–22
  long-term, 122–23
Telecommunications network, 37
Transactions costs, 116–17
Transmission technologies, 36
Transnational corporation (TNC), 139,
  153, 174, 178, 182
Treaty of Rome
  and cross-border services, 214–15
  and dominant undertakings, 222–24
  and network access, 230
  and network provision, 213–21
  and public undertakings, 218–19
  and regulatory tools and sanctions,
    224–25
  and television broadcasting, 214–15
  and terminal equipment, 225–30

V
Videotext, 53

W
Whipsawing, 1, 31, 89–90
Williamson, O.E., 113

Wilson, Woodrow, 142
World Administrative Radio Conference
  (WARC), 177
World Administrative Telegraph and
  Telephone Conference (WATTC),
  140, 143, 150, 178

DATE DUE

~~APR 08 1995~~		
~~NOV 1995~~		
~~MAY 0 5 1996~~		
~~DEC 8 1997~~		
		Printed in USA